CRITIC OF CIVILIZATION

L. CLARK KEATING

CRITIC OF CIVILIZATION

GEORGES DUHAMEL AND HIS WRITINGS

UNIVERSITY OF KENTUCKY PRESS

PREFACE

FOR MORE than fifty years the name of Georges Duhamel has been known to the reading public of France, and hardly one of those years has passed without the publication of a new book by him. In the last three decades his major reputation has been won as a novelist, but in the early days of his career he also wrote plays and poetry. Honors have come to him in full measure. He is a member of the Académie Française, whose chairs are reserved for forty distinguished men of letters, and of the Academy of Medicine, in which his labors on behalf of the medical profession have won him a coveted place. He has been the recipient of prizes. He has edited the *Mercure de France,* one of France's best-known literary journals, and he is a past president of the Alliance Française. At eighty-one he is still at work, with no apparent thought that his career as a writer is over.

It is regrettable that such a writer should be known abroad for scattered articles and a few books only. His books have been reviewed as each has appeared, but there have been few attempts to summarize his work, none of them comprehensive. There has been a recent tendency even for French critics to damn him with faint praise as the nearly forgotten relic of bygone decades, a judgment that is neither sensible nor fair. Ironically, as a young man Duhamel himself displayed a like attitude toward his elders, in the fashion of young readers and critics everywhere, who are prone to desert aging giants in favor of newer, more controversial figures. Thus, while Duhamel is still in possession of his powers and just as he is approaching greatness, he is neglected at home and abroad. As time passes, his work is certain to be admitted, however, to the shaky pantheon of literary immortality. In the United States he has already been recognized in some circles, and the productions of Duhamel and his contemporaries are discussed in university classrooms. These studies are impeded, however, by the paucity of up-to-date critical evaluations.

My own interest in Duhamel stems from first reading him in a textbook edition of *Confession de minuit* and has continued with extensive reading in his other works. Later, in 1950, while on an academic mission, I had an interview with M. Duhamel in Paris. He was most cordial as we discussed his work and wished me luck when I mentioned that I was interested in publishing a book on the ensemble of his work. As time has passed, I have become more and more convinced that a book on the writings of Duhamel should appear in the United States, and that what he has to say about the twentieth century has more and more cogency.

In the present study the overall importance of Duhamel has been evaluated in an introductory chapter, followed by a detailed discussion of his work. In the critical synthesis of his writings I have adopted a topical rather than chronological arrangement, although within a given topic the items have been arranged chronogically. Duhamel's early publications were mostly poetry, drama, and literary criticism, and these have been separated from his later, maturer work. Indeed, except for literary criticism, which provides a continuous thread, these early genres do not reappear in his writings. Because the First and Second World Wars were to call forth some of Duhamel's finest writing, a separate chapter is devoted to the books inspired by them. The character Salavin, to whom Duhamel devoted five books and who may be regarded as his contribution to the analysis of contemporary frustration, is likewise treated in a chapter apart. Two chapters are devoted to the Pasquier Chronicle, which many critics consider his major work. His other writings, creative, polemic, and casual, seem to fit into rather well-defined categories, as a glance at the table of contents will show.

My especial thanks are due to the research fund of George Washington University which helped me with funds and with clerical assistance as I made my first attempts to find my way through the maze of Duhamel's published and republished books and articles.

Thanks are also due to the many friends and colleagues who have been kind enough to listen to me and to encourage me as I have discussed Duhamel and his work.

L. Clark Keating

CONTENTS

INTRODUCTION

GEORGES DUHAMEL has led a full life and a fruitful
one, firmly dedicated to human values. During his long
career he has striven to be a leader of humanistic thought,
expressing his philosophy in a wide range of activities as
well as in varied literary forms. Because his is a literary
life and his works are his greatest monuments, a "study"
of Georges Duhamel is necessarily a study of his various
writings. But Duhamel believes that the artist must
influence the world in his turn and that it is not enough
for this influence to be expressed only in his creative
works. A complete evaluation of Duhamel must therefore
include an evaluation of his success in this wider realm,
his total contribution to an awareness of our human
dilemma.

Duhamel the man would not wish to be separated from
Duhamel the writer, nor could he be, for the complex
interactions between his life and his writings are clear
for all to see. He has reacted sensitively to the main

currents, cultural, political, and artistic, that have influenced the twentieth-century world during his lifetime, and there are forces in these currents, on the other hand, that have emanated from the words or the actions of Georges Duhamel.

He moves out into the world in the cause of humanism, but he moves always under the lilies of France. This is one of his most distinctive features. He is a loyal Frenchman, so devoted to his country that at times he has been guilty of an absurdly sentimental chauvinism that excuses French mistakes because they are French. At the other extreme, this loyalty makes of him an idealist who demands of his country that it embody the best in twentieth-century civilization. A keen interest in other nations has grown out of his love for France, for he believes that an educated man should know the world in general and the countries close to his own in particular. Such knowledge, he says, will enrich oneself and one's nation. His travels have taken him around the world many times, and his commentaries on his travels have extended his influence beyond the frontiers of his own country. Everywhere that he has gone, he has won a reputation for a sane humanism, a belief that man must control the machine that he has invented, that he must never put expediency before principle, and that he must regard the dignity of the individual as the most precious possession of the race. In the name of this doctrine he has everywhere urged men to resist encroachments on their freedom of thought and action.

His national pride did not blind him during the period between the First and Second World Wars to the unpleasant truth that France and the world at large were beset by many perils. He was among the few who saw, as many commentators have done recently, that the First

World War was as senseless as it was wicked, and that the blow it dealt to Western European civilization might well prove fatal. Because he said this, he was called a pessimist and a Cassandra, and the name-callers, trained less soundly in the classics than Duhamel, spoke more truly than they knew. They were using Cassandra as a symbol of error, but in this they erred themselves: Cassandra's tragedy was not that she was wrong (she was not), but that she was not believed.

Until the political situation in Germany made it impossible for him to do so, Duhamel carried on a serious campaign for Franco-German *rapprochement*. When Hitler manufactured a European crisis, Duhamel was forced to desist and to warn his countrymen of what was going on in Germany. This he did in books, pamphlets, and speeches on the radio. Meanwhile, the inner balance of his mind was such that he began and carried on the writing of the *Chronique des Pasquier*, a work in which the crises of his own time were relegated to the background. His concern with the present was coincidentally displayed in other writings. In the midst of the Second World War, after his own brief participation as a surgeon, he went back to his study of civilization and considered calmly and reflectively the theoretical bases of man's rise from savagery to a civilized state. As the occupying forces forbade him any kind of professional activity, he took refuge in writing so that the war years were productive and ultimately fruitful ones for his literary career.

Since the Second World War Duhamel has continued his career with no diminution of his activity. He has traveled widely and lectured at home and abroad. He has been a member of countless prize juries, has collaborated conscientiously with the four academies of which he is a member. He has demonstrated his conviction that mankind is one and world civilization indivisible by espousing the cause of the United Nations—although noting its defects—and by trying in various ways to help Europe to maintain her cultural leadership in the free world. But he has preferred to tilt at the windmills of modern life as an individual, refusing perhaps wisely to become, like his character Patrice Périot, so involved in collective action that his influence as an individual is lost.

The value of the individual is the thread that runs through all of Duhamel's writing and through all of his other actions as well. From his early poems to the latest production there is visible, though in varying moods and means of expression, the theme of the importance of the human heart and its imperishable values. This is all the more remarkable when one considers the astonishing variety of subjects that he has dealt with. How, one asks, can he venture to express himself so firmly on such a range of matters?

Duhamel cannot pretend to expertness in all the fields he writes about, and of this he is well aware. But he has insisted on his right, as a citizen of the world, to share his chief preoccupations in speech and in writing. Of the concerns of the literary man, the practice of medicine, and the role of science in modern life, he speaks with wisdom as well as passion. In other fields he is no more than an enlightened and articulate layman, and we listen to him with the degree of acceptance that the cogency of his arguments and the state of our prejudices and knowledge will permit.

But even if he possessed the knowledge that would enable him to do so, how can a serious novelist find time to talk about the contemporary scene? One would expect his time to be taken up entirely with his creative work. This is not so in Duhamel's case. Writing is his hobby, his avocation, his joy, as well as his serious vocation, and he makes a careful distinction between creating, which he considers the most difficult task imaginable, and writing merely to express opinions, which he finds as easy as breathing. Incidental essays, whether in the form of books, pamphlets, or articles in the newspapers, belong in the latter category. At times he has also taken pleasure in writing expository footnotes to his novels. Sometimes this explanation takes the form of an account of his hero's evolution, sometimes it combines a description of his purpose as he conceived it with the procedures he followed in developing the purpose. Sometimes he has turned away from literary concerns to write thoughtfully about the status of the writer in contemporary France or the problems that confront the writer in performing his job.

He has devoted time, energy, and much eloquent prose to the tragedy of man's dehumanization in a mechanized world. As he turns from the posture of the novelist, literary critic, and academician to that of an analyst of man's problems, his manner of writing changes also. Because he is suspicious of professional reformers with doctrinaire assumptions about what is good for their neighbors, he is careful to avoid any tinge of their cocksureness. However firm his convictions, he will not speak with the serene superiority of the dogmatist. As he writes to point out the folly of our ways or to admonish the world for its own good, he is aware that his readers may suspect his motives, as he himself suspects the motives of self-appointed do-gooders. The result is that in his polemics Duhamel always strives to persuade. With but rare exceptions he refrains from easy generalizations. The world's dilemmas trouble him, yet he will not become a pessimist. Things he denounces frequently, persons rarely.

This continuous stream of "noncreative" writing has

not interfered with the steady production of Duhamel's serious, imaginative works. Creative writing, he believes, is a high calling whose demands are severe, and it deserves and must receive the writer's primary attention. The writer's opinions, to which he is entitled as an individual, must be kept separate from his creativity, because creative work is incompatible with reform. Duhamel's mission in the name of humanism appears in his novels but only in its broadest sense, as one of man's eternal concerns, for he feels that only eternal concerns are worthy of a serious writer's attention as a part of his creative work.

In the solid and consequential literary pyramid that Duhamel has built, the immovable base is his group of war sketches. His service as a surgeon in a frontline hospital during the First World War produced his vivid descriptions of the horror of its sights and sounds, his repeated, intense cry of anger at the useless killing, and his grim humor that no one has equaled. Of the thousands of war-inspired volumes, all but a few are forgotten, and of that few, *Vie des Martyrs* and *Civilisation* are still in a class by themselves. Duhamel was not alone in considering the First World War a lapse into the morality of the cave man, but he was unique in the manner of his protest.

In the postwar years, the anger of the wartime surgeon gave way to irritation, disillusionment, and frustration, and these were reflected in his writings. Now came the story of the self-tortured Louis Salavin, henceforth to be reckoned as one of the notable characters of fiction. Salavin, no less than Lieutenant Dauche or Sergeant Bouin of the war sketches, was trying to find himself in a perplexing world. He never succeeded in finding the formal religious faith that he sought—any more than has Duhamel—but he did, like his creater, find some meaningful spiritual satisfactions. The concerns of the wounded soldier, the victim of a senseless strife, are identical with those of Salavin. Each wants most of all to live a happy life. Caught though he is in conflict, some of it of his own making, Salavin, then, epitomizes the postwar desire of all men for harmony.

When readers met him for the first time, Salavin was puzzling, even irritating. Many resented Duhamel's suggestion that he is an example of twentieth-century man, for he is not a man in whom we like to see ourselves. In the last three or four decades, however, the presence of the Salavins of this world has been pointed out to us with increasing insistence. He is one with his brothers in misery who grope through the pages of Mauriac, Malraux, and Camus, and we can now identify ourselves with Salavin in a fashion that seemed impossible in the nineteen-twenties. For this increased awareness we have several contemporary writers to thank, but we must acknowledge the place of Duhamel as a pioneer in the treatment of social incompatibility in the twentieth-century novel.

Duhamel's next great success was the *Chronique des Pasquier*. In an essay on the novel Duhamel had declared that his domain was to be that of psychological realism, and the Pasquier family gave wide scope for experiments in that field. In the ten-volume work the story of a family became the point of departure for an exploration of the progress into the middle class of a family situated just below it. The canvas that Duhamel chose was broad. He used the numerous minor characters of the Chronicle to portray the aspects of the *bourgeoisie* that he instinctively disliked, but for the most part the family dominates the action. The money problems, the quarrels, even the faithlessness of Papa Pasquier, awaken a responsive chord in the reader, who tends to equate the Pasquier experiences with his own. Above all, the force and exuberance of the Pasquiers is remarkable.

Laurent Pasquier, the central figure, sees the world as a disordered place, and Duhamel has him declare that he wants to find a balance. It is not clear just what form this equilibrium, or balance, advocated by Duhamel, is expected to take, but seemingly Laurent strives for a world in which the forces that make for human happiness will at least counterbalance those that make for bitterness and despair. Despair Duhamel has always wished to combat, but the eternal skeptic in him, fostered by his early scientific training, requires that his views remain tentative. When necessary he discards yesterday's truth as incompatible with today's knowledge, and he is even willing to hold simultaneously two theories that might to another man seem mutually exclusive.

Of one thing Duhamel is certain: Pascal was right in assigning to the feelings a preponderant place in the scheme of life. Reason, though not subordinate to emotion, must work in harmony with the nonrational forces in man, and in this collaboration reason will not always be the senior partner. His insistence on the feelings that the reason is not aware of has led some critics to classify him as an intuitive writer and to claim that he is false to his scientific training. Others have rejoiced that a scientific education could prove so adaptable to a life dedicated to the exaltation of the spirit. Both views are extreme. Both imply a continuation of the now outworn concept of a quarrel between science and religion, a quarrel that a great many scientists regard as having long since been settled on a basis of mutual esteem, or at very least, an agreement to disagree. In harmony with this view it is not surprising to find a biologist and physician in the company of poets and prophets, since his views and theirs may be complementary.

The blending of intellect and intuition in Duhamel's

writings has led his severer critics to ask to what extent he may be considered intelligent. Among his detractors are men who feel that no man of first-class intellect would be willing to be counted among the intuitives. But this is merely a way of begging the question. To argue, as many do, that Duhamel's occasional errors in judgment, his prejudices, and the often chauvinistic quality of his patriotism are proof of weak intellect is patently absurd. As soon might one accuse all one's political opponents of stupidity, for Duhamel, whether one agrees with him or not, always displays a keen and analytical mind. He is fond of talking about the influence that the laboratory and the hospital have had upon him. He also emphasizes the deep imprint of his classical training, and both influences are marked indelibly upon all his books.

Duhamel is a man to be reckoned with. No artist in an ivory tower, he has come into the market place to espouse the causes that he believes are just. Wrong in detail sometimes, but right in principle, he has attacked his fellow men on their own behalf, as a doctor attacks disease. He has been for six decades an exponent of fine writing as well and has contributed enduring characters to the literature of France and the literature of the world. He has been by precept and example a leader of the writing craft in his country. As he has grown older, he has broadened his point of view to include political considerations. Most important, he has drawn the attention of the world, and especially that of his fellow countrymen, to the necessity for focusing man's attention upon himself. He has harped endlessly, but necessarily, on the need to distinguish between material progress and human progress, and he has done so at a time when materialism appears to be well in control. His bitter campaigns have made the decline of humanism a live issue in an epoch when the spokesmen for the nations have often registered their contempt for man, at a time when men have put their trust in the test tube and the assembly line rather than in the mind that created both. Whether we agree with him or not, Duhamel is, if we would heed him, the voice of our conscience, and in these days of atomic power the human race can ill afford to forget its conscience.

PART I

THE CREATIVE WRITER

IL ME FAUT, avant la minute de l'oubli, compter, peser, évaluer toutes les montagnes, tous les fleuves, les forêts pleines de senteurs et les cités fourmillantes où jouissent, besognent, souffrent mes frères aimés, mes frères amers, mes frères effrayants, les hommes.

1

THE YEARS OF APPRENTICESHIP

SHORTLY after the turn of the century a young student of medicine and biology named Georges Duhamel settled in bachelor quarters at 5 rue Vauquelin, on the Left Bank in Paris. Among his few articles of furniture was a modest piano; his library consisted mainly of a battered copy of Littré's French Dictionary and seven volumes of the Larousse *Encyclopedia*. His monthly budget of sixty francs, small even for those days, had to be eked out by odd jobs such as tutoring foreign students and writing articles for a medical encyclopedia for a few sous per page. Duhamel's health during his student days was not good. He had been exempted from military service on account of it, and even in later life he was to be a frequent visitor to nose, ear, and throat specialists. But like most impecunious students the world over, Duhamel was pleased with his lot. He had escaped from the well-loved but restraining arms of his family and was on his own. The world seemed a bright and wonderful place, and his new-found freedom a guarantee that he would enjoy it fully.

The Duhamels came from old peasant stock of the Ile-de-France region, but the family, when Georges was born on June 30, 1884, was already Parisian to the core. Father Duhamel was a middle-aged medical student, avid of self-improvement, who moved his family about with disconcerting frequency. The apartments occupied by the Duhamels, now in one section of Paris, now in another, seemed crowded for a family of five children, three of them boys. As a student in the local school, Georges was attentive but not brilliant. He was a quiet boy of peaceful disposition, already interested in medicine and literature. He lost his religious faith early and turned increasingly to science for an answer to life's questions. During these boyhood days he dressed poorly, and his myopic eyes peered out through glasses that have very nearly become his trademark. After attending the *lycée,* he entered the medical school of the University of Paris and enrolled concurrently in classes at the Institute of Biology.

The days of the young student of science were filled with activity. Attendance at lectures, experimentation and study in the medical and biological laboratories, observations at clinics and amphitheaters were the daily routine. He ate a hasty lunch in a nearby cafe, sometimes alone, sometimes in the company of fellow students. More often than not supper consisted of fish and fried potatoes bought at the corner delicatessen to be taken home and eaten on the sixth floor at 5 rue Vauquelin.

Most evenings were devoted to study in one of the libraries near the university, usually the hospitable reading room of the Bibliothèque Sainte-Geneviève, near the Panthéon. Free evenings were frequently devoted to the reading or discussion of books, for literary interests were already beginning to claim more and more of Duhamel's time. Like most young French intellectuals he knew and loved the French classics. He also had a lively interest in current literature, counting among his friends at least half a dozen young men who intended to conquer the world with their as yet unwritten masterpieces. Such a man was Charles Vildrac, who was to become his lifelong friend, collaborator, and brother-in-law.

Duhamel and his friends often called on distinguished men of letters. Formal gatherings, however, they tried to avoid, for the adulation that such masters as Mallarmé and Leconte de Lisle expected of those who came to their soirees had made organized coteries and literary *salons* unpopular with many young writers. This dislike of formal groups also extended to cafes, despite the success of the famous *Chat noir* and its imitators. Duhamel and his friends had both a healthy confidence in their own ability and a natural desire to retain their freedom of thought and action. A sure way to lose that freedom was to tie themselves to the acknowledged leaders. Hence, their readiness to join any literary or social circle was in inverse proportion to its stability, regularity, and formality. Few literary men of the day were unselfish enough to win the friendship of Duhamel and his friends on these terms, but the hospitable poet René Ghil was an exception. He and his wife, by their open-handed and undemanding hospitality, made their home an appreciated, though only occasional, center of discussion.

Another reason for Duhamel's reluctance to become an habitue of any one circle was that most of them were

conservative in their literary and artistic tenets. The
established men of letters, who in their youth had come
together to advocate new techniques in writing or painting, tended in middle age to resist the innovations proposed by the younger generation. Such a progression was
possibly inevitable, but the reaction of the younger men
was to look upon their elders as stodgy and to avoid
contact with them. Duhamel was already ardent in
championing the new techniques in poetry, and he could
see no point in seeking the company of men who would
belittle every new idea. There were plenty of young men
who shared his enthusiasms, however, and it was not
difficult to complement the strenuous routine of the
laboratory and hospital with sociable and happy hours
among those who shared his literary tastes.

In 1904 this pleasant schedule of alternating study and
relaxation was interrupted for Duhamel by a serious illness. He had contracted rheumatic fever, and at the
appearance of the first symptoms he was taken home to
be watched over by his father. In a few weeks the crisis
was over, but the experience so upset him that he was
thereafter more than ordinarily conscious of the value of
good health.

Two years later Duhamel's friendly association with
fellow students and kindred spirits crystalized into the
experiment in communal living known as the *Abbaye*.
The story of this venture has often been told by the
participants as well as by literary historians and was later
made the theme of Duhamel's novel *Le Désert de Bièvres*.
He has also described it in detail in the third volume of his
memoirs. In brief, beginning in 1906 and for more than
a year thereafter, Duhamel joined Charles Vildrac, later
a distinguished playwright, René Arcos, a novelist-to-be,
Albert Gleizes, an aspiring artist, and Henri Martin-

Barzun, a future critic and essayist, to live in a large house that they rented in Créteil, a suburb of Paris.

Expenses were to be met by operating a printing press, and so a secondhand machine was bought and a professional printer was found to teach the young men how to run it. In the course of this operation the members of the Abbaye, and Duhamel in particular, became expert typesetters. Printing orders were hard to come by, but the participants managed to print and distribute a number of books, including original works of their own in which established firms were not interested. Financially, however, the venture was a failure. Perhaps if some of the participants had devoted more time to the work, the enterprise might have succeeded in spite of their inexperience. As it was, nearly all the members of the group were occupied with their studies or other activities. In Duhamel's case the extra work load at Créteil had to be fitted into the heavy schedule of a candidate for the *licence ès sciences* and the doctorate in medicine. The happiest moments for everyone came on Sundays, which were given over to recreation and to musical and artistic entertainments attended by family and friends from Paris. Among the frequent visitors was Louis Farigoule, not yet known as Jules Romains, and the young and attractive actress Blanche Albane, who was to become Duhamel's wife.[1]

The literary significance of the Abbaye as a kind of school for writers has been widely discussed by the critics, since the subsequent careers of the members of the group have been brilliant. From their own accounts, the Abbaye's founders plainly regarded their sojourn there and their share in its activities as important in their lives. Duhamel, for his part, says that his participation in the experiment made him realize how difficult are the problems of harmony even among young men of good will. Despite their intelligence and their good intentions, the men of the Abbaye could not wholly resolve their day-to-day difficulties. In recollecting the state of mind brought on by the failure of the Abbaye, Duhamel has one of his characters say:

Au fond, l'idée d'une association humaine qui ne serait pas subie, mais demandée, mais acceptée avec joie, ce n'est pas absurde. Nous sommes des intellectuels, nous autres, c'est-à-dire de mauvaises têtes. Notre échec ne prouve rien pour la foule des autres hommes.[2]

In the year the Abbaye was dissolved, Duhamel received his degree in science. A year later, in 1909, he was awarded his medical degree, and in the same year he married Blanche Albane. Already the idea of abandoning science and medicine for a literary career had occurred to him, but science offered a way of earning a living while he acquired the basic skills of the writer. Thus when a post was offered him to work in a Paris laboratory on the biological activity of colloids, Duhamel accepted, and for five years he was so occupied. His wife, meanwhile, appeared regularly in plays at the Odéon Theater, which was then under the direction of André Antoine, the celebrated producer of new and experimental material.

The acting career of Duhamel's wife might of itself have sufficed to keep him interested in literature, but actually her vocation simply provided added stimulus to a choice that he had already made. Duhamel's first published book was a volume of poetry entitled *Des Légendes, des batailles*, which had appeared in 1907 under the imprint of the Abbaye. We learn from Duhamel's memoirs, however, that this was not his first composition. The impulse to write had come upon him early, and by the time he reached manhood he had already destroyed some juvenile efforts in poetry and prose. *Des Légendes, des batailles,* which was the first work that he thought worthy of presenting to the public, is disappointing, for it reveals few of the qualities that were later to make Duhamel famous. It opens with a preface in which he alludes patronizingly to Paul Verlaine and Francis Jammes and derides academicians and their honors. Shakespeare is mentioned admiringly, and there are a few harsh words for political democracy. Duhamel was obviously already a man of strong opinions.

The poetry is of uneven quality. Occasionally there are charming and unaffected lines, but much of the material is trite. There are verses disparaging women, and some that are atheistic in tone. There are clumsy, hyphenated words, like "doute-enfant-terrible," and pretentious turns of phrase. Decidedly, Duhamel had not yet come to the maturity that, he says in his preface, he had wished to attain before publishing, and it is perhaps significant that he has never reprinted this work, which has now become rare.

Duhamel's second book, which appeared in 1909, was another volume of verse, entitled *L'Homme en tête.* This was a kind of epic with symbolistic overtones. Using the life of the hero, Anthrope (*i.e.,* man), Duhamel tried to write an allegory of man's existence, which he divided into "Le temps de l'enfance," "L'Annonciation," and "L'Epreuve." At the time Duhamel was being influenced by the *vers libristes,* and hence he did not observe the usual rules of French prosody. His poem was further complicated by obscurity. The consensus was that the poem fell far short of excellence.

Duhamel's third volume, *Selon ma loi* (1910), is mainly composed of short lyrics in the *vers libre* style, treating traditional themes. We read of love and the loved one, of the loved one's absence and presence and the lover's reactions. In a section called "Servitudes" there is a pre-occupation with the interaction of two personalities that foreshadows the subject of a later novel, *Deux hommes.* For the rest, the poems express conventional sentiments and, though competent, are little more than that. Several of the critics attributed considerable talent to the new poet but expected better work from him later on. Duhamel's major biographers, César Santelli and Pierre-Henri Simon, writing several decades later, gave these early poems little space but avoided pronouncing a harsh judgment on them.

From the beginning, all Duhamel's literary enterprises were related. While writing poetry, he was establishing himself as a poetry critic. The short volume *Notes sur la technique poétique,* written in collaboration with Charles Vildrac and published in 1910, attempted a comprehensive view of the state of French poetry. The collaboration was the result of a warm friendship and a sharing of interests. Vildrac, like Duhamel, was a man of warm sympathy. Like him he had little patience with timid writers and old-fashioned forms. The resulting work was therefore an attack on conventional verse. Forthright and self-assured, as befitted a manifesto, the book scoffed at the partisans of rhyme and the timid innovators who were content to write in *vers libérés.* In brief staccato paragraphs the authors talked of the infinite possibilities of free verse, and of rhythm, chant, and caesura. Rhyme, they informed their readers, might occur occasionally if it were not obtrusive. Using identical words to rhyme is not only permissible but desirable, and alliteration and assonance may be freely employed. All the illustrative poetic passages were taken either from the works of contemporary *avant-garde* poets or from the authors' own works.

The truculence of Vildrac and Duhamel is revealed in this book in a dogmatic pronouncement like this:

> Aujourd'hui, les gens qui défendent la versification régulière avec le dogmatisme et l'intransigeance glapissante d'un Dorchain sont aveugles ou imbéciles.[3]

So much for Dorchain. Here is a condemnation of rhyme:

> Tout en reconnaissant que dans cette geôle sont nés des chefs-d'œuvre *incomparables,* nous ne mesurons pas sans étonnement le trou de souris par où un Baudelaire dut passer, avec ses ailes . . .[4]

These harsh words must have grated on many an ear. Even in retrospect, when we excuse them on the familiar grounds of youth and inexperience, they seem sharp and irritating.

Two years later another volume of verse established at last Duhamel's right to speak as a poet as well as a critic. In *Compagnons* are some of the simplicity and directness that Anglo-Saxons admire in Housman and Frost and a Whitmanesque love of humanity, which was lacking in his first verses. Like Romains, who was sponsoring a form of togetherness called *unanimisme,* Duhamel was mindful of his close relationship with his fellow men, and in these poems there are occasional verses like these:

> Et s'il est un coin
> Où tu aies vécu des heures violentes
> Et où l'air encore garde ton empreinte,
> Ne vas pas ailleurs.[5]

There is also much material here, as in *Selon ma loi,*

that foreshadows later work. These lines from "A un pauvre homme," which are reminiscent of some of the lonely characters in his fiction, are not the least poignant in the collection:

> Et ces événements médiocres
> Qui charpentent ton existence,
> Qui te sont des événements considérables,
> Qui sont pour toi les seuls événements du monde,
> Les trouverai-je négligeables tout à fait?[6]

Similarly, the poem "L'Inconnu" describes a man to whom the poet had never spoken, but whom he had encountered and observed daily for years. He tells of the unforgettable moment, never to be recaptured, when at last they spoke to each other. This theme of the difficulty and fragility of human relationships recurred in the novel *Deux hommes.*

All the poems in this collection display more nostalgia and tenderness than had Duhamel's previous verses. Here, for instance, is the poet's view of happiness:

> Vous, mes compagnons! O vous, tous les hommes!
> Laissez-moi saisir ce bonheur perdu,
> Laissez, et si mes mains tendues ne me suffisent,
> Aidez-moi donc pour l'atteindre et le posséder.
>
> Aidez-moi donc, et lorsqu'elle sera conquise,
> Cette joie qui pour vous, peut-être,
> Ressemble à peine à de la joie,
> Je veux rendre à chacun de vous,
> Sous les espèces qu'il préfère,
> Dix fois le poids de ce bonheur
> Que je consens à vous devoir.[7]

This is good poetry, as most of the critics agreed, and the public hoped for more like it. Duhamel did not disappoint his admirers, but the First World War had to come and go before he published another book of verse, called *Elégies* (1920). The poems in this volume treat rather successfully some of the themes encountered elsewhere in his writing. Elegy XI speaks of happiness as a fragile gift, a theme that recurs in his novel *Confession de minuit*. Elegy VII is a pleasant reminiscence of a hike through Alsace-Lorraine, later described in his memoirs. Elegy VIII recreates the story of climbing a church steeple, later retold in the novel *Le Combat contre les ombres*.

Several years later Duhamel gathered together some previously published poems under the title *Ballades* (1926). Most of these poems dealt with the events of the years 1914–1918, and they portray with equal magnificence the emotions expressed in the prose sketches of the war. César Santelli may have exaggerated a bit when he called them the finest poems in the language, but the fact that they have won a secure place in the anthologies attests a poetic power that appeals to many readers. The "Ballade de Florentin Prunier" in particular achieved broad popularity. Observing Prunier's mother watching at the bedside, the surgeon was moved to write with a sensitivity that will always be one of Duhamel's outstanding characteristics:

> Il a résisté pendant vingt longs jours
> Et sa mère était à côté de lui.
>
> Il a résisté, Florentin Prunier,
> Car sa mère ne veut pas qu'il meure.
>
> Dès qu'elle a connu qu'il était blessé,
> Elle est venue, du fond de la vieille province.
>
> Elle a traversé le pays tonnant
> Où l'immense armée grouille dans la boue.

Son visage est dur, sous la coiffe raide;
Elle n'a peur de rien ni de personne.

Elle emporte un panier, avec douze pommes,
Et du beurre frais dans un petit pot.

.   .   .   .

Il a résisté pendant vingt longs jours,
Et sa mère était à côté de lui,

Comme un vieux nageur qui va dans la mer
En soutenant sur l'eau son faible enfant.

Or, un matin, comme elle était bien lasse
De ses vingt nuits passées on ne sait où,

Elle a laissé aller un peu sa tête,
Elle a dormi un tout petit moment;

Et Florentin Prunier est mort bien vite
Et sans bruit, pour ne pas la réveiller.[8]

After publishing these poems, Duhamel turned away from writing verse. In so doing he reacted as had many a writer before him—like Daudet, Maupassant, Bourget, and Mauriac, to name but a few. He had found poetry the most convenient and congenial form for the sensitive young writer, but as he matured he was led more and more to express himself in prose. Henceforth he by no means lost his interest in poetry, and the lyric vein that was the chief charm of his verse was inevitably utilized in his prose, to which it contributed greatly. Obviously, Duhamel was not one of the great poets, but in a few of his best verses he succeeds in stirring his readers. Obviously, too, the discipline imposed upon the poet by the rules of the medium was invaluable to the the far greater writer of prose that emerged.

During the prewar years Duhamel had been engaged in literary criticism, mainly in the field of poetry, and as a result of his studies he published three critical works in as many years. The first of these appeared in 1912 entitled *Propos critiques*. Here were gathered his articles published during the previous year in the short-lived periodical *Vers et prose*. His style in these articles is terse and epigrammatic, and its effect is lively and provocative. It is the poet, not the subject that makes a poem, he says, and he defends some of the unusual topics of modern poetry by declaring that "a 'subject' becomes poetic in the hands of an artist, which was not especially so before and may cease to be so hereafter."[9]

In two chapters on Jules Romains he asks a fair hearing for his friend. He declares that he does not particularly like the word *unanimisme,* but he asks that the doctrine of solidarity with one's fellow men at least be listened to. He defends Romains' now famous novel *Mort de quelqu'un* against the attacks of Henri Ghéon, a little-remembered novelist of the day. A chapter apiece is devoted to the work of his two friends Charles Vildrac and René Arcos. In the first of these he gives illustrations of the poet's work and his reasons for admiring it. In the second he speaks favorably of Arcos and recalls his pleasure in reading him. He confesses: "I feel a certain reluctance to argue when I am dealing with a poem that I like."[10] But his analysis achieved the principal aim of a review, awakening an appreciation of the value of the poems.

Duhamel's next critical volume, *Paul Claudel* (1913), concerns the great poet and diplomat whom he was one of the first to admire deeply, but whom he had never met. The book is friendly to its subject. The first chapter, "Philosophe," attempts no simplification of Claudel's complicated views. Like all poets, Claudel strives, he says, for self-expression, and in his God-centered life, progress toward happiness is measured in terms of progress toward

God, for in God alone is true happiness to be found. In the chapter entitled "Poète, écrivain," he sets out to prove by excerpts from the poet's work his remarkable metrical virtuosity, his wealth of metaphor, and his skill in handling words. He is enthusiastic about Claudel's magical poetic effects and the difficult and sometimes obscure means that he sometimes employs to achieve them.

In his discussion of Claudel's plays Duhamel has much praise for the dramatic use to which the poet has put his lyricism. He likes the development of his characters, of whom there are often a considerable number, and he calls attention to the apt but often odd and even vulgar names by which they are called.

This critical essay, with its praise of Claudel's achievement, is a pleasant and charming book. Viewed as an attempt to elucidate a complex subject, it is disappointing. By reading Duhamel's views, our admiration for Claudel's genius is increased, but our understanding of his obscurities is not.

Les Poètes et la poésie, which appeared in 1914 on the eve of the First World War, is a much better book. Duhamel had taken upon himself the formidable task of evaluating all the poetic output in France during the years 1912 and 1913, and he confesses that the mountain of reading his preparation involved had left him fatigued, though not discouraged or intolerant. He divided his book into two parts, the first dealing with poetry in general and the second with individual poets. The purpose of these essays was to communicate the pleasure and displeasure that the reading of poetry, good and bad, might be expected to give to an intelligent reader. For Duhamel there is but one great rule of poetic art: "to feel something, to think something and to compress one's thought as much as possible."[11] His own critical outlook he sums up in the following:

Je crois avoir apporté autant de parti pris dans le blâme et dans la louange. Loin de m'en accuser, je serais tenté de m'en prévaloir, sûr comme je le suis qu'en matière littéraire il n'est d'opinion valable que relative et particulière.[12]

Feeling and self-expression, he says, not documentation and research, are the poet's tools. Precision in measurement is the way of science, but though himself a scientist, Duhamel warns poets against imitating the techniques of the laboratory: the poet's role should be that of interpreter of the emotions. He should perceive, feel, and recognize great truths so that his fellow men may encompass them.

The second part is taken up with critical essays on well-known poets such as Rimbaud, Mallarmé, Verlaine, and Jammes, whom Duhamel enjoyed. Lesser lights are handled more roughly, and he is occasionally merciless in his attack on someone he regards as insincere. Duhamel had feared that the essays would not fit smoothly together, as each had already been published as an individual article, but this fear was groundless. However, the essays rise to few heights and add little to our familiarity with their subjects.

This was not Duhamel's last book of literary criticism, nor the last time he was to write of poets and poetry, but his career as a systematic critic of poetry was drawing to a close. His next task on behalf of French poetry was undertaken in the role of anthologist. In 1923 a Leipzig publisher asked him to prepare an anthology of French verse for German readers, and as a part of his self-imposed mission to minimize Franco-German tensions Duhamel agreed cheerfully. For his book he made a selection among the poets from Villon to Baudelaire. Most of the favorites are there. One finds Malherbe's "Consolation à M. Périer sur la mort de sa fille," Vigny's "La Maison du berger," Musset's "Ballade à la lune," and Hugo's "Tristesse d'Olympio." Everything considered, this is a workman-like job, and the preface, which was published in France in the magazine *Europe*, is an excellent short discussion of French poetry.

During the apprentice years poetry and criticism were not the only forms of literature Duhamel tried. As he had married a talented actress, what could be more fitting than for him to write a play in which he might see his wife cast in the leading role? His other literary endeavors had brought him into contact with the theater and its people, but it was Jules Romains who introduced him to André Antoine, the aging but still enthusiastic experi-menter who had become a state theater manager. Shortly after the meeting, Duhamel offered Antoine the manu-script of a play entitled *La Lumière*.

Antoine accepted the play, and its first performance took place at the Odéon Theater on April 8, 1911. The subject was the psychology of the blind, which was to be of lifelong interest to Duhamel, and which later led him to accept the editorship of a magazine in Braille. The simple plot deals with Bernard, blind from birth, who had a difficult disposition. He was admired greatly by Blanche, a young girl who lived with his family. She too had defective eyesight and had to be spared close work and bright lights. In a moment of selfish exaltation Bernard tried to "see" through Blanche's eyes, and he forced her to stare at a brilliant sunset in order to describe its colors to him. The result was temporary loss of vision for Blanche, who had to bandage her eyes for a week. Subsequently, while walking in the woods, Bernard and Blanche were caught in a storm, and the latter became terribly frightened when they lost their way. In abject terror she snatched off her bandage and recognized the path. Simultaneously a lightning flash did irreparable damage to her vision. She would never see again. After this incident the two young people spent most of their time together, and after a declaration of love by Bernard they decided to be married.

This play calls to mind the similarly intuitive characters of Maeterlinck. There is also, as with the Belgian master, a corresponding lack of action and a tendency to lengthy dialogue. Although written in prose, the play contains many fine lyric passages and some genuinely pathetic situations. Antoine liked the play, but the critics, even those who were kindly disposed toward the experimental theater, were harsh in their judgments. Maurice Boissard in the *Mercure de France* declared that *La Lumière* was "the most boring spectacle in existence,"[13] and Duhamel's succeeding plays fared little better at his hands.

A year later Duhamel submitted to Antoine another play, *Dans l'ombre des statues,* and again his wife was cast in the leading role. The first performance was on October 26, 1912. Once again the conflict is psychological. Robert Bailly, son of a famous scholar, had had to live in the shadow of his father's fame. As the play opened, Robert was readying himself to speak at the unveiling of a statue to the dead *savant.* No one save Alice, whom he loved, had an inkling of Robert's distaste for the speech he must deliver. His frustration at never being able to express his real self had been a well-kept secret. Then suddenly he found that he was in fact the son of the artist, Florent Lavaud. Reacting violently, first in grief and then in joy, Robert was recalled to duty by his mother. As the play ended, Robert was still a prisoner, still living in the "shadow of the statue."

This play shows definite improvement over its predecessor. The characters are better drawn, the dialogue is more natural, but several defects are conspicuous. Robert's tempestuous revolt and quick return to duty, for one thing, are too quickly accomplished. The minor characters are too numerous. For these and perhaps for other reasons the critics did not warm to Duhamel. Antoine alone was deeply impressed, and he thus described his enthusiasm at the first performance:

Saisi par la beauté de l'œuvre, je n'avais pas hésité à m'engager publiquement dès avant la représentation, à annoncer qu'un écrivain de première grandeur était né. . . .[14]

The public, usually heedful of Antoine's pronouncements, was not carried away.

Duhamel's third effort was a play in verse entitled *Le Combat,* performed at the Odéon on March 14, 1913. The plot concerns a feudal family, represented by the patriarch, aged ninety, his son Vincent, a hypochondriac, aged sixty, and his grandson, aged twenty-five, who has been stricken with tuberculosis. The action is simple: Gérard read his death sentence in his doctor's eyes, and determined to devote his remaining days to building a dike to control the river. The rest of the play describes his progress in the undertaking, which was directed by an architect and admired by Gérard's fiancée, Anne-Marie. But the ultimate success of the project, although in reality inspired by the dying Gérard, was attributed to the sagacity of Vincent. When at last the dike was complete, just in time to prevent a flood, everyone deserted Gérard, whose unselfish vision had made the work possible.

The minor personages in this drama, a group of local peasants, perform some of the functions of a chorus, commenting with little comprehension on the action as it progresses.

The outcome of the play would appear to suggest the

irony that in this imperfect world friends of society frequently receive neither thanks nor credit for their sacrifice. This theme had been explored with more success by Ibsen in *An Enemy of the People* some thirty-one years earlier.

These three plays were the extent of Duhamel's dramatic work written and performed before the First World War. The verdict of P.-H. Simon, and of nearly everyone else, was that at most these plays presented a promising young dramatist who had not yet reached the height of his powers.[15]

The next and best of Duhamel's plays was a one-act comedy called *Lapointe et Ropiteau.* In it two soldiers tried to outdo each other in describing the seriousness of their wounds, and although the subject sounds more pathetic than funny the result was in fact a hilarious farce. Even in the face of death, says this play, the human ego proclaims its importance, and as we laugh at Lapointe and his comrade, we laugh at ourselves.

After the war Duhamel did not at once renounce the theater. His next play was written because of an appeal from the ingenious and imaginative producer Jacques Copeau. The four-act comedy, *L'Œuvre des athlètes,* was played at the Théâtre du Vieux-Colombier on April 10, 1920. The leading character, Rémy Belœuf, a hack writer and editor of the magazine *L'Œuvre des athlètes spirituels,* is a charlatan and parasite who reminds us of Tartuffe. The victim in this case is a druggist named Auboyer, who invites Belœuf and his followers into his home. Almost at once the Auboyer daughters Mathilde and Léa become infatuated with the intruder. Their brother Denis is the only skeptic in the family. This farce has little or no plot, and in truth no conventional beginning or end, but its dialogue is sprightly at times. Its

reception by the critics was hardly enthusiastic, and
Duhamel was to risk their judgment but twice more.

In 1921 a one-act comedy, *Quand vous voudrez,* from
Duhamel's pen was staged by the distinguished producer-
director Georges Pitoëff in Geneva. This play also has
some comic lines, but its reception was mixed.

Despite his relative lack of success Duhamel made one
more trial of his dramatic powers. His play *La Journée
des aveux* (1924) presents a dreary scholar, Héglin, who
had decided to give his fortune to the supposedly happy
Foulon family, whom he was visiting and whose domestic
felicity he admired. He discovered before long that the
daughters of the family were in fact desperately unhappy,
that his host was untrue to his wife, and that his supposedly ideal family was in reality a pathetic example of
domestic discord.

Although this play has truly dramatic qualities, the
public and the critics were unimpressed, and Antoine
himself is authority for the statement that Duhamel became so discouraged that he renounced the theater.[16]
Whether this is fact or speculation, more than a little
bitterness appeared in Duhamel's description of the trials
of the dramatist in his essay "Sur le théâtre," which he
included in a collection of satires published in 1922. Here
he pictures the poor author, happy to have finished his
drama, being hounded by theater people from stage-hand
to soubrette, all of whom assume they know more about
the play than the author. The impresario will settle for
nothing less than a completely new version, and when at
last the badly manhandled work is performed, the critics
pounce on it and tear it to pieces. These sentiments were
probably not entirely autobiographical, for Duhamel had
dealt with sympathetic producers, but much of what he
said had its roots in behind-the-scenes reality. Certainly

his commentary was symptomatic of a general dissatis-faction with the theater, which he left after the produc-tion of *La Journée des aveux.*

Four years later Duhamel came more seriously to grips with the stage and its problems in a long paper entitled *Essai sur une renaissance dramatique* (1926). In the nineteenth century, as he sees it, none of the great French writers had won his reputation in the theater. Even Hugo, who aspired to be a national dramatist, was far more famous for his poetry. Toward the end of the century and shortly thereafter the experiments of Antoine and pioneers like his friend Copeau turned public attention once again to the theater. Problems of stagecraft were studied. New approaches to play production were tried, and excellent new techniques resulted. Prose had to displace verse, since the classical verse drama, in Duha-mel's view, does not suit twentieth-century taste. In the field of comedy he considers Molière still a valid model. Foreign plays may be studied with profit, especially Shakespeare, whom he called (one wonders why) an author of "Latin formation." Shaw, Ibsen, and Synge he regards as too un-Latin to influence France very much.

Duhamel holds that for far too many dramatists the theater is a mere substitute for the pulpit and lectern. In this he detects the influence of Ibsen, whose followers, although lacking the master's genius, nevertheless aspired to repeat his success with theme plays. Duhamel believes that such writers of didactic drama are mistaken as to the real function of the theater, and he observes that "there is more true philosophy and original depth in ten lines of Spinoza, Spencer, or Bergson than in the four or five heavy acts of a play,"[17] though if he himself has read much philosophy the evidence of the fact is not very obvious in his works, dramatic or otherwise.

Duhamel sees in Maeterlinck an equally bad influence, for he inspired other writers to clutter the stage with grottoes and never-never lands. Both his errors and those of Ibsen must be expunged. The new French drama, like the new fiction, must turn to realism to survive.

It is fruitless to speculate on the reasons why Duhamel's own contributions to the theater were so modest, especially since in his more comic efforts his verve is undeniable. Did he simply lack dramatic skill? Many critics said so. If he had persisted would he have become a more skilled craftsman? Most critics hoped so, but there can be no satisfactory answer. Chronologically, some of the plays were written after he had won fame as a writer of prose. But in a real sense his writing for the stage must be classed with his prewar efforts, as the work of the apprentice years. Had Duhamel been able to adapt to the theater the mature talent of his wartime prose, he might well have produced a masterpiece. But it was not to be. As we have seen, no less a friend than André Antoine himself suggested that the adverse critical reception that greeted his last two plays drove Duhamel from the theater. The fact remains, Duhamel chose to become a bystander. His work as a writer was to go on. His theater has become armchair drama, no longer staged. Perhaps it is just as well. As P. H. Simon says: "Son œuvre n'était point faite pour les feux de la rampe, mais pour la lumière de la lampe."[18]

2

THE IMPACT OF TWO WARS

FEW EUROPEANS expected war in 1914. Most people thought the Kaiser was bluffing, just as a later generation shrugged off the fulminations of Hitler. Duhamel has given a convincing account in one of his novels of the shocked disbelief with which most Frenchmen greeted the outbreak of hostilities. The second reaction for most, however, was a patriotic urge to enlist. Everyone expected a short war. Like all doctors Duhamel was automatically a member of the military reserve, and despite previous exemption from the service, he enlisted immediately. He was to be stationed close to the front in a mobile surgical unit. For no less than fifty-one months he was seldom out of earshot of the guns, and he tells us that during his war service he treated some 4,000 wounded men and performed more than 2,000 operations. Thus the scientist of the research laboratory became a practicing physician overnight.

As the war went on, the inadequate medical equipment of the French army improved until, by 1918, the mobile unit to which Duhamel belonged, and which in 1914 had consisted of a single motor vehicle, was composed of a fleet of trucks comprising operating rooms, X-ray equipment, and radium therapy units—a complete field hospital on wheels. The men who served in this and similar front-line hospitals, mobile or not, had a nightmare schedule—eight hours on and eight hours off most of the time. After a battle the wounded arrived in unmanageable numbers. Amputations, gangrene, infected wounds, stenches, groans, and ever-present death were for more than four years Duhamel's daily experience. Few who endured such a life remained unchanged by it, and Duhamel was stirred to his innermost core. His reaction as a sensitive, educated man was inevitably philosophical as well as psychological. The primary, inescapable fact of life was suffering, suffering that the surgeon, as he probed for shrapnel and disinfected ugly wounds, must often cause in order to heal. Most of the sufferers were mute, uncomprehending, and uncomplaining, and the medical men at the front came to understand, as others could not, how suffering made all men brothers.

One day Duhamel observed a look of anguish and pity on the face of a stiff-necked, arrogant German sergeant as he heard another wounded man cry out, and he was moved to write:

Depuis j'ai souvent pensé qu'il existe une véritable langue internationale, une langue universelle. Je me demande si les

animaux eux-mêmes y demeurent insensibles. C'est la voix
de la souffrance. Croyez-vous qu'il y ait des hommes vraiment
incapables de la comprendre?[1]

From these physically and emotionally exhausting duties,
Duhamel drew inspiration for the four prose works that
he managed to compose during the war. Two of these
represented an attempt to formulate a philosophy of life
that could satisfy himself and appeal at the same time to
a few of his fellow men by providing a humane answer to
the questions on the lips or in the hearts of the dying.
The other two books were an expression of protest against
the war and its cruelty, presented in the form of short
stories or sketches. In them he addressed himself particularly to noncombatant bystanders, in the hope that
civilians might share the horror and the frightfulness of
the war and that they might achieve at least some slight
concern for the suffering of the soldiers. None of the four
books was *belles lettres* in the accepted sense, least of all
those of protest, which were written at white heat. Of the
two books of sketches entitled *Vie des martyrs, 1914–1916,*
and *Civilisation, 1914–1917,* the first appeared in 1917.
The second was published a year later under the pseudonym Denis Thévenin.

There was no immediate public reaction. *Vie des
martyrs* created a slight stir, but not until *Civilisation* had
appeared and been identified as a work by the same
author was widespread notice taken of Duhamel's achievement. He then experienced his first enthusiastic public
acclaim. The Goncourt jury awarded him its prize, and
with this award came unwelcome fame. In peacetime to
have won so smashing a critical victory would have
seemed a just reward, but to the wartime Duhamel, the
surgeon and witness of suffering, public recognition seemed
less important than getting his message across. Having

written the sketches in his little cubbyhole, two steps
from the ward where the wounded lay, he found it dis-
tasteful and a little shocking to find himself mainly praised
for the literary quality of his work. He had wanted all
men to become eyewitnesses to war's brutality, and he
found it disconcerting to hear people say "What pathos!
What wonderful writing!" Such praise for a man who felt
deeply was too trivial to be borne. He had not intended
his stories to be entertainment, and mere successes over
the teacups of Paris were abhorrent to him. He was
equally astonished to learn that his first book was looked
upon by the military and civilian authorities as useful
win-the-war propaganda, because it tended to accustom
people to suffering. Such a purpose was the very anti-
thesis of his desire, and he cried out in anger:

> Pour que le sacrifice ait toute sa portée, toute sa significa-
> tion, il faut qu'il soit, jusqu'au bout, très amer, que la coupe
> soit réellement vidée jusqu'à la lie,—la lie comprise.—Il faut
> qu'on ne s'y habitue pas.[2]

Despite the sincerity and the sharpness of this declaration, Duhamel's literary skill in creating *Vie des martyrs*
and *Civilisation* continued to win him a wide reputation
as a raconteur. What was meant to be protest became a
notable artistic triumph. In addition to the Goncourt
prize, *Civilisation* won a special award of the French
Academy, though in effect the book does not stand alone.
Together with its companion volume it forms an unbreak-
able whole, a critique of war that is all the more powerful
for being indirect.

Duhamel is indisputably magnificent in these pages.
The pathos, anger, and frustration he made his readers
feel as he described the agony of the wounded are unsur-
passed in war literature. And the most terrible thing

about the sketches is the reality of their horror. This is all true! The vignettes of the dying men—the cheerful ones who died in the belief that they were getting well, the pessimistic ones who recovered, the beardless youths and tired old men who hovered on the brink of death—are awful in their cumulative effect. The nine sketches of *Vie des martyrs* and the sixteen of *Civilisation* have an overwhelming intensity from first to last.

The suffering of Croin, with his blinded eye, is described in one of the many horrible scenes that surgeon and nurses had to look upon daily:

Quand j'approche mes doigts de son œil crevé, Croin fait un petit mouvement en arrière.
—N'aie pas peur! lui dis-je.
—Oh! je n'ai pas peur.
Et il ajoute avec une fierté tranquille:
—Quand on a vécu à la cote 108, on ne peut plus avoir peur de rien.
—Pourquoi recules-tu donc?
—C'est l'tête qui se recule tout seule. Moi, je n'y pense pas.[3]

The war to which Duhamel introduced readers was no drum and bugle parade. He wished to show what went on at the front, to shock civilians out of their acceptance of the war and the soldiers' part in it. He was telling the people at home that their husbands, sons, and brothers would never be the same again, that they were no longer the carefree men and boys they had been:

Ils racontent tous la même histoire. . . . La guerre ne les a pas trop changés. On les reconnaît tous. . . .
—Etes-vous sûrs de les reconnaître? Vous qui venez de les regarder, êtes-vous sûrs de les avoir vus?
Sous leurs pansements, il y a des plaies que vous ne pouvez imaginer. Au fond des plaies, au fond de la chair mutilée,

s'agite et s'exalte une âme extraordinaire, furtive, qui ne se manifeste pas aisément, qui s'exprime avec candeur, mais que je souhaiterais tant vous faire entendre.[4]

Duhamel writes of death as one who has faced it daily, but who is not and never can be reconciled to it. Here is Mercier's story:

Mercier est mort. Ses pupilles s'élargissent solennellement sur un abîme vitreux. Tout est fini. Il ne sera pas sauvé.

Alors, des yeux du mort, sourdent de grandes larmes qui lui coulent sur les joues. Je vois ses traits se crisper pour pleurer pendant toute l'éternité.

Je garde encore, de longues minutes, la main du cadavre entre mes mains.[5]

Or, even if death does not come, putrefaction and decay are none the less present. Fetid odors and unpleasant sights have a large place in these pages. Nothing terrible is omitted. Yet Duhamel refuses to hate the enemy. Such folly he leaves for nonparticipants. He comes nearest to expressing hate as he meditates upon the foolish passions of those behind the lines. But in the last analysis he feels only a contemptuous sort of pity for them. Is there hatred in war? he asks, and answers:

Hélas! j'ai rencontré la haine; mais ailleurs, loin de de ces campagnes tonnantes, loin des flammes et de la colère du combat. J'ai entendu des cris de haine: ceux qui les proféraient se trouvaient presque toujours éloignés de l'action, de la souffrance et du péril. Voulaient-ils donc donner le change? Cherchaient-ils des excuses? Espéraient-ils remplir, avec ces clameurs, le vide de leur existence et de leur âme? Croyaient-ils faire oublier leur inefficacité? Je ne sais. A coup sûr, ils étaient à plaindre.[6]

The rhythm of war, as its sights and sounds penetrate the hospital, is thus memorably described:

Le grondement de la guerre, la rumeur des convois en
marche, les secousses épileptiques de la canonnade, tous les
sifflements et les halètements de la machine à tuer arrivaient
jusqu'aux fenêtres et les secouaient avec une fureur épuisée,
comme arrivent au fond d'une crique les vains échos des
tourmentes du large. Mais ce bruit était familier à l'oreille
comme la pulsation même du monde misérable, et l'on ne
s'ennuyait pas dans la chambre de Revaud.[7]

Little or nothing is said by Duhamel about his attitude
towards war, yet his loathing for it is implicit on every
page, and ultimately the reader feels less pity for the
innocent victims of the monster than for himself as a
member of a race so tender and brave yet so horribly
uncivilized as to wage a modern, mechanized, and fratricidal war.

Two stories, one in *Civilisation*, the other in *Vie des
martyrs*, commend themselves to critical attention. The
first of these Duhamel published separately in a magazine
in 1918. This is the story of Lieutenant Dauche. The
narrator, who is described as a convalescent officer, has
learned from an attending physician that his friend, the
delightful Lieutenant Dauche, is condemned to death
by the presence in his brain of a piece of shrapnel
that cannot be removed. The narrator then described his
uncomfortable association with the doomed man, to whom
he could not tell the secret of his imminent death. On one
occasion, horror-stricken at Dauche's cheerful formulation
of plans for the future, he exclaimed: "You are fortunate
indeed to dare to make plans in times like these." Then
while he was trying to think of a way to make up for his
clumsy slip, Dauche innocently replied: "Don't we all
make plans merely by letting our hearts beat? We must
defy the future if we don't want to be afraid of it. . . ."[8]

There could be no happy ending. One day as Dauche

and his friend were walking together, the former's death
convulsion began, and he had to be carried back to the
hospital in his comrade's arms. After Dauche's death his
friend remarked:

> Il paraît que Dauche fut enterré dans le petit cimetière
> enclos de branches de bouleaux et de sapins morts que l'on
> aperçoit du village de C . . . dans un aride champ de sable
> blanc. Je n'ai pu me résoudre à l'aller visiter là. J'emportais
> avec moi une tombe plus profonde et moins vaine.[9]

The sketch called "Discipline" treats another side of the
war, the tragicomedy of regulations and military rank.
The narrator this time is Léon Bouin, in civilian life a
teacher of mathematics. He found himself condemned
to four days of confinement for failing to carry out an
assignment that had been given to another man of the
same name. Protest was useless. An order had been
issued. That order had to be obeyed even if it took the
wrong man to do it. At about the same time Bouin over-
heard a conversation between two of the illustrious doctors of the hospital. One had been a renowned obstetrician, the other a member of the Academy of Medicine.
They were talking together as they made ready for a visit
from their military superior, a physician of whose civilian
accomplishments they had no great opinion. This irritating situation led the eminent obstetrician to the following observation:

> La discipline . . . n'est peut-être pas une vertu française.
> Mais, Dieu soit loué, nous en possédons d'autres; et, à lui seul,
> notre esprit critique, par exemple, notre esprit critique si fin,
> si parfaitement incisif et délicat vaut bien, permettez-moi de
> l'affirmer, toutes les pesantes qualités de nos ennemis.[10]

Let those who will submit blindly to discipline, said he.
Medical men would not. It was decided that the inspect-

ing physician would get a courteous reception but without distinction as to rank.

When finally the inspecting physician appeared, in full-dress uniform, and criticized the methods of the hospital's illustrious but undisciplined practitioners, poor Bouin, himself a victim of the rules, expected an outburst. Instead, he heard the once-haughty medical officers answer every remark of the visiting inspector with an obsequious "Yes sir, yes, Inspector, sir." Thus the unlucky Bouin not only served undeserved days in the guardhouse, but saw with dismay his superiors bow to an authority they pretended to despise, in a tragicomic attitude of humility.

This sort of ironic twist, which at most elicits a wry smile from the reader, was about as close to humor as Duhamel allowed himself to come in these sketches. The author did see the ridiculous, even the funny side of the conflict at times, but in these two books he seldom permitted anything to break the tension or relieve the cumulative effect of horror.

In the last chapter of *Civilisation* Duhamel came closest to summing up his attitude toward the war. His spokesman, a sergeant in the medical corps, pronounced an anathema upon our times. His summary is bitter, and seemingly without appeal:

Je hais le XXe siècle, comme je hais l'Europe pourrie et le monde entier, sur lequel cette malheureuse Europe s'est étalée, à la façon d'une tache de cambouis. Je sais bien que c'est un peu ridicule de sortir de grandes phrases comme cela; mais bah! je ne raconte pas ces choses à tout le monde, et puis, autant ce ridicule-là qu'un autre![11]

He then described the obstacles in the way of setting up and maintaining an efficient stretcher service. He talked about the wounded and their treatment and spoke of X-ray machines and sterilizers. For several years these mechanical devices had been the surgeon's indispensable tools. By their means he had frequently won victory over death, yet as he contemplated these splendid steel and nickel-plated monsters the sergeant was moved to exclaim:

J'ai bien regardé l'autoclave monstrueux sur son trône. Je vous le dis, en vérité, la civilisation n'est pas dans cet objet, pas plus que dans les pinces brillantes dont se servait le chirurgien. La civilisation n'est pas dans toute cette pacotille terrible; et, si elle n'est pas dans le cœur de l'homme, eh bien! elle n'est nulle part.[12]

With this declaration of the primacy of humane values the book ends. Duhamel did not forget this statement, nor did he allow his readers to do so. He has often referred to it as a fair statement of his position.

A year after the war a complementary volume appeared, entitled *Entretiens dans le tumulte*. This was the first of Duhamel's many polemic works. Using the device of conversations between Cauchois (himself) and various friends and acquaintances he attacked directly the problem of war and the postwar world. Once again he proclaimed the importance of the human heart, contrasting its intuitions with the kind of knowledge that, coupled with manual dexterity, is able to invent the automobile and the machinegun. Duhamel reasoned earnestly in these pages, but his frontal attack on war and its inhumanity is less effective than are his simple yet terrible accounts of the sufferings of the wounded.

Of more importance were the thoughtful essays which Duhamel had published in periodicals during the war, and which he reissued in book form as *La Possession du monde* in 1919. These essays tried to answer, as did the *Entre-*

tiens, the basic questions that every soldier wishes to have answered. Has life a purpose or meaning? If so, what is it? Is there a technique for acquiring happiness in this imperfect world? Even while performing operations, Duhamel was meditating upon man's destiny, asking himself what, if any, are the permanent values of life for twentieth-century man. His thoughts, written during the few hours when he could lay aside the surgeon's rubber gloves and gauze mask, provide thought-provoking and poetic reading.

In *La Possession du monde* Duhamel preached man's need to seek spiritual values. Happiness, beauty, love, and self-development he saw as indispensable to the individual. They might be discovered by a definite technique: first by a willingness to listen to the infinite, and then by a conscious sharing of one's happiness and spiritual resources. This reaffirmation of spiritual values by one who had lost his childhood faith was addressed to all men. In fact, the universal need to find some sort of comfort, with or without religious faith, would be one of Duhamel's constant themes throughout his work. It is also to be noted that in this reaffirmation he used, without attempting redefinition, words generally associated with religious belief. Apparently he was willing to let conventional definitions suffice, though the context in which he used the words was outside formal religion. For this he was severely criticized by Roman Catholic writers.

Duhamel's position was that of the scientifically educated man who had begun, under the stress of war, to reevaluate and to criticize the aims and achievements of science, particularly insofar as it had claimed to be a panacea for society's ills. Henceforth, the role of science in the modern world would be a major preoccupation of his thought, evolving into a kind of esthetic humanism.

In *La Possession du monde* he pointed out that the most important thing in life was the individual soul, and that with this soul science could have little or nothing to do. From this he turned to a consideration of individual happiness and attempted to inventory the means of achieving it. This, he said, was the "goal of my life, and of all humanity, the goal of all the living world." "Happiness," he said, "is not only the end and reason of life, it is its mainspring, it means of expression, and its very essence. It is life itself." So long as the tuft of lilies shall tremble in the month of April upon the ruins of the world, let us repeat in our innermost heart, "Oh happiness, my tears tell me that you are my goal and my reason for being."[13]

These affirmations were all the more true for Duhamel because the war had robbed most men of their chance for happiness. He therefore wanted to persuade them to seek within themselves and in their fellows a rediscovery of values. Happiness begins at home, he said; therefore let us know ourselves, our neighbors, and our universe. Riches and poverty are not determined by the possession or lack of material things, but by the degree of our knowledge of eternal values, which are the only real ones. "The world is given to all men to be possessed in totality by each one with the aid of all."[14] Without a knowledge of our fellow men, he went on, and without a love for them, we have no happiness. We must turn to the world. In it there is no single object that may not be a potential source of happiness. "That man is truly rich for whom life is a perpetual discovery."[15]

Among the greatest gifts to be attained by striving for them is an appreciation of beauty. If we begin to think that beauty has gone out of the world, it is no longer in our hearts. Everything speaks to us of beauty, for art is a way of life. Art, which creates beauty, is the supreme

gift that men give to each other of their discoveries and
their riches. He who "possesses" Rembrandt or Beethoven
has no reason to envy the great and the powerful. In so
speaking, Duhamel was reflecting more than the usual
cultural interests of the educated European. His own
concern for art and music was an active one, as we shall
see.

Even grief can make us rich, Duhamel continued, for if
we experience no sorrow, we never mature. We cannot
renounce grief, nor can we renounce renunciation itself.
In this world we have two immense realms of refuge, the
future and the past. No one can dispute with us our
world of memories, and so it is with the future. We must
welcome visions and dreams of the time to come, for by
possessing a great dream we are ourselves made great.
Only in these ways can we acquire grace, the mysterious
quality that will give us happiness, the greatest gift life
has to offer. To enforce this point of view he quotes and
then expands Bergson's description of intelligence:

M. Bergson a dit, de l'intelligence, qu'elle est «caractérisée
par une incompréhension naturelle de la vie», on pourrait
ajouter: et par une incompréhension complète du bonheur,
qui est le but de la vie.[16]

Duhamel wrote these pages as he wrote his sketches,
with all the horror of war around him. In his cramped
hospital quarters he must have longed for ordinary com-
forts, but he thoughtfully resisted the temptation to
identify comfort with happiness. He wished France to
avoid this mistake, which, he feared, had already been
made in England and America. He said:

Les peuples anglo-américains, si ouverts cependant à toutes
les révolutions morales et religieuses, se sont appliqués à
dévier de son sens primitif le simple bien-être jusqu'à l'identi-

fier avec le luxe confortable. C'est une façon de donner un
aspect moral à la jouissance, de transiger honnêtement avec
les corruptions de l'argent.[17]

Later Duhamel was to return to this theme of comfort and
launch an attack upon it. At this stage in his thinking he
was more concerned with finding a positive means of
circumventing materialism than with combatting it. Even
so, some critics found *La Possession du monde* not quite
satisfactory.

There were, of course, sympathetic reviews, and from
this time on, Duhamel could always count on the whole-
hearted admiration of a number of critics. This much
the war sketches had earned him. But there were some
who were skeptical and even hostile. The critic of *Le
Temps,* Paul Souday, resisted the temptation to lump this
book with the war stories. In fact, he accused those who
said they liked *La Possession du monde* of not having
read it very carefully.[18] For himself he found its doctrine
too vague and added that Duhamel lost his footing when
he tried to philosophize. Georges Palante, a critic with a
psychological-sociological orientation, wrote in the *Mercure de France* that despite the lyricism of Duhamel's
periods he quite failed to inform his readers what life and
the science of life consisted of.[19] But Duhamel's severest
critic was the frequently bilious conservative Henri Massis. In an article entitled "Le cas de M. Georges Duhamel," in the *Revue universelle,* Massis savagely attacked
the whole framework of the book.[20] He accused its author
of facile and ill-founded optimism and summed up the
thesis of the work as a sort of Jamesian pragmatism with
overtones of Christian Science, for which he had no high
regard. This was an extreme view. The majority of the
critics liked *La Possession du monde.* From a vantage
point of twenty-seven years later, P.-H. Simon remarked

mildly that after all something more than a common love of Beethoven would have to be found in order to bring about Franco-German *rapprochement,* and he sums up:

. . . les instincts égoistes enracinés dans la chair de l'homme ne se laissent aussi facilement conjurer. Mais peu importe. Ce qu'il fallait entendre, ce que les lecteurs de 1920 ont entendu dans ce livre généreux, et ce qui lui laisse aujourd'hui une actualité poignante, c'est le réquisitoire lucide et passionné contre l'orgueil de l'homme fabricant des machines, contre *«l'intelligence calculatrice et démoralisante»;* c'est l'invitation à destituer la civilisation scientifique du rang d'idole à celui de servante.[21]

The above statement hits the mark fairly well. *La Possession du monde* was hardly intended as a complete philosophy of life. At most it was a signpost along the way, and simply as a kind of surgeon's journal it was one of the most remarkable books to come out of the First World War.

Duhamel had by no means said his last word about the First World War. In 1928 he returned to his most effective kind of attack, the short sketch. His short stories and reminiscences this time were entitled *Les Sept dernières plaies,* a title that he took from the Bible. A few of these sketches he had published earlier. His purpose in giving them to the public as yet another war book was stated at the conclusion of one of the stories. He wished, he said, to remind those who had too willingly forgotten it of the historical period 1914–1918, and of its meaning for mankind. He wrote:

J'ai grande tristesse à remuer une fois de plus ces souvenirs. Ils sont trop simples, trop nus, trop vrais, pour émouvoir une société qui ne veut point guérir de ses plaies, mais seulement les oublier. A quoi bon parler encore de la guerre? A quoi bon parler d'une chose qui n'intéresse plus personne?[22]

Despite this mood of discouragement, *Les Sept dernières plaies* is an excellent book. It takes us back to the bitterness of Duhamel's earlier sketches. It dwells ironically on army red tape and the muddleheadedness of the professional military, but although it is well-written, even superbly written at times, its author does not often succeed in generating the intensity of the earlier war sketches.

Duhamel was well aware of the uneven quality and variable reliability of most war books, and he discussed the question in an excellent short essay, *Guerre et littérature* (1920). He believed that books by eye-witnesses to the First World War would not often appear after 1920, although a few admirable exceptions might turn up. War as such, Duhamel suggested, makes no contribution to literature, for although a few *chefs-d'œuvre* may be produced by the participants, the conflict itself is not decisive in developing their talent. At most, war gives men experience that they later draw upon in works of imagination. Nor is participation a guarantee of truthfulness. Actual combatants in a war can and often do write false books about it, whereas men far from battle may contribute works of value, purely through vicarious participation. Still others, including some who have taken part in a war, remain unaffected by it and continue to write as if nothing like it had ever happened to them. Everything considered, Duhamel feared the effect of such war books as might yet be written. He forsaw that war fiction might in time appear again and transmute the actual, terrible conflict, even in the minds of old soldiers, into a legendary, even a glorified adventure. He had seen and understood, though he could not approve, Romain Rolland's attempt to maintain a humane yet critical attitude toward the war in his *Au-dessus de la mêlée*, but as a participant himself Duhamel could not then and would not later allow the war to legitimize itself in peoples' minds, even in retrospect.

During the years between wars Duhamel's thinking, like that of many intelligent persons, was to undergo several changes. For a time, while the treaty of Versailles was in force, he turned briefly toward a philosophy of absolute pacifism. In a magazine article he resolutely opposed international violence, declaring in the following terms that he would support no future war:

Je suis tout à fait certain qu'il y aura de nouvelles guerres, et prochaines et inexpiables. Je ne suis plus à l'âge où l'on espère de réformer le monde. Mais j'entends me réformer moi-même, refouler mes impulsions pures et simples, fonder raisonnablement mon désaveu de la guerre, de toute guerre, sans distinction, sans pieux sophismes.[23]

Elsewhere he reiterated this position, going so far as to say on one occasion: "Peace at any price, that is what we must say and keep on saying."[24]

The reasons for Duhamel's pacifism are not far to seek. Everywhere in Europe a revulsion against the prospect of another war gripped those who had been close to the last one. This was the most obvious source of pacifism, but there were other causes too. Duhamel shared the general disillusionment over the failure of the war to achieve a peaceful world. He began to regard the treaty of Versailles with irritation, because he saw in its harsh terms the seeds of future conflict. The treaty of Lausanne, which followed, seemed equally unsatisfactory, and Duhamel protested against the mass migrations for which it provided. European hopes for the League of Nations were likewise being frustrated by the weak organization that emerged. Disarmament, which Duhamel saw as the key to a permanent settlement, was not forthcoming, and even in France members of the prewar ruling clique were still in power. In his bitterness Duhamel addressed a dead comrade who had once been afraid of the changes the war might bring:

> Il n'y a rien de changé à la façon des peuples de régler les grandes choses humaines. Je vous le répète, dormez tranquilles: on ne vous a pas défiguré votre Europe. Elle est toujours l'Europe des Cimbres et des Teutons, l'Europe de la Saint-Barthélemy et des autodafés.[25]

As Duhamel's pessimism regarding the world situation increased, he multiplied his comments concerning the frightfulness of war and the indifference of mankind. He spared no shaft of irony to excoriate those who failed through selfishness or lack of imagination to understand the immensity of the scourge of war.

As a contribution to international and particularly to Franco-German *rapprochement* he made several visits to Berlin and other German cities, and he delighted in affirming before German audiences that like Goethe, the great German, he wished to be a good European. He thought of his *Anthologie de la poésie lyrique française,* published in Leipzig in 1923, as a specific contribution to international understanding, and in his introduction he stated his belief that ignorance of the culture of other nations makes us more susceptible to prejudice and an easier prey to armed conflict than we would otherwise be. He also reverted to this theme in a book of essays, entitled *Délibérations* (1925), in these words:

> Ce sont les œuvres d'art qui éveillent la curiosité et entretiennent l'affection. C'est surtout par Dickens, par Hardy, par Wells, par Kipling que je connais l'Angleterre. Si j'aime la Russie, c'est à cause de Moussorgsky, de Borodine, de Tourguenev, de Dostoievski, de Gorki.[26]

Thus Duhamel hoped that literature, music, language,

and an exchange of culture would help to create international understanding. His wide travel, he believed,
helped in this process, for he tried to be a bridge between
the countries he visited and his homeland. Long before
the Common Market made the concept of continental
unity popular, he had developed the theme, emphasizing
the role of Europe as a defender of civilization.

In 1928, in a speech to French school teachers (later
published as *Entretien sur l'esprit européen*), Duhamel
discussed the colonial problem as it affected Europe's
leadership. He held for the most part to the nineteenth-
century point of view that colonies are part of the "white
man's burden." Colonies, he said, provide a meeting
place for East and West, and this is an important function,
for if the West does not control the East, Europe will be
menaced by the "colored peoples" of the Orient. These
unprophetic and backward-looking words are about the
nadir of Duhamel's political views but coupled to them,
surprisingly enough, is a magnificent plea for the triumph
of the European spirit.

In the meantime Mussolini and his fascism were gaining
ground, but like many others Duhamel seems to have
failed to perceive his significance. His eyes were turned
mainly toward Germany, and he continued his efforts at
bridging the gulf between that country and his own.
He had not accepted at face value accounts of Germany's
immediate and total conversion to political democracy in
1920, but he hoped that an honest confrontation of the
two nations through cultural exchange might help to keep
the peace.

During the nineteen-twenties Duhamel did not yet
consider communism a menace to western Europe, although as an individualist he repudiated its collectivist
principles. On his return from Moscow, which he visited
in 1926, he wrote:

. . . si le communisme apparaît, à l'individualiste que je suis et veux demeurer, passible de maintes corrections, si le communisme, en bien des points, me blesse et me révolte, je m'incline devant la révolution. Je l'accepte et je la salue.

. . . si le communisme doit, un jour, s'étendre sur toute la face du monde, c'est que des millions d'hommes l'auront appelé de tous leurs vœux, c'est que d'autres hommes auront, par leurs excès mêmes, fait en sorte de le rendre inévitable.[27]

Then mindful of his part in the First World War, he added that he would join in no preventive war against communism. Neither would he pin his hopes on a dubious collective security. For him the individual was the only key to peace, and he made a character in one of his novels say:

. . . vous pouvez changer ce qu'on appelle le régime, vous pouvez remplacer la classe au pouvoir, vous pouvez tout changer; si vous ne me changez pas, moi, par exemple, moi, Salavin, eh bien! vous n'aurez rien changé du tout.[28]

Duhamel's individualism thus caused him to reject communism, and in a brief literary essay of the year 1934 he also declared his hatred of dictatorship of the Fascist variety, but playing down the possibility of collective action against both sorts of tyranny, he seems to have rejected or, at least by implication, to have shown little faith in a practical solution. To rely, as he said he would, upon the conversion of individuals was a rather futile strategy to use against the totalitarians who were recruiting and arming followers by the millions. Thus, like many other pacifists, Duhamel found himself in the famous dilemma of hating war too much to be willing to organize armed resistance against the enemies of the peace.

The coming to power of National Socialism in Germany, however, brought about a sharp change in his thinking.

He was forced to discontinue his labors in behalf of
Franco-German understanding. By the time he published
Mémorial de la guerre blanche in 1939, the political situation had become acute, and he said that although he did
not ultimately despair of Germany, there would be, until
the end of National Socialism, no civilized entity called
Germany to deal with. Hitler's hypocritical tears over
the plight of his "unredeemed" Germans outside the Reich
aroused Duhamel's anger, and he began his book by
imagining as a *reductio ad absurdum* that by 1945 the
German chancellor would be protesting against the mal-
treatment of German nationals in New York and Aus-
tralia. Hitler's concern, he said, about the fate of three
million Germans who lived under the democratic rule of
Czechoslovakia did not extend to the ten million Germans
at home who had been thrown into concentration camps
merely because they opposed National Socialism. Hitler's
torchlight parades and screaming harangues grated on
Duhamel's nerves as they did on those of other civilized
persons. Yet, much as he disliked the ranting spokesman
for German world conquest, he preferred the German
leader in the role of open imperialist to that of cynical
diplomat grinding beneath his heel the well-meaning
Chamberlain and the dignified Masaryk. In both roles he
saw Hitler as a threat to peace, but like many others he
was inclined to regard him as a self-deluded maniac with
a gift for oratory.

To the Germany of Goethe and Wagner he continued
to pay his respects. As he saw it, the great German
culture had renounced its tradition for a time. In its place
was a regime that he despised for having turned its back
on humanity. He wrote:

Il ne faut jamais oublier que le premier acte du parti
national-socialiste a été de brûler des livres sur les places

publiques. Un régime qui brûle des livres a péché contre l'esprit. Il est juste que l'esprit se détourne de ce régime.[29]

Toward Russia, which at that juncture he merely mentioned in passing, he had a more fearful attitude than formerly, but he still regarded the Soviet Union as a less immediate peril than Hitlerite Germany. Japan, he thought, would also cause trouble, for he expected the Japanese to raise an army and pursue their conquest on the Asian mainland with modern weapons. For such weapons in the hands of a ruthless power he had acquired a healthy respect, and he confessed that the incredible technical advances in the methodology of killing had forced him to renounce his earlier pacifism. Nonresistance, he decided, was not a practical measure for this century, and so he said:

> Nous raisonnons en philosophes de l'ancien temps quand nous disons que l'on ne vient jamais à bout d'un peuple courageux, sûr de sa cause, résolu fermement au martyre. Il faut nous rendre à l'évidence: avec des avions, des poisons, des tanks et des mitrailleuses, on vient à bout de tout, parce que l'on peut tout atteindre et tout détruire.[30]

Because he was aware of the brutality of the Nazi concentration camps, he was impatient with those who still held to the kind of pacifism he himself had once professed. He was indignant at novelist Jean Giono's remark that he would rather live one hundred years as a lamb than one day as a lion. Still, public consciousness of danger was awakening all too slowly, and Duhamel's attitudes were unpopular in 1938. There were still many Frenchmen who, though they feared war was coming, hoped that it might somehow be avoided if they merely dismissed it from their minds. *Mémorial de la guerre blanche* was therefore a timely book. It challenged the group that stood for peace at any price, of which Duhamel had been a member, to reconsider its position. Duhamel insisted that the principle of force, symbolized by the Maginot line, must inevitably fail and that reason must ultimately triumph, but meanwhile, France should follow a single course of action: remain calm and dignified and work hard in sight of the aggressor.

However, the political situation continued to deteriorate. Duhamel came to fear that his "Descartes line," as he called it, which stood for the imperishable values of French civilization, might be overcome by the "Maginot line." He came to believe that war was imminent, and while waiting for it to come, he began to write a month-by-month account of the position of France as it seemed to be evolving in the year 1939. These reflections he published in 1940 as *Positions françaises,* and they furnish an interesting picture of French intellectual processes in the crucial months preceding and immediately following the outbreak of hostilities. In them he goes further than before in reversing his pacifist views. He states flatly that he has changed his mind entirely about absolute pacifism. He even characterizes his earlier attitude as a "rather brief Tolstoyan fever which gripped me after the experience of the First World War." In the twentieth century, he says, it is impossible to maintain such a position even though one hates war and has everything to lose if war comes. Here is his declaration as of 1939:

Si je me permets de faire à ce sujet une déclaration personnelle, c'est que le vrai pacifisme doit changer de nature et de démarche avec les événements. Je suis non seulement pacifique, par philosophie, par expérience et par goût, mais je le suis encore pour maintes raisons personnelles. J'ai des fils en âge de porter les armes. J'ai, dans ma maison une vieille mère intransportable. J'habite ordinairement une grande ville exposée. Je suis vulnérable de partout. La guerre, quoi qu'il arrive, serait non seulement un échec pour la pensée de toute ma vie, elle serait non seulement la négation de mon œuvre; mais elle m'atteindrait sûrement dans tout ce que j'aime au monde. Et c'est bien pourquoi je dis: que les pacifistes résistent, qu'ils s'arment pour résister. Tout le reste, à l'heure actuelle, n'est que sophisme, sottise, fausse manœuvre, erreur tragique.[31]

Here was part of the inescapable logic that was forcing pacifists into militance just one year after the cession of the Sudetenland to Hitler. The Germans had become victims of their own Frankenstein, but Duhamel was still able to summon up respect for them as a people. "The Germans," he said, "are among the small number of peoples who have contributed to the building up of western civilization."[32] After the war Duhamel expected to be able to address himself once more to a Germany cured of the "madmen and pathological leaders who [are] taking her to disaster."[33] He denied categorically the frequent assertion that National Socialism represented a wave of the future. For him it symbolized rather "the distant past, ancient man, the cave man, man still a prisoner of his primitive animal nature."[34]

When the war began, there was no abrupt change in Duhamel's thinking. He continued his apparently unhurried, event-by-event discussion of the international situation. He saw the war as a crusade to "deliver Germany from a criminal government, to restore her to her true genius, and bring her back forcefully into the concert of cultivated peoples."[35] Many pages here are eloquent, all are tolerant, and this at a time when few Frenchmen troubled any longer to distinguish between Germans and Nazis, as the caissons rolled through Poland to the accompaniment of dive bombers. Duhamel, however, continued to make this distinction not only in writing but over the air in his series of radio broadcasts, for he became at this time one of the leaders of French broadcasting.

The attack on France brought Duhamel close to suffering again. From May to July, 1940, the academician and man of letters found himself once again a surgeon in a hospital. This time, instead of being sent to a mobile unit near the battle area, he was stationed in a converted convent far from active fighting but not far, in the aerial war of 1940, from German bombs. His little volume *Lieu d'asile* describes this experience, and once again across his pages parade the mutilated, the amputated, the dying, and the bewildered. This time, instead of the poilus and the few displaced civilians of 1914–1918, the injured are all civilians, women and children mostly, young girls and their grandmothers. There is the same tenderness and pathos here that affected the readers of *Vie des martyrs* and *Civilisation*. This time too Duhamel's horror is accompanied by a vast pity. Here is the portrait of Madame Pochet:

Quand je l'ai vue sur son brancard, Mme Camille Pochet m'a, dès le premier coup d'œil, donné l'affligeant spectacle d'une personne à l'agonie. Elle portait, épinglée sur sa chemise, une petite fiche médicale sur laquelle on pouvait lire ce diagnostic alarmant: fracture du bassin. D'ailleurs Mme Pochet semblait plongée dans une prostration profonde: il était impossible de lui arracher un mot. Mais il n'était pas difficile de lui arracher des cris et elle me l'a bien montré.[36]

And this is a description of the demented M. Krauset:

M. Krauset a souffert d'un gros phlegmon de la main, car les fous souffrent dans leur chair, comme les autres hommes. Je lui ai ouvert son phlegmon et j'ai posé un pansement. Il accomplit son éternelle promenade en tenant droit devant lui cette main bandée de blanc. Avec une maladresse obstinée, il s'efforce de dénouer et d'arracher son pansement.

Je sens bien que M. Krauset ne nous quittera plus désormais. Il va continuer, en ronchonnant, de trébucher à travers mes pensées, comme le fantôme ridicule et tragique de cette extravagante époque.[37]

Artistically Duhamel's achievement is on a plane with the sketches of the First World War. By that achievement he could add nothing really new to his reputation, but he proved that at fifty-six, as at thirty-four, he was capable of deep feeling and of translating his emotion into moving and beautiful words. Certainly his volunteer service in the hospital added to his stature as a human being. After twenty-nine years as a writer he showed himself still capable of working as a humble practitioner of medicine, and if he has often written and spoken from the point of view of the physician and biologist, he has amply demonstrated his right to do so.

Lieu d'asile concludes on a note of hope. A child has been born in the hospital and is named Peter; mindful of his country's future, Duhamel wrote tenderly, suiting the style to the subject:

> Pierre, tu es pierre et sur cette pierre fragile nous rebâtirons notre patrie. . . .
>
> «Un petit enfant nous est né!» Il est né comme doit naître la France nouvelle, il est né d'une créature blessée, brisée, sanglante, mais fière encore, forte encore et résolue à triompher de sa misère.[38]

The paraphrase of the Bible is also noteworthy. Duhamel is ever aware of the poetic and symbolic appeal of Biblical language and of its usefulness to the writer as a form of universal discourse.

The year 1940 was a tragic one for France, but we can

detect in our author no note of discouragement, nor any hint of hatred. The German occupation forces refused Duhamel permission to publish *Lieu d'asile* unless he would agree to put in a few words in their behalf. This he refused to do, and it was not until 1944 that his sketches finally appeared.

With the demobilization of the French army in 1940 Duhamel returned to Paris, which, for personal and patriotic reasons, he refused to leave thereafter. For the duration of the occupation he wrote clandestinely and lent his support to the civilian resistance. Three books were written during this period, including *Chronique des saisons amères, 1940–1943*, which was published in 1944. In the first two parts of this book Duhamel mused upon the problems of civilization—how it developed, of what it consists, and how amidst war and man's destructive impulses it continues its evolution. The third part describes the experiences of typical French people as they try to attend to business and family concerns in occupied Paris, despite curfew, rationing, material shortages, the blackout, and the hated presence of German soldiers. These excellent descriptions recall the tramp of Nazi boots on Parisian pavements and the lurking brutality of the Gestapo and SS. Duhamel avoided appealing to emotion, describing instead the monotony as well as the tragedy of living in an occupied city.

His third book dealing with the war is *Tribulations de l'espérance* (1947), a journal commencing with the months just preceding the liberation of Paris in 1944 and continuing for more than two years afterward. By this time Duhamel was refusing to distinguish any longer between Nazi and German. He denounced the enemy's oppression in all its forms—anti-Semitism, concentration camps, forced labor, torture, and police methods. But although he was convinced that Germany as a whole was guilty, he was equally convinced of the folly of wholesale retaliation by the victors. He called for the swift punishment of guilty individuals whoever and wherever they might be. In a later novel about the war he was moved to examine at his leisure the mentality of a war criminal; for the time being he was less concerned with the analysis of the guilty than with their swift punishment.

As the Nuremburg trials got underway, Duhamel began to be impatient with the delays of justice. The slowness and thoroughness of the prosecution appeared ridiculous to him. Documentary proof of guilt, he thought, was everywhere at hand. He had himself seen it in photographs, in motion pictures, and in real life, and although he did not advocate lynch law, he said that now if ever was a time for quick justice. In conclusion he expressed the fear that a third war would come and that in it the Germans might once more find themselves on the wrong side.

At the moment of the bombing of Hiroshima Duhamel did not comment in his journal on the atomic bomb, but toward the end of the book he reflected that the use of such a weapon would certainly become world-wide and might result in the destruction of mankind. In future conflicts, he thought America would bear the brunt of the attack.

Many of Duhamel's chapters express his gratitude for the arrival of peace. He is aware that peacetime problems can be as difficult to solve as those of war, but the return of peace will give western Europe a better chance to work out its destiny. He concludes with sharp words for the bungling by France's legislators, an expression of confidence in General de Gaulle, and reinforced faith in individual man.

As we read the pages that Duhamel was inspired to write as the result of his observation of and participation in two major wars, we cannot but admire him. Through his diaries and commentaries we are able to watch his evolution from the seeker for happiness of *La Possession du monde* to the Tolstoyan pacifist of the postwar years and finally to the disillusioned observer of Hitler's legions. He was not plagued by a petty consistency, and freely admits this. He has kept little from us. His books are a progress report on one man's conscience. Certainly, Duhamel was not a major prophet. Neither was he a cynic. He was a sensitive, intelligent man forced against his will to witness the progressive deterioration of the European political situation and the onslaught of a second and more terrible conflict than the "war to end war" of 1914–1918. Yet he never despairs of man. In his war sketches he was far less calm. Into *Vie des martyrs* and *Civilisation* and the later *Lieu d'asile* he put the force of his protest. In these books and these alone did the sight and sound of suffering cause him to blend deep feeling with unrivaled prose, and the result was realistic literature in its finest expression.

3

THE LIFE AND DEATH
OF LOUIS SALAVIN

IN 1920, coincident with the appearance of the *Elégies*
and but shortly after the publication of the idealistic *La
Possession du monde,* Duhamel offered the public a one-
volume narrative entitled *Confession de minuit.* This was
a strange story about a strange man, unlike anything its
author had yet done. It dealt with the mental processes
of a perplexed and bewildered character named Louis
Salavin.

Putting down the book after the first reading, many
persons were hard put to understand either the main
character or the author's purpose in describing him. But
if the picture seemed incomplete in this volume, the

reader did not need to complain, for four subsequent volumes have continued and concluded the story. In these five books and a single short story devoted to Salavin's adventures, the reader has been given the opportunity to explore the recesses of Salavin's heart and mind. In addition Duhamel has furnished in "La Vie et mort d'un héros de roman" a detailed commentary on the genesis and development of Salavin's character as he meditated upon him and wrote down his life story. With the passing of time the Salavin novels have become one of the solid bases of Duhamel's reputation as a novelist, and we are therefore fortunate to be able to study both Salavin's character and the manner in which imagination brought him into being. In retrospect it is also interesting to see that in this series Duhamel was a pioneer in the study of the twentieth-century psychological outcast and that the kind of study here attempted has since had a surprising vogue. Subsequent novelists like Sartre and Camus have based much of their reputation on this kind of character.

Louis Salavin, the hero and narrator of the confession, introduces himself as he stands in a bar at midnight telling a stranger the story of his immediate past. His beginning is arresting. Salavin says that he was dismissed from the employ of the firm of Socque et Sureau for yielding to an irrational impulse to put his finger on Mr. Sureau's ear lobe. In so doing Salavin had not stopped to imagine Sureau's possibly violent reaction. The latter, as it turned out, went into a tantrum and threatened to call the police. Salavin then tells about his return home, describes the humble tenement where he lives, and relates the unexpectedly calm reaction of his mother to the story of his dismissal. The remainder of the book describes Salavin's unhappy attempts to keep his self-respect as he successively gave up all efforts to find a job, forwent his daily shave, and smoked far too many cigarettes. Meanwhile, by his shiftlessness and the progressive deterioration of his habits, he made himself and his mother miserable.

A peculiarly Dickensian episode in the midst of this futile existence is Salavin's encounter with a one-eyed derelict named Lhuilier. Mistaking Louis for a homeless vagrant like himself, the latter ushered him into an establishment where the jobless could earn a few pennies for bed and board by copying wrappers. Lhuilier's kindness made a deep impression on Salavin, for although he realized that Lhuilier's acceptance of him as another down-and-outer was hardly a compliment, he was touched by his spontaneous fellow-feeling for someone whom he supposed to be similarly homeless and hungry.

As *Confession de minuit* draws to a close, we find Salavin still in the unhappy mood that led him to confess his dissatisfaction with himself and his mode of living. Yet his greatest unhappiness was caused less by circumstances than by qualms of conscience. While visiting his old friend Lanoue, Salavin had been seized by a fleeting desire for his friend's wife, Martha, and this thought, which another man might have dismissed as ephemeral, and therefore unimportant, upset him. He wished to punish himself for an evil thought even though it was unaccompanied by any overt act, just as Sureau had wished to punish him for an action that was in itself innocent, though unusual. Taking the thought for the deed, Salavin decided that he was an unworthy friend, and he fled from Lanoue's apartment to wander aimlessly around Paris for several days, oppressed by a sense of guilt and a misery too great to take home. Such is Salavin's first account of himself.

The style of *Confession de minuit* foreshadows that of Duhamel's maturer years. His manner throughout is lyric and graceful, and makes much of the beauty that can be found in ordinary things even in the populous quarters of Paris. Sounds and colors generally thought unpleasant are shown to have a beauty all their own. Salavin says this about the odor of the stairwell in the apartment where he lives:

J'aime l'odeur humble et fade qui rôde, avec les courants d'air, dans cet intestin de ma maison. Si je ressuscite dans cinq cents ans, je reconnaîtrai cette odeur entre toutes les odeurs du monde. Ne vous moquez pas de moi; vous chérissez peut-être des choses plus sales et moins avouables.[1]

Similarly, the gutters of the steep Parisian streets, whose waters run down into the city's vast underground sewer system, are thus charmingly described:

Et puis, le ruisseau chante quand même sa petite complainte. Cela me fait penser à des prairies, à des fleuves, à des pays que je ne connaîtrai jamais. C'est de l'eau civilisée, de l'eau pourrie. De l'eau, de l'eau malgré tout! La mer, les grands lacs, les torrents dans la montagne! Si vous passez rue Lhomond, le soir, assez tard, à l'heure où les bruits de Paris s'engourdissent et s'endorment, vous entendrez, au-dessous de vous, tous les égouts de la montagne Sainte-Geneviève qui chantent doucement, comme des cataractes lointaines. Ce sont les cataractes de mes voyages, à moi.[2]

Salavin, who enjoys these humble sounds and smells, is no ordinary man. Even his view of happiness is unique. In an episode of some length he reveals his preoccupation with it. One day, despite unemployment and despair, Salavin felt himself suddenly possessed of a joy so powerful, so overwhelming that he could not bear to keep it to himself. In order to share his effervescent spirits with

someone, he hurried to the apartment of his friend
Lanoue, and with him and his wife he began the "expendi-
ture" of his joy. Then, for no good reason at all, he felt
his good spirits begin to leave him as suddenly as they
had arrived. He says:

> La nuit était venue depuis longtemps, et la lampe, et la
> fraîcheur, quand, sans la moindre raison apparente, sans la
> moindre raison intelligible, une chose nouvelle apparut en moi.
> Il y eut un instant précis où je m'aperçus que j'étais un peu
> moins heureux qu'à la minute précédente. Voilà! Je ne peux
> pas vous exprimer cela plus clairement. . . .
> J'eus envie de crier, d'appeler à l'aide, au secours, comme
> un matelot en détresse sur un esquif avarié. C'était bien
> inutile: la solitude s'élargissait autour de moi, ténébreuse,
> impénétrable, mortelle.[3]

Elsewhere Salavin tells us that in his whole life he had
never known more than four or five hours of real joy. In
the main, a modest contentment had been his lot, the
nearest to happiness that he could come. This frailty of
human happiness is one of Duhamel's favorite themes.
Happiness, he thinks, is easily expended. Unheralded it
comes, and it must be hoarded and used up gradually.
This idea is foreshadowed by passages in *La Possession
du monde* and in the prewar *Propos critiques*. In the latter work Duhamel says of a character in one of Chennevière's plays that he was "too weak to allow himself to
expend safely any large quantity of joy," so evidently
the idea of the fragility of happiness had long been with
him. In Salavin's case this was but one of many curious
thoughts, the forerunners sometimes of curious actions,
which made it difficult for readers to bear with him.
The remark was often made, "What a pitiful creature
Salavin is."

The temptation to dismiss Louis Salavin must be

resisted. His problems and the problems of those like him are always with us. As our environment grows more complex, there is every reason to believe that the little man everywhere finds himself increasingly confused, and being aware of his confusion, he is also aware how far his achievements fall short of his aspirations and expectations. He then becomes in real life a counterpart of Salavin, a failure all too conscious of his failure. Salavin tells us on one occasion: "I do not try to be odd; I am not different from other men." Yet when a mood of despair is upon him, he says: "I spent the whole night hating myself."[4]

The critics, noting Salavin's capacity for self-castigation, inquired what manner of man his creator had called into being, and Duhamel answered:

Salavin est un homme moderne, un homme quelconque, mais en qui des hommes venus de tous les points de l'horizon moral, en qui des hommes différents par l'âge, le métier, la condition sociale, la nationalité, la race, peuvent à certaines heures et s'ils sont de bonne foi retrouver quelque chose qui leur soit humblement ou mystérieusement commun.[5]

Some of the critics, however, have not accepted this view. Salavin's alleged lack of balance has attracted the writers of scholarly monographs, and the persistence of the view that Salavin is mad, or at least slightly mad, has annoyed Duhamel to the point of a categorical denial. He says:

Médecin, je ne considère pas Salavin comme un malade et surtout pas comme un paranoïaque. J'entends qu'il n'y a pas lieu de traiter Salavin. Ou alors que l'on traite dans des maisons de santé tous les hommes qui souffrent sous l'effort de leur pensée.[6]

This disclaimer is clear, but a French dissertation on

Salavin is, nevertheless, entitled *Georges Duhamel: le clinicien dans l'art du roman.* In its pages Salavin is treated as a psychopath.

All question of illness aside, many critics did not take to Salavin. If the introspective Salavin was ignorant of psychoanalysis, his creator was not, and because Salavin has come to exist in the twentieth century, men are prone to call his worries complexes, his desires libidos, and his ideals delusions. Duhamel has said that he is the "petit-neveu de l'Hidalgo,"[7] but most people are even more persistently reminded of Jean Jacques Rousseau and others among us whose problem is an alienation from the society in which they live.

The mixed reception of *Confession de minuit* and of its unusual, perplexing protagonist probably results from a number of things. The novel marked, for one thing, a sudden shift in the direction of Duhamel's writing. The introspective Salavin with his mental agonies was far removed from the wounded heroes of *Vie des martyrs* and *Civilisation.* To many the simple suffering and the moving realism of the war sketches had conveyed a message. But what message did poor, tortured Salavin convey, himself no victim of war, no victim of anything except his own uncertainties? He seemed *sui generis,* with no relation to the rest of mankind. The public was not yet ready to accept the "outsider" as a character in fiction. Moreover, what seemed obscurity in the intent of *Confession de minuit* was augmented by the fact that when the novel appeared it had to be taken as complete. There was nothing to indicate that Salavin's confession was to be the cornerstone of a larger work. When Duhamel later took the public into his confidence, he confessed that when he began writing the Salavin story, he himself had not been sure how it would turn out. Initial critical judgments, then, lacked the complete picture which we are now able to see with the whole series before us; they lacked too, perhaps, the fuller understanding of the Salavin type of character which we now have and which Duhamel himself helped to create.

In a book of short stories called *Les Hommes abandonnés* (1921) Duhamel included another piece about Salavin, with the title "Nouvelle rencontre de Salavin." In this short narrative he shifted to the third person. Salavin has returned to Lanoue's apartment and has seduced Martha. Disconsolate, he thinks to wander away from the scene, only to be awakened by the bartender of the cafe where he made his confession, and to discover that he has been having a bad dream. This account, excellent as an independent sketch, fits admirably into the larger narrative.

The second long narrative, called *Deux hommes*, followed three years later in 1924. *Le Journal de Salavin* came in 1927, *Le Club des Lyonnais* in 1929, and the final volume, *Tel qu'en lui-même*, in 1932. This is the full cycle, and in attempting to evaluate it the critics had to revise some of their earlier judgments.

Deux hommes is the story of a friendship, an unsuccessful one, in which Salavin finds out the difference between good intentions and good conduct. A chance encounter in a cafe has led to an association with Edouard Loisel, a happily married and successful chemist. Salavin meanwhile has also married. His wife is Marguerite, the loyal seamstress who was his neighbor in the tenement. The beginnings of the friendship between Salavin and Loisel are commonplace enough. Loisel deserted his usual table companions at lunch to sit with Salavin, and they began to talk. As their acquaintance progressed, they felt each other out, moving cautiously but inevitably to a complete understanding. They wished to share each other's lives in every respect. They talked about each other to their wives and finally arranged a family get-together. Salavin cheerfully ate lobster, knowing that it would disagree with him, and his wife, who was unaccustomed to wine, drank it at dinner.

As their friendship deepened, Edouard became more and more Salavin's benefactor. He arranged for him to get a job at the plant where he worked, and when Salavin's son was ill, he sent him to the seashore for a vacation. As Edouard became more and more successful in his work, he was named director of research in his laboratory, and his salary was doubled. Salavin the while was still Salavin. He seemed not to progress materially or spiritually. He felt a compulsion to tell Edouard all about his past mistakes, his self-torture, and self-deprecation. The latter, on the other hand, could not refrain from sharing with his friend all his joys and triumphs, and Salavin found it increasingly difficult to enter into Loisel's happiness without envy and irritation.

The crisis in their friendship came when Salavin at last reproached Edouard for trying to be his benefactor. Edouard, who had noted Salavin's increasing moodiness and had blamed himself for it, said: "Louis, what have I done to you?" This question, tactlessly repeated, at last drew forth a brutal answer from Salavin:

Je ne t'ai jamais rien demandé. Tu m'a obligé d'accepter tout. Pour que tu sois toi, il me fallait tout accepter. Tu m'as contraint d'être faible, pour pouvoir, toi, être fort. . . . Sous prétexte de tout me donner, tu m'a tout pris, même mes rares heures de liberté, même de l'amitié.[8]

Edouard was severely shaken by these accusations, and his friendship with Salavin came to an end. But Salavin watched his former friend leave with sadistic pleasure. Had he not warned Edouard that he was incapable of friendship? Was it his fault that Edouard had insisted on being his friend?

There is an epilogue in the form of Edouard's reflections. On learning of the death of Salavin's boy, he wrote his former friend a letter but received no reply. As he thought about their past relationship he said to himself:

«Nous sommes deux hommes intelligents, généreux, malgré tout, et bons dans notre faiblesse. Nous souhaitons que la concorde et l'harmonie régissent toutes les actions des peuples; et, pourtant, nous n'avons pu mettre à l'unisson nos deux voix.

«Eh bien, c'est à recommencer!

«Je recommencerai! Etre toute franchise, toute loyauté, toute droiture, voilà mon grand, mon unique désir. Et je veux croire que ce désir de pureté n'est pas la seule pureté des hommes.»[9]

In other words, Duhamel asks his reader to believe that in this unsuccessful friendship he is to see reflected the essential problem of human relations. To do so he must accept the assumption that Edouard and Louis are truly representative. But even if it is true, as some psychologists insist, that all of us are neurotic to some extent, there remains by common consent, or at least by custom, a dividing line between the normal and the slightly abnormal person. We have all known someone like Salavin as he appears in *Deux hommes,* but some readers find their credulity strained to hear it said that Salavin's problem epitomizes that of all ordinary friendships. The broken relationship between these two men points up the obstacles in the way of amity, but their failure also appears as a special case. The Salavin of the midnight confession provokes more sympathy than this one. His dilemma, as he tells about it, appears to be without a solution within the framework of everyday life. Here is the way he looks to himself:

> Monsieur, vous allez prendre de moi une idée qui a bien des chances d'être fausse. Vous allez penser que j'ai un sale caractère, que je suis misanthrope. Moi, misanthrope! C'est absurde! J'aime les hommes et ce n'est pas ma faute si, le plus souvent, je ne peux les supporter. Je rêve de concorde, je rêve d'une vie harmonieuse, confiante, comme une étreinte universelle. Quand je pense aux hommes, je les trouve si dignes d'affection que les larmes m'en viennent aux yeux. Je voudrais n'avoir pour eux que des paroles amicales, je voudrais vider mon cœur dans leur cœur; je voudrais être associé à leurs projets, à leurs actes, tenir une place dans leur vie, leur montrer comme je suis capable de constance, de fidélité, de sacrifice. Mais il y a en moi quelque chose de suscéptible, de sensible, d'irritable.[10]

Finally, with the full realization that Salavin and his troubles were to be with him for some time, Duhamel began the third book of the series, the *Journal de Salavin*. Here we follow his pathetic hero another step in his quest for a new and different self, or at least for a working relationship between his old self and a godless universe. As in the beginning Salavin is once more the narrator. He tells us that he has resolved to become a lay saint, and to keep a record of his progress.

Lest his diary fall into profane hands, he began by substituting the word *tourist* for the word *saint*, further to conceal his purpose; then, feeling that this practice made his efforts ridiculous, he decided to refer to "saint" by its initial letter only. As we read the journal, we come to realize how difficult it is to achieve sainthood in these times. A partial retreat from the world appeared to offer certain advantages, and so Salavin left his wife and mother for a bachelor retreat. Once a week he visited his family.

In this new phase Salavin's philosophy was based on helping his fellows. He intended to lend a hand whenever and wherever he could, but he discovered to his astonishment that the people he tried to help were as ungrateful for his intervention as he had been when Loisel did him favors. At the office his quest for sainthood was ill-timed and ill-received. Among his fellow-workers were a pimply-faced young man named Jibé Tastard and a nasty fellow named Arbelot. After tolerating the latter's sneers for a time, Salavin reduced him to silence by the unsaintly procedure of throwing an inkwell at him. Then he apologized but realized with mingled sorrow and relief that Arbelot thought him a hypocrite.

Jibé, who was a sneak thief, proved similarly unsatisfactory as an object of saintly deeds. Salavin replaced the sums Jibé stole from the petty cash and so earnestly desired to effect his reformation and cure that even after Jibé was dismissed, he continued to give him money out of his own pocket. This he could little afford to do. Besides, he knew that Jibé was spending all his money in the pursuit of vice.

Salavin's attempts to do good in his apartment house were likewise doomed. His gruff landlady resented his would-be kindness in bringing up her bottle of milk every morning ("I wonder if the fellow who tampers with my milk spits in it," she mutters to herself), and his attempts to help a hopeless drunkard were similarly unappreciated.

Salavin's crisis of conscience came when he learned through another employee, Max Aufrère, that the products of the Cilpo, or Pasteurized and Oxygenized Milk Company, were not oxygenized at all. This fact, dropped nonchalantly by Aufrère, shocked Salavin. He felt that the public was being cheated and that he was helping in the deception. His honest if naïve reaction was to write to the police. The countermove of M. Mayer, Salavin's employer, was no less forthright but far less naïve. When the police showed him the letter, he did not discharge Salavin. Instead, he gave him a job in his own office, where he could keep an eye on him and keep him out of mischief.

Hard on the heels of this incident, Salavin played an unheroic role in a theater panic. Sainthood forgotten, he ran for the door as did everyone else, trampling people as he went. More than anything else, this reaction disillusioned him as to his actual goodness. Still he refused to accept himself. In anguish he cries out: "This is the way I am and yet I cannot accept myself thus. I cannot make up my mind to be Salavin forever. I must be helped so that I may change."[11]

At this point Salavin decided to appeal to the ministers of religion. He knew that faith would not come if he merely willed it. He must be shown the way. He wrote to a Protestant minister named Croquet, who was recommended by Aufrère. Unfortunately, the pastor proved to be a kind of businessman-psychologist, hurried, brusque, and impersonal. His experience with the Catholic confessional was equally unsatisfactory. The priest to whom he confessed was uninterested in his plight and turned him away with minor penance and routine consolation. A second encounter with the confessional was more fruitful, and he decided that the young Abbé Pradelles, who heard his story and prayed with him, was indeed a saint. In greater despair than before, he turned back to his unsaintly self. As a final, hopeless gesture, he gave the erring Jibé, now far gone in degradation, his only overcoat.

Shortly thereafter, Salavin contracted pneumonia. With his last remaining strength he found himself listening to the babblings of the vagabond Lhuilier, who turned up in the bed next to him in the charity hospital.

In this story, more poignant by far than either *Confession de minuit* or *Deux hommes,* Salavin seems more human than before. His gropings for sainthood, bizarre though they appear, are somehow more credible than were his actions as son, husband, and friend. His search for goodness, and his unshaken belief that it is possible to acquire it, touch a responsive chord in the reader. He found to his astonishment that in a world where people are only relatively honest and relatively decent, the man who tries to be absolute in his loyalties is at a disadvantage. The world appears to reject him with as much force and even more scorn than it reserves for the absolutely dishonest and indecent man. The resulting discouragement, which the saints of all ages have had to face, Salavin in his weakness could not bear. The suffering he inflicted on his wife and mother by leaving home and the worry he caused his relatively honest employer Mayer were but a few of the unhappy results of Salavin's conduct. And his own sense of failure was greater than ever.

From the critics came protests that they had had enough of Salavin. François le Grix, perturbed at Duhamel's treatment of the religious problem, wrote a long analysis of *Journal de Salavin,* in which he discussed the quest for sainthood without religion.[12] He took Duhamel to task for superficiality and a lack of real understanding of religion, but he liked the book on the whole. Robert Kemp was impatient with Salavin, saying irritably: "Why can't Salavin tell a villain from an honest man?"[13] César Santelli, always more sympathetic, wrote many years later:

La vérité est que le *Journal de Salavin,* s'il nous contraint à penser, à discuter avec nous-mêmes, n'en reste pas moins une œuvre taillée à même la vie, avec une galérie de personnages si vivants et si proches de nous que je vous défie, non pas seulement de fermer l'ouvrage avant d'en avoir lu le dernier feuillet, mais de ne pas le rouvrir aussitôt pour revivre telle scène qui continue à vous hanter.[14]

Journal de Salavin is in many ways the best volume in the series. Here more than elsewhere Salavin is truly human. It is perhaps a little unusual to touch one's employer's ear, and even less so to break up a friendship deliberately, in neurotic fashion. It may be even less usual to attempt sainthood, but the significance of Salavin's outlandish conduct is easier to accept in this volume. In some way or other every man faces the problem of ideals and how to relate them to reality, and though Salavin never finds a solution, Duhamel's description of his struggles contributes something to our understanding of the problem.

The fourth volume finds Salavin once more at home, having abandoned sainthood to live with his family. Through his former associate, Max Aufrère, he is introduced to the Club des Lyonnais, which gives the book its title. On the rue des Lyonnais an ill-assorted group of revolutionaries, including Communists, fellow travelers, and mere curiosity-seekers, meets in a cobbler's shop. Legrain, the old cobbler, has turned revolutionary in order to work for a better world for his talented sixteen-year-old daughter, who is dying. The Communists, of whom there are a half dozen, are well drawn. We have met them elsewhere, some in the newspapers, some in real life. Among the hangers-on is an apparently robust playboy, César Devrigny, whose sole aim in life is the pursuit of women.

Salavin was greatly attracted to the Communists. He

enjoyed being among people who unlike himself had strong convictions. Meanwhile, Aufrère was trying to pull him in the opposite direction. Aufrère's own philosophy consisted mainly in not having any. He pretended that he was a mere spectator at the show of life. For Salavin, whose moods seldom permitted him sufficient calm to be a dispassionate observer, Aufrère's point of view was as much a revelation as the convictions of the Communists.

Duhamel gave this story a more complicated plot than those that went before it, putting Salavin this time in the context of a conspiracy. The Communists needed to have a check cashed by someone not suspected of party affiliation. Devrigny, when asked to do it, showed his cowardice by running away. Aufrère, true to his role as a spectator, at first refused, but yielded to an appeal to his vanity. At this juncture Devrigny found out that he had syphilis, and despite Salavin's attempted consolation he slit his wrists and died. The police, meanwhile, began to close their net around the Communist cell, and all those who had frequented the cobbler's shop were arrested, including Salavin. The lodgings of everyone in the group were turned upside down, and when Salavin's apartment was searched, his mother was so shocked that she suffered a fatal heart attack. Marguerite, bewildered by these latest and least comprehensible doings of her husband, was in despair.

Outside the Communist conspiracy, and much more important to the reader who is interested in Salavin's progress, is the continued theme of Salavin's determination to change his soul. Just what change did Salavin contemplate? He explains this specifically as follows:

Je suis en possession de tout mon bon sens. Vous comprenez bien qu'il ne s'agit pas de changer d'âme avec Pierre ou avec

Paul. Il s'agit d'une expérience raisonnable. Mon âme, c'est quarante années d'habitudes, quarante années de menus événements, de pensées, de gestes, quarante années de paroles, toujours les mêmes. Ce que j'appelle mon âme, c'est une carcasse, usée déjà plus qu'à demi, avec des poils, des plis, des cicatrices et des durillons. C'est un canapé que vous ne connaissez pas, mais qui n'est pas dépourvu d'expérience.[15]

Salavin has defined his soul in understandable terms. He is not using theological or psychological jargon. He is giving a common-sense definition of his ego and personality, the essence that makes him Salavin instead of Aufrère or Devrigny, and it is difficult for him to see how this can be changed.

At least Salavin has made some progress. If he cannot accept himself, now he at least knows himself better. He knows that he is not responsible for his wayward thoughts. He has turned his back on the kind of torment he felt when he harbored a momentary desire for his friend's wife. He says:

Mais je ratifie rarement mes pensées par mes actes. Ratifier ou ne pas ratifier ses pensées par ses actes! Il m'a fallu des années pour assigner à la vertu cette humble définition. «En vérité, celui qui a regardé la femme du prochain avec désir, il a déjà commis l'adultère dans son cœur. . . .» Mais non! mais non! J'ai souffert pendant vingt années à cause de cette maudite phrase! Tout le monde regarde avec désir la femme du prochain. La vertu est, précisément, d'enfermer tout ça dans son cœur, avec les autres saletés.[16]

This was at least a modicum of consolation.

This fourth book is the first to give much attention to subsidiary characters, all of whom are well contrived. The groveling of the conceited Devrigny when he discovers his disease is excellently portrayed, as is the nonchalance of Aufrère.

As usual the critics were divided. R. Bourget-Pailleron, writing in *Opinion,* called the Communist cell an out-growth of Duhamel's trip to Moscow.[17] Benjamin Cré-mieux, in *Annales politiques et littéraires,* said he was dis-satisfied with Salavin's queerness, but added hopefully that he seemed less abnormal with each succeeding volume.[18]

The title of the next and final book, *Tel qu'en lui-même,* is borrowed from a line of Mallarmé's famous sonnet on Edgar Allan Poe. In this volume, Salavin's adventure reaches its decisive and final phase. As the story opens we meet three new characters, Louis D'Argoult and his wife Gertrude, enroute for Marseille with their child. Their seat companion on the train is Simon Chavegrand, whom the reader recognizes as an outwardly altered Salavin. Simon is clean-shaven, wears no glasses, and has dyed his hair.

An unchecked impulse, reminiscent of Gide's *acte gratuit,* and quite like the whim that made Salavin touch his employer's ear, led Simon to throw himself on the railroad track to save the D'Argoults' child from an on-coming train. This act earned him the unsolicited friend-ship of the parents, and the four decided to travel together on the boat to Africa. They finally arrived in Tunis, their common destination. Simon had come to Africa (an area also beloved by Gide, incidentally) to manage a phono-graph shop. Once there, he was drawn into heroic postures. He tried by kindness to win his Arab shop assistant, Moktar, from his evil ways, and he devoted his spare time to caring for native patients in the local hos-pital. Eventually, he allowed himself to be exposed to typhus in order to test a new vaccine, but he left the hospital in disgust when he came to believe that selfish motives rather than a genuine love for humanity had prompted his action. Meanwhile, at the phonograph shop, matters went from bad to worse. Moktar was wanted by the police for his criminal activities, and when Salavin arrived the shop was surrounded by armed men. Salavin stepped out to urge the Arab boy to give himself up, and as he did so Moktar shot him in the leg. The wound became infected, and in desperation the D'Argoults opened up Chavegrand's trunk to try to learn his identity. Finding out that their friend was really named Salavin and that he had a wife in Paris, they sent for her. Marguerite came at once, and with one leg amputated, Chavegrand-Salavin left for home. Once there, in Marguerite's presence, lying on the well-worn couch where he had frittered away so many unhappy hours, Salavin died.

Death is not an unexpected conclusion to Salavin's story. From the beginning it has been apparent that a happy ending for him is out of the question. Salavin was doomed to failure because he was able to follow the Socratic admonition only in part. He knew himself, but he was not able or willing to follow the corollary: accept thyself. Despite his strenuous efforts to escape from self, Salavin could never be other than Salavin, and in this lay the final tragedy.

The emotions aroused in the reader by Salavin's last adventure are pity and sympathy, for once unmixed with irritation. For a curious result of Duhamel's art is that the farther he takes his character from the workaday world, the less abnormal he appears. This Simon Chavegrand is the same Louis Salavin whose tortures were self-inflicted, but as we know him better, our sympathy is less frequently marred by exasperation. P.-H. Simon sums up his own reaction to the series with these words:

Tout se passe . . . comme si Salavin constatait en fin de compte une impuissance de l'homme à se dépasser par les

seules forces de la nature. Son histoire, c'est le drame de la
rédemption de l'homme par l'homme, ou de la rédemption sans
médiateur, ou du salut sans la grace: et c'est aussi l'histoire
d'un échec.[19]

Other critics, writing shortly after the appearance of
the last book, were less charitable. John Charpentier, in
the *Mercure de France,* reviewing the series, dismissed
the work as an attempt at perfectibility through self-
knowledge, an idea he thought chimerical.[20] Henri Massis
repeated his conviction that Salavin's creator was a writer
of power, but repeated also his belief that Duhamel was
confused as to his philosophical position. He ended a
trifle bitterly: "Il y a un peu de Salavin dans M. Duhamel."[21] Gabriel Marcel, the Christian existentialist, wrote
in *L'Europe nouvelle* that at the height of his powers
Duhamel had written himself into a corner, a prisoner of
his success.[22] To soften the blow, he concluded that
Duhamel would probably find his way out. John Charpentier had also confessed an unshakeable dislike for the
character of Salavin. He said that he was glad that he
was dead, and that it had taken all of Duhamel's considerable talent to interest him in Salavin's life story.[23]

The public seems to have thought otherwise. Interest
in Salavin continued to grow even after finis had been
written to the series. Finally, in response to repeated
questions about the origin and development of Salavin's
adventures, Duhamel furnished in *Deux patrons* (1937)
a detailed account of the composition of the novel. He
entitled his essay "Vie et mort d'un héros de roman."
Duhamel here assures us that he did not choose to write
of Salavin. Salavin chose him. And this statement must
be taken literally in order to understand Duhamel's
methods of literary creation, to be described later in his
memoirs. He says that he first conceived of the character

of Salavin in 1914, and he at once wrote out the ten pages
that were to become the first chapter of *Confession de
minuit*. With the outbreak of war, Salavin was laid aside,
though the author dimly felt his presence at his side, and
he believes that during the war years Salavin's character
was ripening in the subconscious area of his mind. "I even
believe," he says, "that the most important part of [his]
life story [was] accomplished outside of the laborious
moments [of writing], in the long intervals of meditation
and waiting."[24] After the war Duhamel started to write
of Salavin again, with the impression that "the five years
of waiting . . . had strengthened and nourished him.
The phantom had taken on density and color. From that
time on, he appeared as I was to see him for a long time
at my side."[25] We are told that there was no model for
Salavin. He was a composite creation whose name was
borrowed from that of the well-known Parisian chocolate
shops.

The short story "Nouvelle rencontre de Salavin" was
written next. After its completion Duhamel thought that
he was done with Louis Salavin. After a short interval
he says that he began to write a story about a friendship
between two men, and "scarcely had I come into the
presence of the two heroes of my projected book when
I discovered with astonishment that one of the two characters was Salavin."[26] He had thought that the *Confession*
and the subsequent "Rencontre" had unburdened him of
the character. It was the intrusion of Salavin into still
another work that made him realize that Salavin was not
"written out" but was destined rather to be the central
character of a long work. Volume then succeeded volume,
and Duhamel further confides to us that he was finally
taken by surprise by the end that presented itself. "I did
not foresee," he says, "that after the last sigh was uttered,

the last line written, I should feel an impulse to raise my
voice all of a sudden, I the silent confidant, and address
myself to the dead man, my wretched brother, the companion of so many years, and bid him a tender farewell."[27]
Salavin, then, had become as real to Duhamel as a person
of flesh and blood. As Balzac once said: "Let us return to
reality. To whom shall I marry Eugénie Grandet?"

Admitting that Salavin was not an admirable character,
Duhamel defends him none the less. Novelists, he says,
seldom write about Plutarchian heroes. He admits that
Salavin is a failure. "The story of Salavin is," he writes,
"in sum, the story of a defeat, and if one judges by appearances alone, the story of an obstinate, repeated, and, one
may say, incurable defeat."[28] This fact he did not consider a valid reason for eliminating Salavin as a hero of
fiction. Again critics disagreed. The critic A. de Luppe
called the Salavin cycle an "œuvre dépourvue de significa-
tion profonde, mais décor plein de vie, où j'aimerais voir
un autre homme que le lamentable Salavin."[29] Harsh
words. Others even complained that it was the novelist's
duty to control his characters, an extreme view, certainly,
which pretends to tell the artist how to create his art.

Time has softened these judgments. Today most critics
agree that the Salavin cycle is one of the solid foundations
of Duhamel's reputation. Whether he is merely to be
accepted as a striking example of twentieth-century man,
as Duhamel hopes, no one can yet be certain. It is prob-
able, however, that if interest in psychoanalysis continues, as it seems likely to do, Salavin will remain alive.
As long, in other words, as our relation to the universe
and to each other is unresolved for us and for all mankind,
so long will Salavin interest us. If Salavin seems to many
persons a man in whom they do not wish to see themselves
mirrored, his character is at least a partial reflection of

some aspect of each one of us. If this is true, Duhamel's achievement is not a small one.

To those who complain that Salavin is hard to live with, Duhamel says: "What about me? I have had to live with him for twenty years!"

4

THE THEORY AND
PRACTICE OF FICTION

DURING the nineteen twenties, while he was writing about Salavin, Duhamel gave considerable thought to the problems involved in writing fiction, and when his theories had taken form, he wrote *Essai sur le roman* (1925), a self-revealing but not altogether penetrating study of the technique of the novel and short story. He opened his essay with a brief résumé of the history of the novel in France from Rabelais onward, commented on the contemporary French novel, and brought into his discussion, for the purpose of illustration, the work of a few writers from other countries.

Duhamel's choice of reading among the best-known

French writers is interesting. Like any literate Frenchman he is well-read in the French novel of the nineteenth century, and he devoted careful attention to the principles and the practice of his immediate predecessors. His analysis of the realism and naturalism of Balzac, Flaubert, and Zola led him to contrast their revolutionary techniques with those in vogue in the present century. He confessed that in his youth he had read adventure stories, a genre in which he believed the English excelled, but that in his maturer years he had been most attracted by psychological realism. Such realism, he believed, was the twentieth-century's contribution to the art of fiction. To achieve it, the writer must have a profound knowledge of the aspect of life he is writing about. He believed that the documentation and research so esteemed by Flaubert and Zola were a poor substitute for firsthand information. Indispensable to the writer, instead, was the kind of experience that stemmed from long and intimate association with the environments and persons that he intended to depict. Admitting that an admiral may write unskillfully of the sea whereas Rimbaud, without ever having seen the ocean, might write competently of it, Duhamel held that such cases were exceptional. He wanted to see what he called the scientific pretensions of naturalism abandoned, along with Balzac's theory of the master passion. Instead, according to Duhamel, modern fiction should strive to create individuals and to study their psychology. Here in capsule form is his doctrine:

Le but suprême du romancier est de nous rendre sensible l'âme humaine, de nous la faire connaître et aimer dans sa grandeur comme dans sa misère, dans ses victoires et dans ses défaites. Admiration et pitié, telle est la devise du roman.[1]

This is a somewhat vague statement of principles,

coupled as it is with a condemnation of nineteenth-century methods, which Duhamel seems to identify with an artificial kind of documentation ascribed to Flaubert and Zola. It is also a strange point of view, for as recent criticism has shown, and as a practitioner as able as Duhamel might have been expected to perceive, Flaubert and Zola cannot rightfully be called superficial in their belief that science, and especially psychology, can be useful for the novelist. In point of fact both men practiced care in their use of research, never regarding it as a substitute for firsthand knowledge.

Duhamel's definition of realism is linked to his personal experience, thus:

J'apprécie, sans nul doute, les ouvrages d'imagination, mais je donne toujours la préférence aux livres qui manifestent une épreuve personnelle, saignante, frémissante de la vérité humaine. Un romancier bien doué pourrait toujours, s'il s'en donnait la peine, inventer une foule d'épisodes captivants ou poignants sur la vie des détenus politiques en Sibérie. Mais à quoi bon inventer, dans notre malheureuse époque? Quelle fiction ne pâlirait au prix de la monstrueuse réalité?[2]

This definition is also clarified elsewhere. Asking what is left for the novelist to depict, he replies: "Man, and an essentially human pathos."[3] Modern novelists, he goes on, should be less preoccupied with apparent reality than with the underlying, hidden reality. They must not waste their time and energy in the brilliant painting of outward appearances. So long as a preoccupation with the inner man, or soul, remains paramount, Duhamel is not too particular as to the external aspects of a novel. The genre too may vary. When he wrote this essay, he believed that the day of the *conte moral* had about ended, though in his later years he was to return to this form again and again. He deprecates the historical novel somewhat, because it takes the novelist away from what he regards as his proper field of concentration. These restrictions excepted, subject matter and technique are of little concern. "The essential thing," he says, "is for the novelist not to lose sight of his goal, which is to search for the eternal truth about man." To accomplish this he advocates a "careful blending of the real and the imaginary,"[4] which is, of course, his own method.

The novelist, as Duhamel sees him, needs a touch of romanticism if he is to be successful, but his primary tool will be a gift for accurate observation of one's own contemporaries, "to be a witness for one's own era."[5] The prime requisite of every good novel, he says, is that it should hold the reader's interest. The true novel is essentially a gallery of portraits; that is, character is all-important. The reader must become attached to, though not necessarily really fond of, the principal character. In these days, he says, we are skeptical of heroes of the Plutarchian sort, and consequently the novelist must write of a credible person:

Un personnage n'est pas représentatif dès la conception. Il peut le devenir. Une grande innocence est sans doute nécessaire à la création d'un personnage représentatif. Le véritable romancier ne dit pas: je vais peindre le Français moyennement instruit, au début du vingtième siècle. Le vrai romancier peint un «bonhomme.» Il se trouve parfois que ce bonhomme représente merveilleusement bien le Français au début du XXe siècle, il se trouve même, plus rarement, que ce bonhomme représente l'homme tout court, l'homme de toujours et de partout.[6]

If the representative element does not eventually appear in a given personage, that personage will be a failure. Duhamel is so sure of this that he confesses having abandoned an idea for a hero because the character he visualized was so odd that he felt certain that he would not interest anyone. This point of view inevitably rules out characters invented solely to prove a thesis. The reader's sympathy must be with the individual in his strength and weakness, in his victories and failures. Admiration and pity are the keys to the success of a novel. Good causes can be furthered in ways other than literature. The novel, Duhamel insists, must not be an ill-disguised forum or a social laboratory, as conceived by Zola. A character, not a thesis, will engender events and thereby determine the course of the action. Some of this is sound doctrine as far as it goes, but it is rather unfair to Zola, who, like Duhamel, practiced better than he preached.

Plot, Duhamel believes, is the first thing forgotten after a reader has laid a novel aside:

L'action des ouvrages romanesques, l'action ou, pour mieux dire, la péripétie, voilà ce que nous oublions tout de suite, à peine le livre fermé.[7]

"What then is left?" he asks, and to his own question replies:

Ce qui nous reste pour toujours, c'est un visage torturé d'espérance, deux mains blanches qui se tordent, un petit carré de lumière sur le parquet d'une chambre. Une odeur, un goût, moins peut-être.[8]

As a kind of footnote to these interesting but rather incomplete statements of his literary credo, we find scattered throughout Duhamel's writings a number of opinions on the foreign authors whose works he has read. The list is not long, but at least he has become acquainted with the most famous of the world's masterpieces. Among the British authors whom he mentions are Kipling, Steven-

son, Conrad, Wells, and Galsworthy, and of older generations, Swift and Butler. Of the early Victorian novelists
the Brontës alone get more than passing mention. He
compliments the British collectively for their psychological insight and for their ability to "cast blinding light
into the darkest recesses of the soul."[9]

Duhamel appears to be even less well acquainted with
American authors. He is fond of Emerson, whom he
sometimes quotes, and of Whitman, who was an early
inspiration to him. There are also occasional references
in his work to Poe and Thoreau. This is apparently almost
the limit of his exploration of the American literary scene,
for he wrote somewhat deprecatingly in 1930:

> Si l'opulente Amérique du Nord rêve d'être, quelque jour,
> une nation souveraine, qu'elle se hâte de susciter, d'inspirer
> un plus grand nombre d'âmes libres et rayonnantes. Whitman,
> Poe, Emerson, Thoreau, c'est fort bien, mais ce n'est pas assez
> pour cent millions d'hommes et pour deux siècles d'histoire.[10]

Nor has time remedied the sketchiness of Duhamel's
knowledge of American literature. In 1948, commenting
on the dearth of French classics available in the bookshops
of North Africa, he dismissed the American novels of
the day in cavalier fashion:

> A défaut de ceux-ci, les gens se mettent à lire du *roman
> américain,* et même à le lire en anglais. Et, qu'est-ce que ce
> roman américain? C'est une bonne marque de roman fabriqué
> selon une formule ou sur les procédés de Balzac, Zola et
> Maupassant. Vous-voyez, l'Amérique a le génie de l'applica-
> tion, même en littérature. Elle donne, là comme ailleurs, une
> honnête marchandise qui risque, si l'on n'y prend gard, de faire
> oublier dans le monde entier, la qualité excéptionnelle.[11]

And in 1950, in a private conversation with the present
writer he referred sadly to our literature as consisting

solely of Emerson, Whitman, Poe, and Thoreau, as if
having fixed these names in his mind, he had never read
any further. The late Professor Fernand Baldensperger,
himself widely read in American literature, of which he
was a great admirer, dismissed this as truly "superficial
ignorance" of American writers.[12]

Among the Germans Goethe gets frequent and admiring
mention, as does Duhamel's friend the late Stefan Zweig.
Among the Russians Duhamel speaks occasionally of
Tolstoi, Dostoevski, and Gorki. Cervantes alone is men-
tioned among the Spaniards and D'Annunzio among the
Italians.

The literature of the Scandinavian countries, especially
as regards the novel, is dismissed in these words:

> Les Scandinaves en particulier, qui nous ont donné des
> philosophes du premier rang, de grands poètes, des drama-
> turges admirables en étaient encore, en ce qui concerne cette
> expérience du réalisme, à faire des gammes et des arpèges.
> Ils sortaient à peine de l'épopée et des légendes.[13]

Yet another phase of Duhamel's outlook as a student
and practitioner of the art of writing is reflected in his
occasional miscellaneous critical essays on French and
foreign writers whom he has particularly enjoyed. None
of these remarks, although they make pleasant reading,
adds much to Duhamel's reputation. In the book *Deux
patrons* he talks of Erasmus and Cervantes, and a second
volume, *Les Confessions sans pénitence* (1941), is made
up of essays on Rousseau, Descartes, Pascal, and Montesquieu.

The subtitle of the essay on Erasmus is "Le Spectateur
pur." After sketching the bare outlines of Erasmus's biography, he characterizes him as a man who refused to
become truly involved in life's problems, hence the word
spectator, with its implied lack of moral courage and

manifest unwillingness to risk personal danger or dis-
comfort in support of a cause. Yet Duhamel says that he
admires the philosopher's intelligence, his love of peace,
and his avoidance of noisy controversy. As between the
cautious Erasmus and the uncompromising Luther, he
declares that he would undoubtedly choose the former.

The second master is Cervantes, whose excellence lay
in the fact that he knew the world, a *sine qua non* for a
novelist. Yet Cervantes like Erasmus disappoints him
by his lack of heroism. We tend, says Duhamel, to
expect a heroic life of a man of genius, but since great
gifts are often given to a man of vacillating character,
like Cervantes, we are bound to be disappointed. As it
was with Cervantes, so it was with his creation, Don
Quixote, and the latter, though sane, is bizarre, to say the
least. From this we can deduce that the apparent failure
of Don Quixote's idealism was much on Duhamel's mind,
and on more than one occasion he makes oblique references to the Don's similarity to his own character, Louis
Salavin.

In the four essays on great French writers Duhamel
seems more at home than with the two foreigners. Pascal
affords him an opportunity to talk on one of his favorite
themes, that of faith versus intelligence. His own loss of
faith at an early age appears to have made him admire
the faith of others, and his interest in Pascal has led him,
he says, to carry a pocket edition of his works.

The essays on Rousseau, Montesquieu, and Descartes,
though pleasant, are of little significance. Rousseau, he
says, is a false witness. His humility hides an enormous
pride, yet despite this fact he is an incomparable artist.
Duhamel admires his skill in arousing and holding a
reader's attention even when he declares what is unproved
and unprovable. Still, a single Rousseau is enough for
this world. We need no one else like him.

The discussion of Montesquieu is subtitled "Le Mag-
istrat frivole." The epithet is apparently justified by the
comment that the great jurist is remembered far less for
his *Esprit des lois* than for what Duhamel refers to—mis-
takenly, one is bound to think—as his "facetious" little
book *Les lettres persanes,* loaded as it is with epigrams,
and as "impenitent" in essence as were Rousseau's *Confessions.*

Descartes is evoked for us charmingly as a "severely-
dressed, mustachioed man with a narrow chest and a dry
cough." Analyzing the *Discours de la méthode,* Duhamel
concludes that Descartes must have reasoned that all the
phenomena of life cannot be explained by the intellect,
since in his later years he undertook the study of living
creatures.

With the passing of the years the body of Duhamel's
casual essays has been slowly increasing. When, for
instance, Jérôme Tharaud was admitted to the French
Academy, he spoke appreciatively of the work of the
Tharaud brothers. A similar occasion brought forth a
thoughtful panegyric of Jules Romains. The deaths of
valued friends and colleagues have also been occasions
for comment. Paul Valéry, long a friend, Henri de
Régnier, a revered master, Henri Mondor, Jean-Richard
Bloch, and many others have been thus eulogized. As
might be expected, however, neither these eulogies nor
the critical essays are especially penetrating. Like most
creative writers Duhamel's skill is best seen in his original
work, and his random criticism is worthwhile only as a
sidelight on his intellectual interests. It is by no means a
definition of his genius.

Duhamel's magnificent wartime sketches led the public
to expect more fiction from his pen. Salavin was one
answer. But Duhamel had no intention of letting his
public image be determined by either kind of writing,

and so, in 1921 he published *Les Hommes abandonnés,* a collection of eight stories, which though it included "Nouvelle rencontre de Salavin" was otherwise different from anything that he had yet done. There is a remarkable virtuosity in this volume. The first story, "Le Voiturier," deals with a horrible murder, as related by a stage driver. This stupid and garrulous man talks about the murder mainly to make conversation, and the reader's sense of horror is enhanced by the narrator's inhuman nonchalance. Similar to this story, in that it too deals with murder and creates an atmosphere of tension, is the seventh story, "Une Expédition." After reading stories like these, we can only regret that Duhamel did not write more like them. In the academician we have evidently lost an excellent writer of murder and mystery stories.

Two of the stories in the book stand in sharp contrast to the rest because of their unpleasantness. The prevalence of superstition in rural communities is the basis for the story "Origine et prospérité des singes." The news is spread about a certain small town that the offspring of a local incestuous union is not a human child but a monkey. This situation, unpleasant enough in itself, is made worse for the reader by the assumed detachment of the village doctor, who tells the story. Even less agreeable, if that be possible, is "Le Bengali," a sketch about a brothel where two sick children share the common bedroom of the place. These stories are reminiscent of Zola at his most horrible or Maupassant at his most sombre. And they are noteworthy particularly because Duhamel has elsewhere scrupulously avoided the cruder effects of naturalism.

"L'Epave" is an adroitly told tale of the efforts of a town's entire population to salvage a cargo washed up on the beach. The greed of each one as he accumulates his little pile of goods is skillfully described.

The remaining stories are quite different from the fore-going and from each other. "On ne saurait tout dire" is a lighthearted account of a walking tour through the Alps, a trip later described in Duhamel's memoirs and used in more than one piece of fiction. "La Chambre de l'horloge" recreates amusingly the atmosphere of an old folks' home as seen through the eyes of a small boy.

Critical reaction to this book was mixed. Marcel Azaïs expressed his personal approval, as did many others, including Edmond Jaloux, but Benjamin Crémieux dis-missed it as unanimist stuff, quite lacking in reality. He thought the stories "constructed" rather than developed, and felt that the characters did not come alive. Most readers now agree that *Les Hommes abandonnés* is an outstanding book and that it deserved more than the faint praise that greeted its appearance.

Some years later, in 1938, Duhamel reprinted some of these stories, together with a new title story called "Le Dernier voyage de Candide." This story shows us an aging Candide, resolved to see the world once more. His travels take him to many lands, and everywhere he finds conflicts, tyranny, prisons, and prisoners. When at last his ship hits the mine of a warring nation, Candide finds himself in the next world. There to his distress the quar-rels of earth are repeated.

Since 1938 Duhamel has stayed away from the short story. For reasons of his own he has preferred the novel in its various forms.

In 1924 Duhamel brought out *Le Prince Jaffar*, a work that in some ways defies classification. Among other things it is the first of his many accounts of his travels, but fiction, local color, Arab tales and legends, and the traveler's impressions are carefully blended to produce a charming book. The peoples whom Duhamel observes, as proud as they are inscrutable, are not far different from their European brothers, Duhamel seems to say. He looks at them all, Jews, Arabs, Europeans, each group with its own sense of community, and happily he refrains from judging them. He paints no moral, attempts no a priori reasoning. He studies local customs, sociology, economics, religion, and morals, and his style in the process is as effortless as anything that has come from his pen.

In the year 1926 Duhamel published his first one-volume narrative, a novel with the title *La Pierre d'Horeb*. Its atmosphere was the world of the hospital and the laboratory, which its author had known so well during his student days. The hero, a provincial named Antoine Rességuier, was a composite portrait whose essential lineaments could have been furnished by real-life counterparts in Duhamel's circle of acquaintances. The heart of the story was a picture of Antoine's reactions to his plunge into the unfamiliar world of Parisian ideas and Parisian amours. A second theme was provided by a group of foreign students, many of them Russians who were more interested in Karl Marx than in their anatomy lessons. Antoine's attempted conquest of women introduces the story of Daria, a Russian girl whom he loved, and Anna, a girl who loved him. The conflicting passions of youth are well described, and the novel may be read rapidly and without flagging interest, but in retrospect the work is more like a trial of Duhamel's powers than a successful novel. Antoine and his friends never achieve the status of major characters of fiction. As recollections of the experiences and acquaintances of Duhamel's student days they interest us somewhat, but we never care very much about them in and for themselves.

Duhamel's third work of fiction during the decade was *La Nuit d'orage* (1928). In this story he set out to study the reaction of a rational, twentieth-century man when confronted with the apparently serious consequences of owning a bad-luck charm. François Cros, a son and nephew of scientists, married Elizabeth, a student of chemistry who shared his tastes, and who was, like him, emancipated from belief in the nonrational. While the couple was traveling in Tunis, they found a relic of an ancient civilization in the form of a small amulet. After their return to France, they showed the charm to François' uncle, a distinguished anthropologist. He told them that their amulet was a bad-luck charm. They dismissed this statement lightly, but shortly afterward Elizabeth fell ill and had to be sent away for a cure. François, though he prided himself on his faith in science and his corresponding contempt for superstition, found himself seized with a kind of nameless dread. Unspoken between him and his wife was the thought, repulsive but ineradicable, that the amulet, dropped by François into an unused bureau, was the cause of Elizabeth's illness. One night François found Elizabeth sitting by the bureau. He feared for her life and sanity but decided that come what might he would not remove the charm. Shortly thereafter Elizabeth fell ill again, and François, in the grip of what he called the totem-fearing savage lurking in every civilized man, decided to remove the charm. Its riddance had become a matter of life and death with him. After ransacking the bureau somewhat frantically, he was relieved to discover that the amulet had disappeared, and Elizabeth, when she learned of its disappearance, started to mend. Some time after her recovery François, still somewhat unnerved by his experience, came upon the amulet in a lower drawer of the bureau. Coincidentally a letter came from the uncle, saying that on consulting the authorities, he had discovered that he was in error:

the charm was a good-luck piece. François was thus faced
with the knowledge that his fears were self-induced, and
as a result, his confidence in the powers of the intellect
was severely shaken.

Interwoven with the central theme was the decision
of François' cousin to renounce the family's traditional
agnosticism in favor of religion. At the same time François' brother Michael decided to withdraw from the
civilized world, thereby turning away from the self-
sufficiency that had always characterized him. François
and Elizabeth thus found themselves in a state of confusion. With the scientific rationalism of their relatives
crumbling around them, they were constrained to recognize that they too had allowed themselves to become a
prey to superstitions they had thought unworthy of them.

Despite the considerable skill that Duhamel displays in
handling this plot, *La Nuit d'orage* is only a moderately
successful novel. It might have been an excellent one if
he had been able to refrain from having his characters
moralize on the novel's somewhat obvious theme. The
result is little more than a tour de force, a novel seemingly
written to prove a point, precisely in the manner that
Duhamel had warned against.

Critical opinions of these three books are particularly
interesting to read. *Le Prince Jaffar* received unanimously
favorable notices. All agreed that it was charming and
delightful, and there was no controversy over it. *La Pierre
d'Horeb* elicited some opposition. Marcel Arland, in a
sharp article in *La Nouvelle revue française* stated his
opinion that the personages were not real and that, everything considered, Duhamel had already said, and said
better, all that was to be found in his new novel.[14] He
also castigated Duhamel for presuming to write on morals.
He thought that the postwar books were disappointing.

The Catholic critic Daniel-Rops noted that this was the first time that Duhamel had dealt with love, and he added that in his opinion the parts of the book dealing with surgery were better than those that dealt with amours.[15] Still others thought that Antoine Rességuier was reminiscent of Salavin and their reaction to him mainly reflected their attitude toward the former.

La Nuit d'orage aroused even more disagreement. The theme of modern persons affected by the presence of a primitive talisman called forth protest when it did not excite downright ridicule. In the course of a lengthy analysis of the novel Henri Bidou remarked, "A world peopled by the powers of evil seems to me less dangerous than a brain capable of fabricating at will an infinite number of such powers."[16] François Le Grix contented himself with the harsh conclusion that Duhamel "always writes apologues instead of novels."[17]

Duhamel turns up once again as an apparently unrepentant writer of a thesis novel in his first single-volume novel after the Second World War. *Le Voyage de Patrice Périot* (1950) has for its protagonist a Sorbonne scientist who has been spending more and more of his time and energy on supposedly worthy causes. No manifesto was without his signature. No peace congress was complete without his presence as presiding officer. And though he lamented the loss of time from his work, he continued to be an activist. He had, unfortunately, no inkling that most of the left-wing groups he championed were simply making an insidious use of his good name to further their devious, usually Communist ends. In his own home, meanwhile, Périot's family of four children was disintegrating before his unseeing eyes. Edwige, who was thirty years old, had married a jealous, narrow-minded man; Christine had become a dialectical materialist who called herself Vera, and was an ardent and active Communist. Hervé, a poet in his early twenties, had his life so tangled with disreputable deeds and persons that he finally committed suicide. Thierry, at twenty the only happy member of the family, was a convinced, ecstatic Christian.

As the story proceeds, the reader witnesses the successive struggles of M. Périot to do his scientific work while he lends his energies to a conglomeration of politically inspired meetings, interviews, conferences, and petitions. His tragedy is that of the well-meaning and impractical idealist, a cat's paw in the hands of unscrupulous demagogues. The theme, which is obvious from first page to last, is that Périot, and scholars like him, could best serve their families and their fellow men by tending to their vocation. By running about trying to serve dubious causes, they achieve little more than to make a mockery of their good intentions. Obviously, Périot is symbolic of Duhamel, for the latter, like his hero, as he tells us elsewhere, has had to fight against the noisy counterclaims of well-meaning partisans of causes, some good and some bad, but all destructive to the peace of mind that a writer must have if he is to do his day's work.

Duhamel's next novel, *Cri des profondeurs* (1951), is from many points of view his best one-volume narrative. The scene is occupied Paris, the story a self-portrait of a minor villain whose downfall is caused by his greed. The protagonist is Félix Tallemand, a Frenchman of collaborationist tendencies who wants to be "en règle," even with God, whose existence he denies. Félix's activities are directed toward controlling the business firm of Dardaille, Winterberg, and Company. His methods are as devious as they are petty. Pretending to help the Jewish Winterberg and his family escape from the Nazis, he let them fall into a trap from which Winterberg alone escaped.

By hiding the refugee in his cellar on the eve of the liberation of Paris, when practically all danger was past, Félix earned a reputation as a hero despite his record of collaboration. This was only a small part of his villainy. By failing to give his half-brother Didier Dardaille his medicine, he caused his death. By preventing his daughter's marriage and asking her not to go into a convent, he cost her her happiness. Yet Félix was timid even in the pursuit of evil. He lacked sufficient courage to be wicked, said Abel Samian, a mysterious go-between who bears some resemblance to Satan. Finally, as Félix lay dying in the presence of Winterberg, whom he had wronged, something in the soul whose existence he denied made him cry out in despair. Something stirred in this materialist, to whom fine sentiments and sincerity were synonymous with hypocrisy.

The outstanding feature of this novel is the character of Félix, a man as tortured as Salavin, and more true to life than Patrice Périot. The story is banal enough in outline, for the Second World War brought out the tyrant and villain in many a mediocre man. But into the telling of this tale Duhamel has managed to put a considerable portion of the kind of pathos he regards as so essential to the novel. He succeeds in making his hateful villain pitiful, too.

Duhamel's next novel, *L'Archange de l'aventure* (1956), is a curious mixture of its author's favorite preoccupations. Apparently unable to make up his mind whether he was writing a novel, a fantasy, a satire, or an essay, he calls the work a novel though it is not one in the Flaubertian sense. The plot is uncomplicated, his handling of it skillful. Cyprien Ricord, a happily married young painter, is accosted by a stranger named Mikaël, who insinuates himself into his home, promotes him as the leader of a new school of painting, transports him to America for a triumphal tour, and then runs away with his wife. Ricord, left alone, recovers his lost faith and rediscovers happiness in the company of his little boy.

In telling this story of the quasi-supernatural Mikaël, Duhamel seems to be attempting a criticism of the modern world and its complications. France, as it appears in this book, has succumbed like other nations to the illusory happiness of automation and the frenzy of getting and spending.

At first glance this novel is even more obviously a tract than *Le Voyage de Patrice Périot*, but by his humorous touch, and his avoidance of outright moralizing, Duhamel makes of *L'Archange de l'aventure* an amusing fantasy. Its message is all the more telling because of the light-hearted manner of the narration.

Judged by its date of publication (1956), *Les Compagnons de l'Apocalypse* was written at about the same time as *L'Archange de l'aventure*. Its theme also relates it to the latter. Yet in manner of narration the two books are worlds apart. This is not as astonishing as it may seem. Duhamel has a predilection for composing books that seem different but have their roots in a common preoccupation and a seemingly common inspiration. *Les Compagnons de l'Apocalypse* is thus an entirely sober and therefore less successful version of the theme that was treated so amusingly in the companion volume. The rather improbable story tells of a war veteran whose small pension enabled him to become an itinerant preacher. After getting out of the army he took to the road in a gypsy caravan. Calling himself Dan Traveler, he attracted a number of men who became his followers. As the group went about from town to town, Traveler preached a call to prayer and consecration in order to save the world from atomic destruction, a prospect he saw foretold in the Book of Revelation. For a time Dan's caravan was welcomed everywhere. Then their fortune changed, and they were scorned and made fun of. At the end of the story Dan died alone, feeling that his pride had taken him too far, even for a minor prophet.

This is an odd story to say the least. Its characters are not fully developed, and neither is the author's purpose. The plot is sketchy and a little absurd. The message, however, is the same as in *L'Archange de l'aventure,* that we live in a topsy-turvy world, that man may be nearing the end of his course upon the planet. The implicit question is whether man may do anything to save himself. Ricord, the artist in *L'Archange,* drifted with the tide and was unhappy. Dan Traveler, in *Les Compagnons,* tried to make his way against the tide, yet he was unrewarded either by happiness or a sense of achievement. The frustration of the author is no less apparent.

Le Complexe de Théophile (1958) continues Duhamel's treatment of the problem of man's salvation. Théophile pours out his story in a narrative reminiscent of Salavin's confession. We find out that he is vain, selfish, introspective, and self-tortured. The slight plot deals with Théophile's relation to the pilot of a Near Eastern airline that employs them both. The airman harbored the strange delusion that the God he worshipped was quite unconcerned with the fate of any human being beside himself. When at last he decided that his God had abandoned him, he consented to crash a plane carrying an important politician. The strange result of the crash was the death of everyone but the politician. Théophile's role of go-between in the negotiations for the accident is the central focus of the story.

This is hardly great fiction, but it is certainly good

entertainment. Théophile, like Dan Traveler, Ricord, and Périot, is lost and helpless, and his search for an anchor strongly resembles theirs. The theme of this, as of the other three novels written since the Second World War, is man's dilemma in a world that his own engines may well destroy. Duhamel has still not lost hope altogether, but as he looks about him, he sees little room for optimism and his writing reflects his mood.

The critical discussions of these postwar novels seem to follow a pattern. Seldom does a reviewer express more than mild disapproval of one of Duhamel's books. For the most part reviews consist of an analysis of the plot that merely tries to present the book to the public. *Cri des profondeurs* had such a long analytical review in the *Revue de Paris*. The reviewer, Marcel Thiebaut, saw the dilemma of Félix Tallemand in the context of an unprincipled villain or *salaud*. He thought the problem fairly well handled but said that Duhamel had complicated his presentation by permitting Félix to be judged solely by his own testimony. Because Félix would not admit his guilt, the reader's comprehension is lessened. Under such circumstances, he said, "we have little chance to understand the matter."[18] Maurice Nadeau in the *Mercure de France* also compared Félix to a Sartrian *salaud*. In this novel Duhamel is more detached than usual from his hero, he said. He seems to content himself with presenting the character and saying: "See!"[19]

Le Voyage de Patrice Périot was reviewed at length in the *Mercure de France* of February 1, 1951. The reviewer regarded the book as a logical progression in Duhamel's life work. He implied that Duhamel had been consciously avoiding certain aspects of life only to find that he could not forever do so. He said:

Un des thèmes qui rôdent depuis de longues années dans ses ouvrages est cette fois empoigné pour lui-même, et devient le centre du roman. Le mordant, l'amertume qui transparaissaient parfois sous le sourire, la bonhomie et la volonté de confiance, ici rompent les digues. La politique, si longtemps contenue, fait irruption à visage nu.[20]

Les Compagnons de l'Apocalypse won more favorable comment for its timeliness than for its quality as a novel. The reviewer of *La Revue des Deux Mondes,* for example, gave a detailed résumé of the plot of the story, which he coupled with a discussion of the circumstances that gave the book its appeal to readers in a period of atomic threats. He avoided completely any judgment on the book as good or bad prose fiction.[21]

Gaëton Picon discussed *L'Archange de l'aventure* in the course of a long discussion of Duhamel's work in the *Mercure de France.* Like most reviewers of Duhamel's books in these latter days, he is less concerned with a value judgment, of the sort to which all of Duhamel's earlier works had been subjected, than with an attempt to assign the book to a category. His name for the work is "un petit traité de morale et d'esthétique abandonné aux détours d'un dialogue romanesque: un conte philosophique, très exactement."[22] The reader is then left to decide for himself whether this book or any other book in the category of *conte philosophique* is to his taste in this century. In his essay on the novel Duhamel had declared that the day of this sort of tale was about over, but in his later years the genre appears to have attracted him as a convenient vehicle for his preachments and his disquisitions on the foibles of mankind.

5

THE PASQUIER CHRONICLE

WHEN Le Notaire du Havre, the first volume of Duhamel's *Chronique des Pasquier,* was published in 1933,
Les Hommes de bonne volonté of Jules Romains had been
on its way for a year, and *Les Thibault* of Roger Martin
du Gard, later to win a Nobel prize, was more than half
done. Duhamel was, of course, mindful of the progress
of these works, but it may be seriously doubted whether
his own undertaking, which has inevitably been compared
with theirs, was prompted by any spirit of rivalry. The
writing of a long work, which might come to be regarded
as his masterpiece, was a logical next step in Duhamel's
career. He had said of lyric poetry that he believed it to

be the literary form best suited to young writers. The theater he had renounced after several near-successes. There remained the field of prose fiction, the theory and practice of which had preoccupied him greatly during and after the writing of the Salavin adventures. Duhamel was approaching his fiftieth year, and in his opinion a good novel is the product of a mature mind. The time had come for a sustained effort, and happily inspiration and the opportune moment had a coincidental meeting.

The opening pages of *Le Notaire du Havre* promise well. In a long foreword we are introduced to the hero and narrator of the story, Laurent Pasquier, who tells us that we are about to read a long memoir dealing with his life and that of his family. As he speaks to us in the introduction, Laurent is looking back on his life from the year 1931, when he is a middle-aged professor of biology. He is, we suspect, the Duhamel who might have been, had he not deserted the laboratory for the writing desk.

It is plain from the very first page of *Le Notaire du Havre* that the personages we meet here are different from the bizarre Salavin. The Pasquiers are a full-blooded and very human family, and their creator has surrounded them with an atmosphere that seems to be made, not out of a segment of reality, but out of life as a whole. It is also plain from Laurent's introduction that although Duhamel may not have planned the book in detail, since it is a favorite theory of his that characters should be allowed to work out their own destinies, he at least had seen the essential lineaments of the Pasquier story before putting pen to paper.

The story opens in the Pasquier dining room in Paris, and no more than a dozen lines are needed before the warmth of the atmosphere, the wealth of detail, and the simplicity of the style have won the reader's sympathetic attention. The Duhamel of the Pasquiers is no longer the dispassionate narrator of *Les Hommes abandonnés,* nor the impassioned one of *Civilisation,* but a mellow and expansive raconteur, seemingly unhampered by any theoretical considerations as to what a novelist should or should not do. This apparent simplicity is, however, an effect of art, as Duhamel later tells us in his commentary on the work.

The Pasquiers when we meet them are a lower middle class family engaged in the struggle for existence, but eager for self-improvement. Papa Pasquier is already past forty, and a belated student of medicine. Madame Pasquier, née Lucille Delahaie, though a trifle careworn and slightly plump, is still young and active. There are four children, Joseph, Laurent, Ferdinand, and Cécile. A second sister, Suzanne, will make her appearance in a later volume.

Two factors outside the family circle serve to activate the plot. A letter arrives from a notary in Le Havre announcing to Madame Pasquier that she is to receive an inheritance from her two half-sisters in Peru. A second inciting force is provided by the antics of M. Wasselin in the next flat. His dishonesty leads to his imprisonment and to the suicide of his lonely and unloved son, for whom Duhamel chose the ironical name Désiré. But truly the prime mover of this adventure and of those that follow, until his death, is the father, Raymond Pasquier himself —irrepressible, unpredictable, choleric.

Immediately upon receipt of the letter from Le Havre, with its news of an impending inheritance, Papa Pasquier dreamed the first of his dreams of grandeur. With the money, which belonged to his wife and children rather than to him, Raymond decided to do great things. Because immediate payment of the legacy could not be arranged, he went to borrow money from his neighbors, the Courtois family. The two Courtois sisters and their brother agreed to the loan, as they were attracted by the high rate of interest that Pasquier offered. Once the money was in his hand, Papa at once invested it in a harebrained scheme that failed completely, so that when the first installment of the legacy actually arrived, he had to use a large part of it to repay the squandered loan.

The Wasselin family's troubles were brought noisily to the attention of the Pasquiers when Father Wasselin took to cursing his son in the hall of the apartment. Later, when this unattractive scoundrel was arrested for embezzlement, it was Papa Pasquier who came to the rescue and played one of his greatest scenes. M. Ruaux, the landlord, came to berate the defenseless Madame Wasselin for her husband's conduct, and Father Pasquier permitted himself a memorable tantrum. Displaying a dazzling virtuosity in his choice of appropriate epithets, he backed the landlord down the stairs and into the street in what is undoubtedly the funniest episode in the entire novel. This done, he calmly went back to the apartment, climbed the stairs, and received on each landing the astonished and excited congratulations of his neighbors.

These are the broad outlines of the plot. Between the lines are etched some unforgettable details. The lives and personalities of the Wasselins and the Courtois are deftly drawn. The latter, with their stinginess and their manias, provide tragicomic relief. Désiré Wasselin, whose father beats him and berates him merely for the sadistic pleasure of it, has but one thought: to hide from the sight of others the sordid and dishonest ways of his mother and father. The Pasquier children do not take on real stature in this volume, but their characters are sketched in roughly. Laurent is an intelligent boy, but a dreamer. Ferdinand is diligent but not very intelligent. Joseph reveals a crude realism, and Cécile her fondness for the piano. The nuances and shadings will appear in later portraits.

Quite outside the story, but affecting the lives of the Pasquiers, is the fabulous notary who writes to the family from Le Havre. Never a participant, he is always an influence on the events that take place. Above all there is the presence of Paris, for Duhamel, like Balzac, and like his colleague Jules Romains, is profoundly moved by his love for the city. The unfashionable street where the Pasquiers live, the Impasse Vandamme, with its plebeian sights and smells, looms large in the narrative. The life of the great city is like an ocean, surrounding and all but submerging the Pasquiers, for this story is above all a story of Paris, and placing the Pasquiers' adventures there was no mere accident. The Pasquier family is thoroughly Parisian, and whatever universal qualities they have are presented in a French and particularly Parisian context. *Le Notaire du Havre* is an excellent book and sets a high standard for those that follow. The Pasquiers do not deprive Salavin of his place in Duhamel's gallery of portraits, but they provide a welcome view of what a skilled writer can do with ordinary and even commonplace persons and places.

Le Jardin des bêtes sauvages made its appearance a year after *Le Notaire du Havre*. The title comes from the Pasquier children's name for the Jardin des Plantes, formerly the location of the Paris zoo. Here they walked and played, as Duhamel and his own youngsters have done. In the chronology of the story several years have passed. Laurent Pasquier is growing up. He is about fourteen years old, and his tragedy as an adolescent, eager to devote himself to an ideal that, for want of a better word, he calls *pudeur,* or purity, is to discover that his father, who talks so much about self-improvement, and self-realization, has a mistress. He also discovered that the mistress, a vulgar woman named Solange Meesmacker, was not the first one and would indubitably not be the last. The discovery of his father's double life changed Laurent's feeling for him into a distrust that was something like hatred. He was further shocked to learn that his practical brother Joseph, whom he was beginning to dislike, calmly accepted the situation. He was even more astonished to learn that his mother, though hurt and saddened by the knowledge of her husband's infidelity, did not protest actively. Laurent was puzzled when his mother explained to him that no inevitable connection exists between intellectual and scientific gifts and morality. Laurent, like most young people, wanted the world all of one piece: he wanted his honest men honest to the core. His is the eternal crisis of the adolescent, which is often brought on by the personal discovery of evil in the world, and Duhamel has described this crisis in a convincing and realistic manner.

Laurent, meanwhile, had become the friend of Justin Weill, a Jewish schoolmate, and together they faced the problems of growing up. Justin was terribly conscious of his Jewishness and was touchy on the subject even with Laurent. He was starting to fall in love with Laurent's sister Cécile, who was developing into a talented pianist. Her teacher was a Dane named Valdemar Hemmingson, who, because he was not a virtuoso, tried to find a musical outlet by tutoring. It was part of his misfortune, and Cécile's also, that he was besides an eccentric who alternately worshipped and scolded his pupil, and the two of them kept the Pasquier household in an uproar with their quarrels. Duhamel was, as we shall see, a musician himself, and this fact enabled him to deal realistically with Cécile and her musical skill.

Meanwhile, Laurent made a clumsy effort to break up his father's relationship with Solange Meesmacker. He visited her and appealed to her to give his father up. Failing in this, he tried to talk his father into changing his ways. He was chagrined to find out that his parent merely sidestepped the issue and refused to discuss it with him. Laurent was no less upset when a plea to his mother to leave his father also failed. Finally, he realized that Papa Pasquier was too strong for him at whatever level he chose to attack him, and for the rest of his father's life Laurent would be frustrated in his relations with this man whom he could not wholly love, yet could not bring himself wholly to despise.

All the members of the Pasquier family show considerable development in this second book. Joseph reveals a passion for money and a cynical attitude toward all else in life. Ferdinand, whose myopia is here emphasized, makes a fool of himself in most things that he attempts. Cécile is more and more an "angel" of music whose life centers about the keyboard of her piano. Little Suzanne makes her first appearance as a toddler. Much of the action revolves around Laurent. It is he who tries to shoulder his father's sins. It is he whose ideals are most shattered by the revelation of the world's wickedness. Mother Pasquier remains more or less in the background, a tender, pathetic figure. Papa Pasquier is a great deal less lovable here, and far less amusing than before, for the reader is made to partake of Laurent's growing antipathy toward him. But in spite of all, Papa emerges triumphant, a dandy and a philosopher, elusive, sinful, and human.

This second volume represents a worthy progression in the unfolding Pasquier story. This time Laurent is the narrator. There is less gaiety here than in the preceding volume, which, despite its moments of pathos, was fairly cheerful. In the time covered by *Le Notaire du Havre* there was no essential threat to family solidarity. In the second volume, despite the healing presence of music, a somber note is struck. Henceforth this note will be heard over and above the harmony that lifts Cécile and Laurent momentarily out of their preoccupations and into the celestial realm of musical enjoyment.

Laurent continued his chronicle in *Vue de la terre promise* (1934), after a lapse of five years. Suzanne was now eight, Laurent twenty. Ferdinand had become an accountant. Cécile was a concert pianist, and Joseph a bustling business man. Father Pasquier had completed his medical studies and had hung out his shingle in Créteil, a suburb from which the rest of the family commuted daily to Paris. The story opens with the receipt of further installments of the children's inheritance, and the pointblank demand of Joseph that he be given his portion, hitherto always preempted by his father as soon as it arrived. Joseph further demanded an indemnity for having given up his studies, and for having had to do his military service. Laurent surprised everyone by asking for a thousand francs in cash. When he got the money, he pocketed it, and later the same evening he invited Joseph to walk down to the river with him. Once there he jumped onto a parapet, out of Joseph's reach, and declared that he was going to tear up and throw away his thousand-franc note. He reminded Joseph, who was wild with rage and cupidity, that he had once sworn to prove his contempt for money by destroying his first thousand francs. Afterward, Laurent tried to make a confession of his action to his senior in the laboratory, Léon Schleiter, who would not even listen to his story, supposing that Laurent wanted to involve him through his confession in some sordid affair. He next tried to tell a fellow student, Hélène Strohl, about it, and finally he attempted to confide in his old friend Justin Weill. When at last he succeeded in making Justin listen, he admitted that he had cheated. Laurent had not really thrown away the thousand-franc note. He had first had it changed into two five-hundred-franc notes and had torn up one of these, keeping the other. Justin was crushed to learn that his friend's *beau geste* was less sublime than he had supposed, and he begged Laurent not to tell his secret to Cécile.

The latter, meanwhile, was continuing her tempestuous friendship with Valdemar Hemmingson, whose mother now called on the Pasquiers to ask in an overbearing manner for Cécile's hand for her son. While this conversation was in progress, Laurent caught Valdemar stealing morphine from Dr. Pasquier's medicine chest, and he then understood at least one reason for the musician's frequently irrational behavior. Valdemar, deprived of the drug, shot his mother and killed himself. To add to the Pasquiers' troubles Papa Pasquier turned out to be responsible for the pregnancy of Paula Lescure, a cousin who was living with the family. When the children managed to get Paula out of town by means of a fake telegram, Papa calmly brought her back and installed her in an apartment in Créteil. These were difficult burdens for Laurent, and so when his friend Hélène wrote to announce her engagement to his brother Joseph, the strain was almost more than he could bear. Sick to death of the family, Laurent wrote to Justin that he had moved into bachelor quarters, and that an unaccountable feeling of peace and hope had come over him.

In this volume, as in the preceding one, we never quite recapture the humor and gaiety of *Le Notaire du Havre,* but Papa Pasquier does have a comical encounter with a horseless carriage, which, with his usual fatuous self-confidence, he thinks he can handle. The result is the wrecking of the contraption and Papa's ignominious return home behind two horses. Memorably comic too is the defeat of the livery-stable keeper who wants to be paid for his ruined gas-buggy. But with the exception of these episodes the tone of the book is seldom carefree. We could hardly expect it to be, for the events related are somber for the most part. Laurent the student has left his carefree days behind him.

The family has grown somewhat older. Only blue-eyed Papa still fancies himself young, and to prove it commits yet another indiscretion. The scenes of the family gatherings and quarrels are as magnificent as ever, and although Cécile tries to remain above the battle, both she and Laurent have come to realize that neither music nor art nor any other occupation can free a person from his family—that, in effect, there is no escape from life. Laurent also has the knowledge forced upon him that his illusions have so far obscured reality that he has failed to see love and happiness beckoning to him, in the person of Hélène. But the reader realizes, if Laurent does not, that there is only partial truth in what he says in a letter about all this to his friend Justin. He says that he has separated from his family in order to love them better, but the reader senses that Laurent cannot escape from the clan so easily.

With *La Nuit de la Saint Jean* (1935), an occasion traditionally associated with odd and unusual happenings, the Pasquier story enters a new phase. Laurent abandons the role of narrator after providing a brief introduction, and the story is told in the third person. The narrative is supposedly derived from a posthumous account of events written by Justin, and given by his mother to Laurent. From his papers we learn that the life of the Pasquiers has not been altered radically since our last meeting with them. Laurent, now twenty-five, is working in hospitals and laboratories. His superior is a middle-aged scientist named Renaud Censier, whom he greatly admires. Laurent is also falling in love with a fellow student named Laure. Father Pasquier, though practicing medicine in a desultory way, is now mainly interested in becoming an inventor. Joseph, already wealthy, and the proud owner of a country estate that he pompously calls La Pâquellerie, lives on a grand scale with his wife and two children. Most of the story deals with events occurring at this country house on the eve of Saint John's Day. The entire Pasquier family has been invited and with them Professor Censier, Laure, Justin, and a Rabelaisian artist named Delcambre. From the beginning things went badly. Laurent tried to woo Laure, only to discover that Censier was also paying attention to her. In the parlor and at the table Delcambre told risqué stories and flirted with pretty thirteen-year-old Suzanne to everyone's annoyance. Cécile offered to marry Justin, who had so often proposed to her, but pride made him reject her offer, which he thought was solely motivated by pity. Censier paid an innocent but untimely visit to Laure's room, only to disappear next day on an unexplained journey of escape to the Orient. Father Pasquier made indiscreet visits to nearby Paula, seated the English governess on his knee, and ended by turning Laurent's Paris apartment upside-down in yet another amorous adventure. Laurent and Laure, their romance broken by the brief intrusion of Censier, were left disconsolate.

There is more than enough incident here and a wealth

of good observation, but the volume does not specifically advance the fortunes of the Pasquiers. The old tensions between Laurent and his father and brother are recreated with all the skill of the previous volumes, but without new intensity. Justin alone, although his role of narrator minimizes his share in the action, seems to gain in stature, and there is more than a touch of grandeur in his unrequited love for Cécile.

Two years passed before the next volume, *Le Désert de Bièvres*, appeared in 1937. This is the story of the founding of a suburban phalanstery by Laurent, Justin, and several friends, an undertaking that recalls Duhamel's part in establishing the Abbaye de Créteil.

The young men of the Bièvres group were an odd lot. There was Bernard Jusserand, who brought with him his wife, Alice; Jean-Paul Sénac, drunkard and master of invective; Testival, a grumpy bachelor; Brénugat, a painter, and his wife, Florence; and Armand Larseneur, a pianist. To these were soon added Monmerqué, a typographer, who came to teach the trade of printing, and a disagreeable housekeeper, Mme. Clovis, whom the group finally had to dismiss for stealing wine.

The aim of the company was to live the life of free men and philosophers, supporting themselves by doing artistic printing on an old hand press. The story opens with a description of their settling-in, when the long-dreamed-of plan was about to become a reality, and continued with the occasion when at last they were able to receive their friends and families at a *fête champêtre*. It closes with the sad story of the quarrels and differences that eventually caused first one and then another of the members to go back to Paris.

The Pasquiers and their trials have receded from the foreground here, although they are by no means forgotten. Joseph, when he appears, is more involved than ever in grandiose but shady financial transactions. Ferdinand is unchanged. Cécile is more radiant and charming than ever. Papa Pasquier is still himself. After a set-to with the police, he came out of jail and, ill but imperturbable, set out to visit his mistress. He was politely contemptuous of Laurent's efforts to dissuade him on the grounds of health and morality. Laurent himself came down with a serious illness, of which his father cured him. Then, to the irritation of his friends, Papa was awarded the Legion of Honor for his development of a vaccine. But the Pasquier aspect of the book, important though it is, remains mainly on the periphery of the narrative, and it comes as rather a shock when the episode of Papa's involvement with the police brings us back to the family at the very end.

The real hero, and the leader of the phalanstery, is Justin Weill, upon whose shoulders fell the cares of housekeeping. His was the spark that kindled the group's enthusiasm, and his were the business acumen and the driving power that kept the establishment going. And finally, in his own mind at least, the ultimate failure was his also, since he was convinced that he should have been able to keep the ill-assorted, undisciplined, and selfish group together. As the community broke up, he felt deeply that if men of supposed intelligence and good will, like himself and his friends, were incapable of getting along together in a free association, then a meeting of minds in the less ideal world of everyday living would thereby be proved impossible. His failure to make others love and respect him enough to follow his leadership, and his inability to make them love and respect each other as he loved and respected each of them, hurt him most. Justin's character emerges stronger here than in any previous volume, for in the midst of his disappointment stands the grandeur of his faith in his fellow men. He was both inspirer and inspired, and he refused to turn away from his ideals.

With volume six, *Les Maîtres* (1937), Duhamel takes us into the world of hospitals and laboratories, which he knows so well. He has cast the book in the form of letters from Laurent to Justin. The latter has temporarily left Paris to work in a factory. The Justin whom we now meet is a new Justin, a touchy, sensitive, and jealous fellow rather than the expansive, poetic and youthful lad we have thus far known. Laurent's letters to him give sad but persistent evidence that Justin almost willfully misunderstands the motives of his friend's actions. The author provides no transition for this new disposition on Justin's part, and we are left to speculate whether his unrequited love for Cécile, followed as it was by the failure of the phalanstery, has embittered him.

Laurent for his part is still an idealist. He is experiencing an admiration almost amounting to worship for the two distinguished scientists for whom he is working. The first, Nicolas Rohner, of the medical faculty, advocates a harsh, uncompromising realism, pure of any taint of mysticism or sentiment. The second, Oliver Chalgrin, is a far nobler character, and by no means less eminent scientist. Rohner, we discover, is a prejudiced and violent man to whom the scientific method is a technique that he is unable to apply to human relations. Chalgrin is more flexible. Although he is president of the Société des Etudes Rationalistes, he confides to Laurent that rationalism may perhaps be incapable of finding the answers to all human problems, and, atheist though he is, he regards the life and personality of Jesus as the crowning glory of mankind. Chalgrin is also astute enough to perceive, as Laurent does not as yet, that under his rationalistic exterior Rohner is an emotional and unstable man, capable

of performing "experiments" that are not far from superstition and antirationalism.

As the antagonism between these two men increased,
Laurent had reason to be disillusioned about Rohner's
integrity. Rohner performed a hasty and heartless dis-
section of the body of his dead assistant, Cathérine
Houdoire, who had died of the disease she was studying,
and when Rohner falsified his findings in order to prove
a hypothesis on the cause of her death, Laurent was
disgusted. The climax of the scientists' quarrel was
reached at a meeting of the Biological Congress. Rohner
had to be coaxed to stay, for he had started to leave on
discovering that Chalgrin was to preside. At the end of
the meeting Chalgrin moved generously and courageously
to end the quarrel, and, apologizing to Rohner for real or
fancied insults, he offered his hand. Rohner refused his
own, and Chalgrin was so upset by this display of hatred
that he suffered a stroke from which he did not recover.

A minor plot is added to the story by the actions of the
self-confessed knave, Jean-Paul Sénac, the drunkard of
Bièvres. He had violated Chalgrin's confidence by letting
Rohner see a hostile article that Chalgrin had written but
was withholding from publication. Sénac's eventual suicide, after Laurent had called him a scoundrel to his
face, brings another emotional upset to a story largely
motivated by the quarrels of the two scientists. Joseph,
Suzanne, Cécile, and their mother appear but infrequently, though we have news of them from time to
time. Joseph pretends bankruptcy and borrows from the
family, and on numerous occasions he infuriates Laurent
by his cynicism and worldliness. At the end of the book
we learn that Cécile is to marry a young scientist, Richard
Fauvet.

Philosophically considered, this volume presents another step in Laurent's quest for eternal values or a

working philosophy of life, a quest that purports to give the story its meaning. As Laurent observed the enmity between his two revered masters, he came to realize that human frailty permits no one, not even a servant of science, to be altogether admirable; that even the best of men have some baseness or weakness in them, whereas the weakest, like his father, have their moments of grandeur. In this, as in previous volumes, Laurent is the dominant figure, for the Pasquier chronicle is far less the story of a family than an account of Laurent's progress toward wisdom.

Cécile parmi nous (1938) takes us back into the atmosphere of the clan to relate the tragic story of Cécile's marriage to Richard Fauvet. The other members of the family come and go, but Cécile and her child hold the center of the stage, and the pages devoted to her love for her son, Alexandre, are touchingly and beautifully written. The villain of the piece is Fauvet. Duhamel has done very well with this character, a detestably ironic intellectual of a sort that he must have encountered frequently in his everyday life. Fauvet is secretly tormented by his own coldness and sterility, but he plays at being *chef d'école littéraire* and man of science, while as a husband he expends most of his energy trying to wound the susceptibilities of his wife. Outwardly, at least, Cécile is above Fauvet's pinpricks, but ultimately he hurts her deeply. His most calculated cruelty, a flirtation with Suzanne Pasquier, within full view of his wife, who is performing on the concert stage, finally brought about the break that Fauvet pretended to dread but seemed subconsciously to desire. The subsequent death of their child dissolved the last bond between husband and wife, and Cécile retired for a time to a convent to recover her strength.

Told in the same volume is the story of Joseph Pasquier's schemes to make money by selling arms to both sides in the Bulgarian-Turkish war. Joseph started a campaign to have the Bulgarian government declared guilty of violating international law. Retouched photographs of unrelated battles were offered to the newspapers as proof of the Bulgarians' use of dumdum bullets. For his purpose Joseph employed the services of his unscrupulous confidential agent, Mairesse Mairal, and the venal pen of a number of journalists. He also attracted the misplaced sympathy of Justin Weill, who was with difficulty convinced of the true situation by Laurent.

Mother Pasquier, when she appears, is still trying desperately to bolster the family solidarity. Suzanne is more attractive than ever. Ferdinand has become an overly domestic and uninspiring husband whose contentment is marred only by his hypochondria. Dr. Pasquier alone emerges triumphant from another of his comic-opera episodes. By now he has left medicine and inventions behind him in favor of literature, and he fancies himself a writer. His first novel, as told to Laurent, is a thriller fit for the pulps, but though he recites it wonderfully, he writes it wretchedly. Justin is once more the easily wounded but impulsive and lovable fellow of his earlier years, though he still has a touch of the irascibility that marks his new social conscience.

Le Combat contre les ombres (1939) was the last volume of the Pasquier chronicle to appear before the Second World War. For the first time the story is told entirely in the third person. Laurent, who is now thirty-three, and a member of the staff of the National Institute of Biology, is faced with political interference with his work. Larminat, the director of the Institute, is a political appointee with no conception of the scientific method. He imposed upon Laurent an incompetent laboratory assistant named Hippolyte Birault, a Uriah Heep with French overtones, who became an ever-present nuisance. Knowing nothing, he thought he knew everything. Not only was he personally unbearable, but by his ineptitude he constantly threatened the work of the laboratory. Larminat reinstated Birault after his dismissal by Laurent, and the latter was thereby forced to the expedient of forbidding Birault to do any work. An impasse had been reached, and Laurent turned to the newspapers to defend himself. Vuillaume, a young scientist with useful connections, agreed to help him publish his views on political encroachments upon science. Article succeeded article. Laurent declared that science must have a free hand. Replies were soon forthcoming, and Laurent found himself the center of a lively controversy. Disillusionment was in store for him, however, when he found out that many persons who pretended to be on his side, including friends and colleagues, were either lukewarm or secretly opposing him. In the end, exasperated beyond endurance, he loses his Pasquier temper, insults Director Larminat, and resigns from the Institute. The last straw is a telegram from Vuillaume, who had urged him to print his opinions in the first place, saying that he has been offered Laurent's position. He insists that either he will refuse it or he will accept only in an attempt to clear Laurent's name. The outbreak of the First World War breaks the deadlock, and Laurent finds himself in uniform getting ready for a quite different kind of combat.

As usual, Duhamel tossed into his main plot a number of subplots, which, in the fashion of a juggler, he kept in motion simultaneously. Papa offers the usual comic relief. His newest enterprise is an office in which he will practice psychological therapy, a move that annoys Joseph, for he fears the social consequences if Dr. Pasquier's quackery is denounced. Laurent is equally dismayed, but for different reasons, because he despises charlatanism in all its forms. The outcome for Papa is a trip to Algeria in the company of his stenographer, from which he returns barely in time to see Laurent off to war. Cécile, now divorced and but partly recovered from the shock of her child's death, appears briefly. Ferdinand worries about the reactions of his father's mistresses to the latter's prolonged absence, a worry not shared by Laurent. Suzanne appears occasionally, and Joseph continues to call a family council whenever their father gets himself into an unbecoming situation.

Justin is more often absent than present, but he never seems very far from the center, because much of the story is cast in the form of letters between him and Laurent. For instance, when Laurent is attacked on all sides, he has to bear the additional burden of reproaches from Justin, who, misreading the newspapers, has mistaken for Laurent's own words some sentiments attributed to him by a careless journalist. When after a series of explanations, Justin is made to understand the true situation, he supports Laurent loyally.

Still another theme is the love affair between Laurent and Jacqueline Bellac, a social worker, who at first refuses and then agrees to become Laurent's wife. This romance is handled a bit stiffly by Duhamel, who, it will be noted, writes of love and courtship fairly infrequently in his novels. All things considered, this volume, despite its many plots and its variety of incident, comes close at times to being a thesis novel. It has warmth and humor, but Laurent Pasquier's irritation sometimes makes him appear to be Duhamel himself, thinly disguised. Such may indeed be the case, for he had once found himself in a situation similar to that in which he placed his character. He was thus introduced briefly and unhappily on one occasion to the unpleasant effects of political influence in the field of science.

The ninth and penultimate volume of the *Chronique des Pasquier* is *Suzanne et les jeunes hommes.* Because the occupying forces forbade Duhamel to publish his book, it was published abroad in 1941. This time the spotlight is thrown almost continuously on Suzanne. The other members of the family are seen from time to time, but only to remind us of their existence or to sum up their status as of 1921. Papa Pasquier, physically old and looking frail, but still considering himself in charge, is inventing a system of philosophy and corresponding with Bergson, a philosopher Duhamel often mentions, but whom he has nowhere discussed in detail. Mother Pasquier is a feeble shadow of her former self. Joseph is deep in money matters. Laurent is an eminent biologist, and Cécile a concert pianist of world renown. Ferdinand and his wife are barely mentioned. With the exception of Joseph and the parents, who appear on a few pages only, the rest of the family is generally disposed of in a sentence or two. Suzanne, whom we have hitherto seen merely as a flirtatious, pretty girl, is given a full-length portrait.

At the end of the First World War, Suzanne went back to her theatrical career. She attached herself by choice to the small art theater of an impresario named Eric Vidame. As the star of the troupe Suzanne expected to play the leading roles. As the story opens, she makes known her wish to play Cordelia in a French version of *King Lear,* but the director passes her over in favor of an untalented Polish actress for the simple but important reason that she is the mistress of the company's purveyor of plays, the aging poet Noël Chérouvrier. In a fit of

pique, Suzanne leaves the theater, and Vidame remarks
cynically that when the time comes he will need but to
crook his finger and the theater-intoxicated Suzanne will
come back to the fold with grateful alacrity. This remark
is borne out by events, but not before Suzanne has
enjoyed a two-month interlude that takes up most of the
novel.

Suzanne's temporary alienation from the theater led
her into the arms of the Baudouin family, whose eldest
son Philippe had courted her for some time. When she
suddenly accepted his oft-repeated invitation to visit his
family at Nesles, Philippe took her home with him. The
patriarch of this remarkable family was Jérôme Baudouin,
a gentle, blinded war veteran, the father of eight children.
His wife and five daughters were all accomplished house-
keepers. Philippe was a well-known painter; another son,
Hubert, was a botanist; and the youngest son, Marc, was
a sculptor. Living with the family were a young cousin
and her illegitimate child, who were accepted on an
affectionate footing with the other members of the household.

The family life of these folk was one continuous
round of hikes, picnics, and garden parties, punctuated
by amateur theatricals and choral singing. In what appeared to be odd moments, the girls cooked, baked,
churned butter, and made preserves. The boys repaired
the house or built additions to the outbuildings. In a
word, the intellectual and manual arts went hand in hand,
and the result was a charming and harmonious family
life. Into this circle came Suzanne Pasquier. Gifted herself, and with gifted brothers and sister, she was not
swept off her feet by the Baudouins' wealth of talent,
but because her own family was not a happy one, she
was impressed by the harmony and affection that pre-
vailed.

Two happy months passed. Then the spell was broken by the arrival of a member of Vidame's troupe, who came to reawaken Suzanne's passion for the theater. She agreed to sail within forty-eight hours for a tour of South America, but before leaving she gave herself to Hubert. He alone of the three heartbroken Baudouin boys went to Paris to try to persuade her to return to Nesles.

Despite the charm of its country setting, this story has several defects. To a degree not found in the previous volumes in the series, Duhamel appears to manage the action. He relies throughout on almost unrelieved exposition for his effects, allowing the characters little chance to speak or act for themselves. The realism of the story is thus weakened. It is further weakened by the presentation of a situation so idyllic that it strains the reader's credulity. As he reads of the peace and concord, devoid of all complication, that prevail in the Baudouin household, one wonders whether this can be true to life, especially since the preceding eight volumes have been devoted to a demonstration that life is seldom happy or carefree. The central problem of the novel is really a very simple one: whether Suzanne, to whom grease paint and klieg lights are as precious as air and water, can give up the theater to live in Nesles as the wife of one of the Baudouin boys. The answer is no, and this fact is obvious from the first page.

La Passion de Joseph Pasquier, the tenth and final volume of the *Chronique des Pasquier,* was published abroad in 1944. Once again Duhamel has brought into the foreground a single member of the family. In 1925 we find Joseph about to take several important steps. He is preparing his candidacy for the Académie française, and he has the cheek to ask Laurent to postpone his own candidacy for the Institut des Sciences. His personal and business affairs are ever more complicated. He is investing heavily in Mexican oil wells. He has a mistress. He has success, but not happiness. His older son, who resembles him, bests him in a business deal. He regards his younger son, Jean-Pierre, as effeminate, because he has expressed a desire to become an artist instead of a businessman. His daughter Delphine is in love with her father's secretary, Blaise Delmuter.

The plot, for all its incidents, is relatively uncomplicated. Joseph has talked too freely to a newspaperman, and the resulting article ruined his chances for the Academy. An English financier bought up his oil wells for a low price on the eve of their most successful production. His mistress was unfaithful to him. His wife, Hélène, refusing to accept his reproaches for her own infidelity, ran away with Delphine to seek refuge in the home of Laurent. His secretary deserted him, and his son Jean-Pierre jumped out of a third-story window. As the story ends, the boy was attended by his Uncle Laurent, who could not say whether he would recover or not.

As Joseph's house of cards comes tumbling down, one cannot help but feel that the catastrophe is not altogether convincing. What occurs ought to seem the logical outcome of Joseph's own actions. Instead, we seem to be witnessing his punishment at the hands of his creator, a punishment for his philistinism. This lessens the realism of the book. Joseph's overly involved business dealings might have been used to bring about his downfall, but the author has failed to use this possibility, even though it would seem hardly credible that so astute a businessman as Joseph could be worsted so easily. Heretofore Joseph's weaknesses have been those of character. To find that he is not even a realist in business comes as something of a shock.

For better or worse the rest of the family have been

disposed of. Cécile is on tour in New York. Ferdinand is still secure though unhappy. Mother Pasquier is living with Laurent and is being tenderly cared for by her daughter-in-law, Jacqueline. Of Laurent himself we have little news except the fact that he has become a professor at the Collège de France. Of Suzanne, no word. Father Pasquier lies buried at Nesles, having died three years before this phase of the chronicle began. His death was ignominious. He died away from home, in the apartment of a mistress. But it was the proud Joseph and not the sensitive Laurent who most bemoaned this fact. Laurent assures Joseph that he is at peace with his father's memory. He has come at last to accept him as he was, and is willing to pronounce a benediction over his grave.

This is the end of the novel as we have it, although Duhamel has refrained from writing the word *finis*. The saga in the aggregate numbers more than 2,500 pages, and was in the process of writing for more than ten years. From the standpoint of size alone the Pasquier chronicle is a large monument to Duhamel's talent. Into its composition went a variety and brilliance that none of his previous achievements can equal.

6

THE ART OF THE
PASQUIER CHRONICLE

IN THE SAME fashion that Duhamel furnished his readers with a commentary on the composition of the *Vie et aventures de Salavin,* he has provided us with an account of the evolution of the Pasquier story. He intended it, he says, to be an imaginary memoir paralleling but not actually describing his own career, and combining reality with fiction. Characteristically, he began to reveal his hand while he was still playing it. In 1934, when the *Chronique des Pasquier* was barely under way, he took his readers into his confidence in an essay entitled *Remarques sur les mémoires imaginaires.* It is typical of him that he thought such an explanation might prove interest-

ing and useful and that he sought to provide it, for
Duhamel's writing is frequently accomplished in two
phases, the creative process and his analysis of it. With
his right hand, as it were, he fashions a work of imagination, and with his left he explains his method and purpose.
Sometimes this explanation takes the form of an account
of his hero's evolution, as in the case of his work on
Salavin. At other times it consists of a discussion of
unrelated matters that have been suggested to him in the
course of writing the major work. At still other times
both kinds of commentaries are offered. *Remarques sur
les mémoires imaginaires* is enlightening both as to Duhamel's purpose in general and as to the procedures he
used in creating the Pasquier story in particular.

In his *Essai sur le roman* Duhamel had given his personal views on the place of the novel in modern literature.
In the *Remarques* he amplifies these ideas and explains
his attitude toward the intermingling of reality and fiction
in a work of imagination. As Duhamel sees it, the narrator
of an actual occurrence is always hard put to confine
himself to objective reality. A modicum of fiction, whether
in the form of embellishment or of unconscious distortion,
usually manages to creep in. This is, or can be, the
beginning of art, an art that is within the reach of the
least creative and least imaginative storyteller. In the
hands of the novelist, the subconscious process becomes
a conscious one, the very essence of creative writing. To
the new "reality" created by the blending of the experienced with the imaginary, Duhamel gives the name
"poetic reality." Because he felt strongly that this is the
only reality that matters to the novelist, he declared that
he would not write his own memoirs. He proposed to
content himself instead with writing the infinitely more
satisfying biography of Laurent Pasquier, his fictional

counterpart. Later he changed his mind and began to set down the story of his life, and in the course of this memoir he has discussed in some detail the proportions of "poetic" and "actual" reality in the *Chronique des Pasquier*.

For Duhamel the characters of his fiction are as real as the people he has known, sometimes more so. He declares:

> Je l'ai dit, je me rappelle très imparfaitement ma vie. Je me rappelle, en revanche, jour par jour, minute, par minute, la vie de Laurent Pasquier, ma créature, mon compagnon imaginaire.[1]

We are thus forewarned that Laurent Pasquier and his family have not been created out of whole cloth. To imagine them the author drew on his own life and experience and on that of his family. To this background he added the adventures of friends and associates and to the mixture contributed a number of purely fanciful elements. The proportions in which Duhamel's art has mixed reality and fancy are of much interest to those who admire his work.

Even superficially the resemblance between the Pasquier and Duhamel families is great. Laurent Pasquier, like Georges Duhamel, is a biologist and physicist, and like Duhamel, his father preceded him by two years in earning a medical degree. The Duhamels and Pasquiers both move about a good deal, in and out of Paris. These are the obvious similarities.

It is also apparent that into the character of Laurent Pasquier Duhamel put many of his own aspirations, perplexities, and passions. It would perhaps be indiscreet to inquire too closely into the possibility that Duhamel's early years were embittered, as were those of Laurent, by his father's follies. César Santelli, however, hints that such was the case, and the author's own statement on the extent of Father Pasquier's resemblance to his own father is as follows:

Avoir eu sous les yeux pendant près de cinquante années, un modéle aussi frappant que Pierre-Emile Duhamel et n'en rien laisser subsister, pour telle ou telle raison de doctrine et d'esthétique, voilà qui serait absurde. Je déclare donc sans détour que j'ai, en composant les figures du père et de la mère, dans la *Chronique des Pasquier,* emprunté beaucoup d'éléments à mes modèles familiers. J'ajoute que, par la suite et le récit prenant de l'ampleur, mes peintures se sont, en bien des façons, éloignées des modèles. J'ajoute encore que les enfants Pasquier n'ont absolument aucun rapport avec mes frères et mes sœurs. Cécile, Suzanne, Joseph et Ferdinand sont les créatures de mes songes.[2]

Father Pasquier, therefore, came to resemble Duhamel's own father less than might be imagined. "I enjoyed myself a great deal with Dr. Pasquier," he says. "My own father . . . was less gay, and less brilliant."[3]

Father Duhamel was apparently no less addicted to fits of temper than his fictional counterpart, for Duhamel relates that once when one of his patients refused to pay for a visit, because he had not sent for the doctor, Dr. Duhamel, Senior, smashed a bottle of medicine rather than let such a miser have the benefit of it. He further relates that his father had a way of looking at other men's wives that greatly distressed his mother.

The other personages in the *Chronique des Pasquier* are also compounded of fact and fancy. The Wasselin family in *Le Notaire du Havre* was borrowed from the neighboring Waterloo family, about whose actual private life Duhamel never knew much. Justin Weill was taken in part from recollections of a school friend who was killed at a grade crossing at the age of fourteen. In his novel Duhamel took pleasure in recreating the boy's life, of which he says:

> Et comme le poète a des pouvoirs discrétionnaires, j'ai décidé, bien des années plus tard, de donner à l'ombre de mon ami cette vie qu'il n'avait point vécue, de le faire durer, jouir et souffrir une ample et riche existence, sous le nom de Justin, l'un de mes personnages, et de vivre avec lui, en rêve, toute cette fervente affection qui nous avait été ravie.[4]

Justin also partook of other models, and Gabriel Adain, the friend of Duhamel's youth, with his touchiness, temper, and changes of mood, must have lent a number of traits to Justin, just as he lent them to many others among Duhamel's characters.

The compounding of reality and fiction thus permeates the entire work, he tells us, and from this we infer that in the *Chronique des Pasquier* there is no character who does not owe one or more traits to persons whom Duhamel knew and whom he has frequently described in his memoirs. What he has said on this subject encourages this assumption. In some cases it has been his pleasure to bolster our assumptions with positive identifications. At other times he says nothing about his models. But of this we can be certain: hardly a person or event is wholly imaginary. He even deprecates whole creation. He has written:

> Le peuple immense des lecteurs a tendance à croire ou bien que les récits des écrivains correspondent à la stricte réalité, «c'est comme ça que c'est arrivé!» ou bien que le créateur a tout sorti du néant. Ces deux opinions contraires sont également puériles. Toutes les histoires des narrateurs ont un œuf à l'origine, cela comme en biologie, *omne vivum ex ovo*. Tous nos récits ont un germe et des racines dans ce qu'on appelle bien vaguement le réel.[5]

Perhaps no phase of the Pasquier story has attracted more attention from those who would like to unravel the tangled skeins of truth and fiction than *Le Désert de Bièvres*, which is from many points of view the finest volume in the series. For many who read the book, it is little more than an ill-disguised history of the Abbaye de Créteil. But such is a superficial view. In his memoirs Duhamel has warned his readers that the separation of the real from the imaginary will be particularly difficult here. The task, he declares, is not even easy for him:

. . . j'ai raconté, dans le *Désert de Bièvres*, une histoire un peu semblable à celle de l'Abbaye. La maison imaginaire est venue tout aussitôt me cacher la maison réelle. Que je pense à l'Abbaye, et c'est Bièvres que je vois d'abord. Pour retrouver le rivage de la Marne, nos saisons, nos querelles, nos espoirs, nos déconvenues, il me faut écarter avec obstination les fictions familières. Je n'y réussis pas toujours.[6]

But even if Duhamel were willing to sort out fact from fiction in all his works of imagination, it is doubtful whether he would do so. It is his notion that "poetic reality," if properly presented, should effectively conceal from the public which elements of the story are real and which are imagined. When the blending process is complete, the real episodes may seem incredible, and the imagined ones may come to be accepted as the most realistic elements of the story. When he wrote his essay on imaginary memoirs, he said that he could still distinguish between the two elements himself, but that as time passed, the imagined part tended to gain on the real in his mind. Later, when he wrote his memoirs, he found it amusing to throw out a few hints about the members of the Pasquier family, but he has never told the whole story. The blend that he has created is his art, and one should not be misled by his candor into thinking that he intends to furnish a page-by-page guidebook or key to the Pasquiers. Duhamel's success must be judged as he wishes, by the validity of the finished chronicle itself. "Far better," he says, "to impart a sense of reality to a fictitious story than to seem to be writing fiction when telling a 'true' story. . . . My greatest wish, when I write a story is that the reader, impressed by its air of truth, should say, as he thinks of me: 'that must certainly have happened to Duhamel.' "[7]

As we examine the lives and the actions of the Pasquier family, we are at once struck by the fact that each one has a dominant trait. In Mother Pasquier the maternal instinct is to the fore. In Papa Pasquier the desire to succeed thrusts aside even the powerful sex drive. Joseph's ambition, though it encompasses all forms of success, is principally an urge to get rich. Timid Ferdinand is the victim of hypochondria. Suzanne is led on by her love of the stage, Cécile by her love of music. Laurent, who is the best imagined of the Pasquiers and the most complex, is motivated in most circumstances by his search for an ideal to which he can dedicate his life. This insistence on a single dominant force in each of his characters comes as a bit of a surprise, for Duhamel had said in his essay on the novel, and also in a preface to *Confession de Minuit,* that characters dominated by a single motive are hardly complex enough for the novel of this century. Yet it cannot be denied that his Pasquiers tend in this direction. With Ferdinand, Duhamel's skill is not sufficient to eradicate the impression of such a development. With Suzanne and Cécile he is more successful, whereas Joseph, Laurent, and the Pasquier parents are most successful of all. All these acquire the kind of independent existence that we demand of the authentic creations of great fiction.

The picture of Papa Pasquier is a masterpiece. He is full-bodied, self-willed, ambitious, and, withal, amusing, and his appearances in the novel are awaited with anticipation.

Duhamel has taken great pains to provide appropriate backgrounds for each of these characters. Each Pasquier —and for this we must thank the master passion—has a milieu of his own with which we identify him. For Laurent we have the world of science and of the laboratory, which Duhamel knows so intimately. For Cécile and Suzanne there is the world of music and of the theater respectively, and these areas are also within the personal experience of the novelist. Such background as Duhamel has given us for the scientific career of Laurent, the musical career of Cécile, and the acting career of Suzanne is therefore entirely convincing. With Joseph he moves into the world of business and finance, and since his experience in these areas is less, his touch is less sure. From the first appearance of Joseph in the novel we see the profit motive as a consuming one. We learn in the successive volumes that Joseph is always engaged in some sort of commerce, that he traffics in arms, buys and sells commodities and properties, and trades in the stock market. We are given to understand that his activities are vast, complicated, and always at least partly dishonest. Yet the total picture is a bit cloudy and slightly incredible. The world of the theater, as Duhamel and his characters know it, is a place of jealousies, hatreds, and quarrels, but also one of real satisfactions. So it is with the laboratory. Human failings are not left behind amid the test tubes of research. Laurent Pasquier experiences violent emotions in his work no less than Joseph in his, and also a certain bitterness that may possibly reflect the actual experience of his creator, Georges Duhamel.

Joseph's financial deals, by way of contrast, come through dimly, like the movements of a water ballet, visible, even interesting, but not sharply defined.

Of the subsidiary characters, Justin Weill is most real. Obviously, Duhamel took great pains in his development, and his friendship with Laurent Pasquier is of central importance in the chronicle. Duhamel chose to depict Justin as a Jew, a fact that enabled him to devote much space to a consideration of the aspirations and ambitions of the Jewish people of France. He was less interested, however, in this problem as such than in the larger question of religion, suggested by Judaism. He seems to attribute to the Jews a keener insight into spiritual concerns than is possessed by the average Gentile, and Justin's presence in a given scene is often a pretext or point of departure for a discussion of the basis of religious belief in modern society. Duhamel has often said that he is an agnostic, but he has also taken pains to make plain that he is sympathetic to the faith of others. In *Vue de la terre promise*, where Laurent and Justin talk of religion at some length, the Jewish concept of a Messiah is discussed in detail. It was Justin's view, though he was not orthodox in his beliefs, that the Messiah might yet come, and for a time he cherished the hope that he might himself embody the prophecy. The idea of a Messiah is also personally attractive to Duhamel, but he believes it unlikely that he will ever return to the faith of his childhood.

Discussions of religion between Laurent and Justin also furnish needed background for a consideration of the problems of idealism in general. Both boys hold fast to a concept of absolute purity, an ideal that they are careful to dissociate from mere sexual continence. Their purpose in life, though difficult or even impossible of attainment, is to devote themselves to an ideal. As Duhamel has observed elsewhere, every man seeks a church. Salavin sought sainthood. The badly wounded soldiers of the First World War sought a salvation that was more than a physical cure at the hands of the surgeon. Duhamel himself has been everlastingly embarked on this very quest, and in the conversations between his two characters, one a Jew, the other a Gentile, he has given interesting treatment to the essence of the problem from the Jewish point of view:

Les plus grands tyrans du peuple sont presque toujours sortis du peuple. Les plus acharnés des antisémites ont souvent du sang juif dans les veines. Et ce sont les métis qui parlent des nègres avec le plus cruel mépris.

—Je ne vois pas très bien . . .

—Excuse-moi. Je rêvais. Est-ce que tu crois que c'est facile d'être Juif? J'ai tous les soucis des autres hommes, plus un souci majeur et constant: je suis Juif. Encore une fois, pardon.[8]

Such other social problems as Duhamel chose to treat in his novel were also made an integral part of the story. He generally refrained from expressing his own opinion as such. In planning this long work he was faced with the necessity of choosing which aspects of French life, in the years from 1905 to 1925, he would treat in detail. He evidently did not plan, as did Jules Romains, or his revered predecessor Balzac, to attempt a complete coverage of the events, imaginary and historical, of the period under scrutiny. He deliberately refrained from taking up the political cries of the period, such as the separation of Church and State, the reverberations of the Dreyfus case, and, later, the problems of reparations and the League of Nations. The Pasquiers and their associates are not unaware of world problems, but these events touch them in much the same manner as newspaper headlines touch the average reader. The news when bad produces a vague worry or a momentary frown, after which the personal concerns of everyday living push the headlines out of the foreground of consciousness. Only when world events materially affect their personal interests are the personages of the novel much aroused by them. Joseph Pasquier, for instance, because he trafficked in arms, was interested in all the wars that occurred. His brother Laurent ignored all but the most catastrophic events—not deliberately, but because the routine of the laboratory and hospital prevented him from taking time to think about them. It was only when the long-threatened European war of 1914 struck and Laurent had to change abruptly from his hospital garb to a military uniform that the happenings of the day had meaning for him. The Pasquier chronicle then skipped from 1914 to 1920, and there is but incidental mention in the next volume of the supposed activities of the Pasquiers during the war years. In his war books the author had had his say vehemently and at length. In his long work he preferred to speak of other things.

The plots that hold our interest in the *Chronique des Pasquier* are complicated ones, and this is surprising, because up to the time that he began this work, Duhamel had not laid major emphasis on this aspect of fiction. Some critics had even doubted whether he had the ability to construct a regular plot. The structure of the earlier plays is sometimes flimsy, whereas his war sketches, by their very nature, precluded the use of complex plots. His postwar short stories and novels were also long on atmosphere and short on structure, and the psychological approach of the Salavin series required a minimum of plot. By way of contrast the *Chronique des Pasquier* is more conventional than any of the earlier works. Whether Duhamel did not know how to construct a plot or merely had never had occasion to do so was answered at once. The distrustful critics were routed, for Duhamel showed himself adept in plot construction, and not in that alone, but in the allied skills of interpolating incidents and the simultaneous handling of several plots and subplots. From the very first page of *Le Notaire du Havre* we are made to feel the force of the unseen but important person, the distant notary, while the deeds of Papa Pasquier and his neighbors, the Courtois and the Wasselins, provide a wealth of incident. Succeeding volumes are no less complex. In only three volumes do the plots appear to be tailored more to the author's purpose than to the ends of the characters themselves, that is, in *Les Maîtres, Le Combat contre les ombres,* and *La Passion de Joseph Pasquier,* in all of which the situations seem a trifle forced. These exceptions aside, Duhamel has created a variety of plots, the equal perhaps of any in the contemporary French novel.

Duhamel himself has tended to give more importance, at least in theory, to certain other aspects of his work. His conviction is that the more lasting effects of a novelist are achieved by the subtler factors of character and atmosphere. He wished above all to succeed in the creation of the intimate, the delicately contrived nuance. For this purpose he had several well-developed and often-repeated devices. One of these is the observation of the tics and manias of his characters, a device that he has used, as Balzac had done, in all his fiction. In the *Chronique des Pasquier* he uses this device with telling effect. M. Wasselin is a nail-biter, and his pleasure in his habit is described in detail. Among the Pasquiers themselves Mama has a convulsive trembling of the jaw when

she is under emotional stress. Ferdinand's myopia is
frequently mentioned. Joseph's tic is a convulsive movement of the jaw, something like his mother's. When he
talked with too much animation, "his jaw twitched in a
spasmodic manner."[9] Papa Pasquier had his own manias,
including an intolerance of the tics and manias of everyone else. In a memorable and amusing passage Laurent
gives a sample of one of his father's rude outbursts:

> Mon père, par exemple, ne pouvait souffrir la laideur. Le
> spectacle du ridicule, chez les autres, le trouvait intolérant.
> La réaction était franche, immédiate, peu prévisible. Nous
> étions dans l'omnibus, un monsieur d'un certain âge, peut-être
> même décoré de la Légion d'honneur, ce qui, en ce temps-là,
> représentait presque un signe particulier, se mettait à bâiller,
> à rebâiller. Mon père, sortant de la réserve, prenait alors la
> parole. L'attaque, en général, était directe. «Allons, monsieur,
> disait-il d'une voix en même temps suave et sifflante, vous
> n'avez donc pas honte de nous montrer tout ce que vous avez
> dans la bouche?»[10]

This too is a distinguishing mark of the *Chronique des
Pasquier*,—its robust and effervescent humor, a humor
sometimes tinged with a gentle irony, and sometimes
unsubtle to the point of boisterousness. For the most part
the humor in this series is provided by the intransigence
of Papa, but it is also provided sometimes by the sober
Joseph and the usually dismal Ferdinand. Duhamel
dispensed by far the greater part of his humor in the first
volume, but there are ironic and funny passages scattered
through the novel. In *La Nuit de la Saint-Jean*, Papa has
his fun at the expense of certain Parisian street names:

> Quand je pense qu'il y a des malheureux pour aller se loger
> rue Pirouette ou Cité Vacheron. C'est à pleurer. Rue Fessart,
> au moins, c'est drôle, ça sonne bien, ça ne manque pas de
> bouquet; mais passage Gatbois! Qu'est-ce que c'est que ce

Gatbois? Qu'est-ce qu'il a fait, ce Gatbois? Un palais, tu entends? Un palais! On me donnerait en toute propriété un palais rue de la Cossonerie ou rue Biscornet que je n'en voudrais pas. Il faut avoir le courage de ses impulsions et de ses répulsions.[11]

Papa's wrath is always good for a laugh. "In his fits of temper he was something of an artist."[12]

The same preoccupation with the odd and grotesque aspects of humanity that furnished humor in the hands of Papa Pasquier is also seen in some of the author's descriptions. Here is Joseph on a visit to the hiding place of his treasure:

. . . mais cette nuit-là comme les autres, chaque fois qu'il descendait dans ce réduit, il se sentait saisi d'une incompréhensible lassitude, et il partait à somnoler, un fil de salive à l'angle des lèvres, les grosses mains abandonnées, avec leurs bouquets de poils, sur les genoux engourdis.[13]

Passages of this sort, which give an intimate if ugly view of a character, can be cited almost at random in all ten volumes, revealing not only a gift of observation but the gift of fine writing and skill in accurate description.

Odors as well as sights are analyzed here, as in Salavin's story. Laurent thus describes the odors that surrounded his childhood:

. . . si je ressuscite un jour, fantôme aveugle, c'est au nez que je reconnaîtrai la patrie de mon enfance. Senteurs d'une fruiterie, fraîches, acides et qui, vers le soir, s'attendrissent, virent doucement au relent de marécage, de verdure fanée, d'aliment mort. Fumet de la blanchisserie qui sent le linge roussi, le réchaud, la fille en nage. Remugle de la boucherie qui tient le «bouillon et bœuf,» fade et terrible parfum des bêtes sacrifiées; note résineuse, forestière de la sciure de sapin répandue sur le dallage.[14]

Duhamel, we see, is not content with mere narration, nor with the mere application of narrative skills to description. The choice of words in the above citation, and their flow, are calculated to recreate the atmosphere, the smells, the scenes of Paris. And at the same time the paragraph appears so artless, so simple, that we are left with the impression—erroneous, of course—that any schoolboy could do as much. As Duhamel has said, he wishes to create in detail the *ambiance* of his characters. We must taste their food with them, smell the symphony of smells that surround them, see the warts and moles on each homely face, and laugh at their own and other people's foibles. It is this intimate quality that, in his opinion, makes both plot and character truly memorable.

The warmth of the Pasquier story, and the humane sentiments with which it is permeated, have led P. H. Simon to compare Duhamel's achievement to that of Charles Dickens, though certainly Duhamel avoids the maudlin sentimentality that was the Englishman's failing. Times have changed in France as well as in England since the time of Dickens and Balzac. Duhamel's chronicle has had to stand with its French and European competitors, when psychological realism is the order of the day. This much he could know with little more effort than reading the novels of his French rivals. Few there are today who deny him a prominent place among French writers of fiction in this century.

Critical opinion has been almost uniformly kind to the Pasquier chronicle. The book was well received abroad. In fact, because of the occupation of Paris, foreign critics were the only ones able to comment on the later volumes. What dissent there was centered on the topical character of the last five volumes. Readers had enjoyed the family as a family, especially in the first two books, and they missed the hearthside scenes when the work came to treat sequentially the lives of Cécile, Suzanne, and Joseph. "Papa Pasquier is sorely missed," said Albert Guérard in reviewing *La Passion de Joseph Pasquier* for *Books Abroad*. Perhaps most readers felt the same, but most were also grateful to Duhamel for giving us the Pasquiers. On this all agree.

7

CHILDREN'S BOOKS, FANTASY, AND SATIRE

NO ONE should be surprised to learn that Georges Duhamel has written whimsical and fanciful books, some for adults and some for and about children, because his creative genius has encompassed almost every other sort of imaginative work. Writing is for him an avocation as well as a vocation, and throughout his career he has spent his leisure hours in writing of a less demanding sort than was required for the production of his major novels. During the First World War, as we have seen, the pen that gave us the magnificent creations *Civilisation* and *Vie des martyrs* was also busy recording the meditations that became *La Possession du monde,* and the sober reflections published as *Entretiens dans le tumulte*. The postwar period was equally rich in minor masterpieces quite outside the main currents of creation that gave us Salavin and the Pasquier family. One might venture to call these productions the literature of repose—at least, Duhamel hints that they are such.

The immediate source of Duhamel's books about children was his own three sons, and, to a lesser degree, the throng of nieces and nephews who visit him in his summer home at Valmondois. Duhamel likes children. He showers them with affection and, so the report goes, spoils them horribly. He regards their presence in the house, even during working hours, as not merely inevitable but as a pleasant accompaniment of his work and of his thoughts. He says that anyone who cannot concentrate when children are present does not deserve to work at all. For him they are a continual source of joy and wonder.

The first of Duhamel's books to take notice of his growing family was *Les Plaisirs et les jeux* (1922), which was written (one wonders how) while he was in the midst of a score of other projects. The subtitle is *Les Mémoires du Cuib et du Tioup,* which refers to the nicknames of his two boys, who were at that time two and four years old. The memoir is cast in the form of random and rhapsodic remarks about the children's development. It is charming and delightful in spots, but its reading public was fairly limited, and was probably expected to be. Only those who are fond of children can even vaguely understand and sympathize with the wide-eyed delight with which the parent-author contemplates the doings of his infant prodigies. Their winsome ways and childish prattle, their pranks and their spankings, are dwelt upon with lavish and loving attention. Here is a passage on thumb-sucking that well illustrates the style of this doting memoir:

Durant sa première année, le Cuib fut un très brillant suceur
de pouce. Le doigt bien engagé, la main repliée, l'index
accroché au nez pour fixer l'ensemble, telle était sa manière.
Elle n'allait pas sans élégance et dissimulait assez bien ce que
l'opération a de délicat, d'intime.[1]

Elsewhere Duhamel remarks that his being a doctor
only made it worse for him when his children got hurt.
His medical training enabled him to envision more horrible surgical implications of his children's cuts and bruises
than would occur to a layman. He satirizes amusingly
the family friend, Barnabé, who is childless yet full of
advice, and contrasts him with the anxious parent, who,
in the midst of repeated crises, must try to find at least
provisional solutions for all problems.

In the course of *Les Plaisirs et les jeux,* Duhamel
examines briefly some of the literature about children
produced in France: Montaigne's famous essay *Sur l'institution des enfants,* the appeal to children of La Fontaine's
Fables and Rousseau's *Emile.* He comments that most of
those who have written about children have spoiled their
observations by a desire to generalize. This, he says, he
will avoid at all cost. His commonsense conclusion, after
perusing a number of books of advice on child-raising, is
that in bringing up one's children it is best to be guided
by daily observation and to forget most of what the
theorists have written. Of the abundance of recent works,
whether written to entertain or to explore seriously the
world of children he has little to say.

From this book we gain the impression that Duhamel
is a sensitive, even an overly affectionate parent, and the
ease and charm with which he writes do much to heighten
his effects. Here, in a memorable passage, is a description
of the coming of the night:

La nuit est si noire, maintenant, qu'elle semble tombée pour
toujours.

Pourtant la maison respire; mais doucement, insensiblement,
à la manière des bêtes hibernantes, engourdies dans leur four-
rure.

Parfois, des profondeurs, monte un bruit léger: soupir des
petits dormeurs, rire ou parole arrachés par le rêve.

Le plus vieux meuble craque une dernière fois, sévèrement.
Et c'est fini. Tout s'immobilise.

Le silence et la nuit se mêlent . . .[2]

Few were the critics who could resist the charm of this
book, and Duhamel therefore had the pleasure of reading
reviews that were almost uniformly favorable.

In a similar vein Duhamel wrote *Les Erispaudants*
(1926), a much shorter memoir about his children. The
point of departure was a game the children were playing
in a corner of the summer garden. The name in the title,
says Duhamel, is of obscure origin, but it seems to have
been applied by the children to themselves to distinguish
them from the adults of the household. By their contacts
with the older people, the Erispaudants reveal that they
are of a different race. There is genuine child psychology
here, much of it presented from the child's point of view,
in a whimsical and amusing fashion. We see the children's
pride, their humor, and, at times, their sadism. The book
is done with sensitivity and quite equals, in its fourteen
pages, the longer *Les Plaisirs et les jeux*, to which it is
frequently appended.

To a related genre belongs another short work of a few
years later (1932). This book, entitled *Mon Royaume*,
describes the adventures of the children once more, including on this occasion a number of nieces and nephews,
as they set up a miniature city-state in the backyard. The
author notes, not without sorrow, that the domain of

childhood is a prey to most of the difficulties that plague the adult world: dictatorship and eventual revolt, laws, fines and punishments, money, and even newspapers. He remarks that although the participants in the game are very young, the main character types have already emerged. Among the children may be found, even at the beginning of their lives, the poet, the logician, the intriguer, the improviser, the drone, and the worker. He talks about education and once more makes fun of childless persons who presume to tell parents the principles of child guidance. For him the basis of an approach to children must be an intimate knowledge of each individual child, gained by careful and accurate observation. He rules out any system that pretends to lay down laws for children in general. He desires adequate motivation for learning and freedom from unnecessary restraints, but feels that they should be accompanied by a modicum of discipline. He would train the memory but encourage independent thought, and he warns that even in applying these rules, what may be good for one child is not necessarily good for another. Thus what began as another descriptive piece about children concludes as a homily on education, remaining all the while informal.

The observation of children and Duhamel's pleasure in their company were not the only aspects of his daily life that led him to write books for and about young people. The events of the postwar period, no less than the events of the conflict itself, set Duhamel to thinking about the meaning and function of civilization, and in two books, which he presented to his children and grandchildren respectively, he presented a humorous and satiric version of his thoughts, first on mechanical civilization, with an application to education, in a story called *Les Jumeaux de Vallangoujard* (1931), and many years later, a story on the effects of the atomic bomb called *Les Voyageurs de l'Espérance* (1953). The first of these tales is a satiric counterpart of a critique of modern life in his book *Scènes de la vie future*, and it treats whimsically the dilemma that the latter book meets head on. The story tells of Professor Pipe, a madcap theorist, who believes that man will attain happiness only after standardization has succeeded in making all men alike. To eliminate individual differences —and, *ipso facto,* the cause of unhappiness—Dr. Pipe and his friends, Dr. Clément ("Dr. Kindly") and Dr. Barbajou ("Dr. Bearded one")—delightful examples of Duhamel's fondness for appropriately absurd as well as absurdly appropriate names—experimented with a set of twin boys. The twins were to be raised by the rich M. Théatine Kapok, with the aid of his Negro servant Bamba. Every attempt on the part of the boys to act as individuals was frowned upon by Pipe (French slang for "visionary," by the way). When it turned out that one boy was near-sighted, it was decreed that both must wear glasses. When it was discovered that one liked science and physical exercise and the other preferred music and languages, Pipe was furious. His method began to succeed only when he sent the boys to Paris to a twentieth-century school. Here all instruction was given by movies, phonograph records, and the like. The use of these devices, together with the twins' eagerness to copy their friend Oscar de Plumapatte, made them begin to seem exactly alike. As a finishing touch to their education, Pipe sent the twins with eight other boys on a three-month trip to America. The results were favorable beyond his hopes. On their return to France all ten boys were as alike as peas in a pod. The professor's theories were vindicated.

Standardization of human beings was a fact. Happiness should then have been an automatic byproduct, but Kapok and Clément began to wonder. . . .

In the preface Duhamel addresses his own children, telling them that he has written the book for them. As if to prove it, the language of the story is uncomplicated. But obviously Duhamel intended more than he said. The book is an attack, oblique but none the less effective, on the misuse of modern inventions, a theme to which he has devoted much time and many pages of eloquent prose. His method in this book is the familiar one of satire. Issues that are seemingly true are shown to be false by extending them to logical but utterly absurd conclusions. Truths and half truths are forced on the reader by the apparent logic of the situation.

A delightful scene in the ultramodern school illustrates the approach:

La gymnastique, dans cette institution remarquable, portait le nom de mécanothérapie. Les élèves étaient installés sur des appareils très curieux qui les secouaient de haut en bas, de droite à gauche, qui les faisaient virer, pivoter, sauter, qui leur allongeaient les bras, leur pliaient les jambes et leur grattaient la plante des pieds.

Après cela, venait la leçon de natation, qui se pratiquait avec démonstration cinématographique, la leçon de conduite d'automobile, la leçon de T.S.F. où l'on apprenait à dénicher Radio-Buda-Pest, à vue de nez et du premier coup, entre cinquante postes émetteurs.

Il y avait encore, selon les jours, des leçons de publicité lumineuse, de rationalisation industrielle, de navigation sous-marine et d'aviation interplanétaire.

—Le vingtième siècle! expliquait avec orgueil M. Pépinsky. Le vingtième siècle, dans toute sa force et toute sa beauté! Ce que nous préparons, c'est l'homme du vingtième siècle!

—Parfaitement, poursuivait le professeur Pipe. L'homme de

grande série, que nous rendrons mathématiquement heureux. Vous illustrez admirablement ma méthode, la méthode pipique.[3]

Duhamel keeps up this pleasant but by no means innocent fooling for pages, suggesting thereby enough thesis topics for a generation of students of pedagogy.

More than two decades later Duhamel was moved by the threat of atomic warfare to write another children's story, *Les Voyageurs de l'Espérance*. The subject is grim: the ultimate fate of mankind when through atomic bombs a chain reaction will have covered most of the earth's surface with water. Surprisingly enough, this tale is entirely without the acidic humor that made the twins' adventure such good reading, and equally without the mood of discouragement that underlay Duhamel's outwardly jocular approach to the foibles of modern education. This is apparently a straightforward narrative, or if it be a subtle spoof, most critics have managed to miss the point.

The numerous members of the Fromond family were among the rare survivors of an atomic disaster. Safe on their yacht, *l'Espérance*, they succeeded in establishing a home on what had been once a mountain peak. They learned that few others on earth had survived but that among the survivors atomic experiment continued. Like Robinson Crusoe, the Fromonds tried to make their new home habitable. They hunted and fished, and thanks to their gardener, they planted and harvested crops. There was even a hint that they might ultimately forge iron and move into the age of metals. But despite their collective knowledge they made no attempt to acquire current for their electrical appliances, nor did they appear to know how to "cannibalize" equipment to repair their machines. Equally strange from the pen of a writer who was himself

an indefatigable hiker and camper, no one in his Fromond
family, although they had been at their new location for
three months, had thought to improvise chairs to sit upon
or a table for their use. Simple omissions like these, which
are not merely isolated examples, make the book more
than a little unrealistic. Besides, stripped of its rather thin
plot, *Les Voyageurs* is little more than an ill-disguised
discussion of several themes: the inability of science to
solve man's most pressing problems, the futility of war,
and the importance of the family as the basic unit of
society. All these matters Duhamel has treated elsewhere,
and treated better. In this instance even the impeccable
Duhamel style cannot save his book from failure: it is dull
as well as farfetched.

From writing books about and for his children to
writing formal satires was but a step. The kinship of
satire and children's literature has been amply demonstrated in history, as when, for instance, both the *Fables*
of La Fontaine and the satires of Swift found a younger
audience than that for which they were intended. Several
years before Duhamel wrote the observations on the
twentieth century that he embodied in his story of the
twins, he had ventured into the field of satire. In 1922,
the same year that his first book about his children
appeared, he published his *Lettres d'Auspasie*. This collection of satires contained the chapters "Sur les Orateurs,"
"Sur les mœurs scientifiques," and "Sur le théâtre." Four
years later these chapters were reprinted with three new
ones in *Lettres au Patagon*. The new satires were called
"Sur les amateurs," "Sur les malades," and "Sur quelques
aventures de l'esprit." In all these satiric essays the tone
is sarcastic, even bitter. "Sur les orateurs" is an attack on
the public's love for oratory, fed as it then was by violent
rightists and dangerous demagogues. Barbadou, the pro-

tagonist, is a popular speaker, willing to speak for or against any cause. The pattern is that of La Bruyère, to whose *Caractères* Duhamel refers.

The second chapter, "Sur quelques aventures de l'esprit," satirizes the plight of a young Frenchman who is looking for a cause and thinks he has found it in monarchism, which was having a pseudo-renaissance at the time. The author pities the young man and tells him that hero worship will provide no answers to his problems. This side of death there are no certainties. The best solution for life's dilemmas lies in "the adventurous quest," continuously pursued.

The fourth chapter, "Sur les savants," describes the trials of a young scientist who writes an important biological monograph only to have it criticized by jealous and incompetent associates. This theme became, of course, the dominant one in *Le Combat contre les ombres*, as we have noted, but in this early satire Duhamel was not hampered by the demands of his novel, and could give full rein to his annoyance at the trials of the scientist in getting his discoveries before the public.

The fifth chapter, "Sur les amateurs," gives an amusing picture of a lover of rare books. We watch his evolution as he changes from a frequenter of bookstalls to the possessor of a valuable collection of rarities. This progression leads to the delusion that his family have been book collectors for generations, and finally he becomes decadently interested in the nail clippings and *sexualia* of the poet Baudelaire. The philosophic conclusion is that we are all collectors in our own way, even including Arnauld, a character who gives away all that he has in order to "collect" the sensation of prodigality.

"Sur les malades" describes the strange case of Professor Bucaille, a hypochondriac who insists on treatment of all sorts. When he is finally cured of his hypochondria, it is impossible to convince him that he has contracted a real illness, and so he dies. This theme of hypochondria, which naturally interested Duhamel as a physician, was later used by him in creating Ferdinand Pasquier.

Duhamel returned again to his satirical vein in *Pages de mon carnet,* a miscellany published in 1931. Here in the midst of chapters on a variety of subjects, many of them reprinted from other books and from magazine articles, he included a satirical discussion of millionaires. Among other things he says that when the Abbaye was in search of manuscripts for its printing press, it was discovered that the richer the client, the less human and more grasping he was.

Two later books have also been products of Duhamel's liking for purposeful and satirical fantasy. The first of these, *Souvenirs de la vie du paradis* (1946), is an imaginary description of heaven, and belongs to the tradition of the fantastic journey. A skeleton plot furnishes support for what is largely a philosophical tale. The hero, Sébastien, found himself in heaven in the company of his guardian angel. Once there he gradually became acquainted with the organization of Paradise. He learned that heaven, like earth, was beset with conflicts of will and desire. The Powers of Heaven did not submit to God's will as one would have expected. God, in a word, had His problems. He was saddened by the plight of the fallen angels and sorely tried by His helpers' attitude toward men. Some were too indulgent, some too severe.

Many of the scenes are colorful and lifelike. Sébastien was upset at finding that his great-grandfather, whom he had looked forward to meeting, was uninterested in meeting him. Sébastien's mother also astonished him. Instead of enjoying eternity, she wept for the fate of her husband, who had not been admitted to heaven.

The apparent conclusion is that heaven, like happiness, is within us, and that an objective heaven, even if it existed, would be unlikely to please us.

The second of Duhamel's later fantastic novels, similar to the foregoing in that it also pretends to explore the after-life, is a fantasy of the year 1960, called *Nouvelles du sombre empire*. Hell, not heaven, is the subject this time. We follow the adventures of a suicide named Lestrangier as he learns the routine of Gehennom, or Hell. The place of punishment is much like earth. In fact, it is the successful machinations of Hell's agents on earth that have given man such playthings as the automobile, psychoanalysis, and the atomic bomb. On the last page we learn that our diarist is to be reprieved. He is to live on earth again. The account of Hell that he has written is a product of days of illness while he was hovering between life and death. Unfortunately, all Duhamel's considerable skill cannot make this fable for adults more than a rather inconsequential *tour de force*.

Akin to satire in their practice of saying one thing while meaning another are Duhamel's nature studies and pseudo-nature studies. Using his garden for a point of departure, he talks about a number of matters that are close to his heart. His impatience with pecuniary values is shown in a characteristic paragraph. When told by a visitor that it is poor economy to make one's own preserves in these days, he replies angrily:

—Ici, monsieur, lui dis-je, nous faisons nos confitures uniquement pour le parfum. Le reste n'a pas d'importance. Quand les confitures sont faites, eh bien, monsieur, nous les jetons.

J'ai dit cela dans un grand mouvement lyrique et pour éblouir le savant. Ce n'est pas tout à fait vrai. Nous mangeons nos confitures, en souvenir de leur parfum.[4]

This paragraph is taken from *Fables de mon jardin*

(1936). For Duhamel the book served a useful purpose. In it he could indulge in reminiscences. He could also criticize society in random fashion. His essays are full of sharp attacks on attitudes of which he disapproves, and the seemingly innocent remarks that he makes concerning the animals, insects, and flowers are directed more often than not toward the conduct of his fellow men. In this book he is once more the poet, though a poet in prose, and in his less angry moods he describes fondly the changing scene in the garden, the bloom and fading of flowers, and the doings of his dog. His zest is good to find in a city man, and the biologist of the laboratory is put aside for the role of descriptive horticulturist.

Not all the critics described the book so favorably. René Daumal thought that *Fables de mon jardin* had some bad implications, and he wrote in *La Nouvelle revue française* that Duhamel's apparent discussion of his garden was but a pretext for imposing his opinions. At this point, said the critic, we must resist. This was a rare dissenting view, however. Most critics liked Duhamel's nature essays.[5]

A companion volume to the *Fables de mon jardin* was *Le Bestiaire et l'herbier*, published a dozen years later (1948), which continues and completes the first volume. The spiders, beetles, and worms, no less than the plants and animals of his country retreat, inspire the author with reflections on man's destiny. Once again there is occasional melancholy, not unmixed with flashes of irony and delicate humor. As in the former book Duhamel is by turns botanist and philosopher. He also suggests occasionally, although the suggestion is belied by his vigorous mind and no less vigorous prose, that he is growing old, and that old age is making it easier for him to accept the world.

PART II

THE OBSERVER AND COMMENTATOR

L'ŒUVRE de ma vie, j'entends ici l'œuvre écrite, celle que je vois déposée sur un large rayon de ma bibliothèque, est en somme un long cri d'alarme. Je n'ai presque parlé que de la souffrance, de la misère, des maladies, des égarements intellectuels, de la guerre et de la mort. Pourtant je jouis d'une réputation surprenante: celle d'un écrivain optimiste. C'est peut-être aussi que je suis, par nature,—c'est-à-dire sans y être volontairement pour grand-chose—assez dépourvu de certain venin, d'un certain esprit d'aggression. Ce fameux esprit est, aujourd'hui, et la moutarde et le poivre d'ouvrages qui, telle la mante religieuse, dévorent ceux qu'ils font jouir.

8

THE PATRIOT AND
WORLD TRAVELER

AS DUHAMEL has wisely observed, a literary work
can best reach universal proportions by depicting feelingly and realistically the men of a given time and place.
This principle he has successfully followed in his creative
writing. Salavin and the Pasquiers, as well as the wounded
soldiers of the war sketches, appeal to foreign readers for
their human qualities, but no one is likely to forget that
these qualities have been developed and nurtured by a
French environment. It is precisely because the creator
of Salavin and Laurent Pasquier put aside any grandiose
notion of depicting mankind and confined himself to
delineating purely French characters that their essential

humanity is apparent to all. Similarly, in the settings of his other novels and in his plays and stories, Duhamel has generally restricted himself to Paris and its environs, and it is the skill and affection with which he pictures that one city that enables him to create for us an impression of reality that arouses admiration in readers who have never been to France. This is as it should be. France is and must be the focal point of most of Duhamel's work. In this he remains within the tradition of French literature from Balzac to his own time.

Naturally enough, not solely in his creative works does Duhamel's deep-seated, tenacious, and all-inclusive affection for his own country appear. Duhamel is French to the core, and his inevitable patriotism is not untinged at times with conscious as well as unconscious provincialism. In a long essay that he published immediately after the liberation of Paris in 1944, entitled *Civilisation française,* Duhamel addressed himself to his downtrodden and prostrate country. His words are a reaffirmation of faith in France and her people and an antidote to postwar defeatism. The essay is beautifully and feelingly written. In it Duhamel goes back to the past glories of the French nation to remind his countrymen that they have much to be proud of. He tells them they have contributed greatly to world civilization in a variety of fields, such as medicine, art, and literature, and that in all fields they have been preeminent. Foreigners were probably not expected to read this book, and those who do find it one-sided, even chauvinistic. According to Duhamel, France is not only the world's most polite nation, she invented politeness. She is not only the most rational, she invented rationalism. She has contrived practically single-handed most modern inventions, such as skyscrapers, radio, and movies. Not only is France outstanding in the arts, but by an almost mystical quality of mind her people enjoy French writers and composers more than non-Frenchmen can hope to do.[1] French colonial enterprises are like no others, for he sees them in their best aspects only. If France has established colonies, he says, it has not been for the usual motives of national and private gain, and "that is why the French colonial empire is like no other. It is not, in principle, a creation of bankers and business men, it is an enterprise of missionaries, teachers, and healers."[2]

The whole of *Civilisation française* is bathed in this atmosphere of patriotic fervor. France is disinterested in all her actions, he says. France is noted for the logical and juridical spirit she contributes to international conferences. Her moral superiority is great: "She has often had to reproach herself for errors and faults, but she has committed very few bad actions, and this apparently modest praise is for a nation major praise."[3]

In 1945 this sort of patriotism was well-timed, coming on the heels of five years of occupation. But Duhamel's overly sentimental view of France was not a new thing. In 1918, when he was much younger, and not yet widely traveled, he had written ecstatically in *La Possession du monde*: "France has always been the land of beginnings and of revelation. It is the chosen land of spiritual revelation."[4] And in *Vie des martyrs* he had claimed for his countrymen the gift of a "naïve grandeur of soul that exculpates for all humanity its greatest crime and forgives it after its greatest fall."[5]

Between wars Duhamel has often returned to his theme of French excellence, extolling even minor aspects of French life. The gourmet in him makes him rhapsodize on the abundance and variety of cheese in France, saying of his fellow Frenchmen's skill, perhaps with tongue in cheek, "From this single ability I recognize and admire the genius of my country, from this single ability I can understand her having produced so many great men in all fields of endeavor."[6]

The non-Frenchman may have to repress a smile at this unexpected juxtaposition of illustrious men and the art of cheese-making, but Duhamel evidently did not think it absurd. He is an enthusiastic propagandist for French food and cooking and is, we are told, no mean cook himself. His interest in food preparation has led him to discuss French culinary excellence in an essay called "Propositions sur la cuisine française" and elsewhere.

An amusing example of the lengths to which Duhamel's love for home and country can sometimes lead him is to be found in his account of his travels in Greece. It seems that while driving through a grim and stony landscape, he was seized with thoughts of France, and he thus nostalgically describes his sensations:

Le sentiment de la patrie n'en poursuit pas moins son irrésistible invasion. Cela me vient—comment l'avouer?—par les reins, et cela monte doucement jusqu'au cœur. Mystère.

—A quoi pensez-vous? me dit Arnauld, affectueux.

—A la France, ai-je répondu tout bas. Oui, à la France, et de façon bien curieuse. Dire que j'y pense est sans doute excessif. Mais il y a quelque chose, ici, qui me rappelle mon pays et je n'oserais même pas vous expliquer quelle région de ma personne cette évocation trouve sensible.

—La France! murmure Blanc.

Et, soudain, tournant la tête:

—Savez-vous que cette route, sur laquelle nous roulons si vite, fut construite par les Français, pendant la grande guerre? Elle n'est pas fort bien entrenue, et même . . .

Je n'écoute plus: j'ai tout compris.[7]

By way of contrast, he has given us in *Géographie cordiale de l'Europe* this sensible and sensitive description of the feelings that his country arouses in him, feelings to which few could take exception:

Je connais bien des choses, bien des êtres, bien des paysages; mais, atteinte et dépassé la quarante-sixième année de mon âge, il me faut déclarer que vivre longuement hors de France ne m'est pas possible. S'il m'advenait quelque jour d'encourir un châtiment mortel, j'avoue tout bas que l'exil y suffirait. J'ai bien assez voyagé, avec, chaque fois, assez d'élan, assez d'ardeur et de confiance pour confesser aujourd'hui cet attachement végétal à mon sol. J'admire les cœurs détachés qui peuvent battre n'importe où d'un rhythme égal. Je sais que mon cœur n'est pas tel. Je n'en suis ni honteux ni fier; c'est ainsi.[8]

For all his attachment to his country, Duhamel was not, as he says, prevented from visiting other lands. His natural curiosity and his fondness for studying the ways of men have taken him into nearly every country in the world. Everywhere he goes, he talks to as many people as he can, visits as many important institutions and as much else as he is able, and on his return to Paris gives an accounting of his observations in a book or essay. In these travels he is handicapped to a degree by the fact that, as he himself freely admits, he is equipped with no more than a smattering of foreign languages. But his skill in asking questions, even through an interpreter, and his shrewdness of observation, make amends for this lack. It is part of his philosophy that an educated man should know the world in general and the countries close to his own in particular. Such knowledge, he says, will enrich oneself and one's nation. He declares: "The study of our neighbors is our duty if we wish to be enlightened con-

cerning ourselves. To study, love, and celebrate the
virtues of foreign countries is to work toward our own
enrichment and to take cognizance of all human greatness."[9]

Duhamel's first serious European journey, except for
hiking expeditions in Switzerland and Italy as a young
man and a brief trip to England in 1914, was to the newly
formed republic of Czechoslovakia in 1925. On his return
home, he described his visit in an essay called "Prague,"
in which he expressed the opinion that although he neither
knew nor understood Czech, he could somehow feel the
soul of the people as he mingled with them on a walk
through the city streets. "We have been in Prague only
two hours," he said, "but we have the feeling of penetrating at once, and deeply, into the soul of this people."[10]
He was to call this sort of intuition to his aid quite often
during his subsequent journeys. In this instance his heart
was warmed. His report on Czechoslovakia was favorable.
He liked the Czechs and was hopeful of their eventual
political success.

In 1926 Duhamel undertook a far more important
journey when he headed north to Finland and Russia.
Two books were to result. The first, *Chant du nord*, was
a brief, idyllic account of Finland, to which he was later
to return and of which he would write again. The second
volume was an account of some 258 pages, called *Le
Voyage de Moscou*. Although this book is not, and was
not intended to be, a sociological treatise, it has more of
the appearance of a serious study than the brief essays
on Czechosolvakia and Finland. From the first page the
tone of the book is one of serious and impartial observation, and Duhamel appears to have been eager to learn
something good about the nation whose political regime
he profoundly distrusted.

As befitted the product of a man of letters, *Le Voyage de Moscou* (1927) was written primarily as an account of an intellectual adventure. He visited hospitals, museums, schools, laboratories, libraries, and theaters, and much that he saw he admired. He thought life was decidedly better than it had been under the czars, and everything considered, the trend of culture seemed to be upward. He tried to judge the Communist regime by its fruits. In literature he found surprising riches, though he deprecated a tendency for the state to tell young authors what kind of writing, whether realistic or romantic, was expected of them.

To the extent that he could do so, Duhamel avoided any serious discussion of politics or the political implications of communism. He said in the introduction to his book:

Pour l'homme qui montre quelque souci de l'homme, un voyage en Russie est, avant tout, une occasion exceptionnelle de méditer avec fruit sur les expériences sociales, de cultiver son opinion sur la conduite et l'avenir de l'espèce.[11]

Knowing that such an above-the-battle posture would not be popular either in France or in Russia, Duhamel felt obliged to declare his opposition to communism, basing his objection on its denial of individual liberty, but he also maintained that the most sensible attitude was to look upon the revolution as a *fait accompli*, without indulging in wishful thinking as to its imminent overthrow. Communism, he said, would come to France only if circumstances made it inevitable, and if enough people wanted it. This statement, like the book itself, was ill-received in the U.S.S.R.

As a picture of Soviet Russia in the nineteen-twenties, Duhamel's account is interesting but by no means unique.

French journalists, writers, and even tourists before him had given cogent reports on the situation there in the first decade after the revolution. If Duhamel's contribution is useful to us, it is primarily for its revelation of the depth of his concern for any and every attempt to change the course of the world with a view to human betterment. He was in his overall view neither optimistic nor pessimistic, but simply eager to inform his fellows of the progress of man as he confronts this perplexing century.

In 1931 Duhamel gathered into a single volume under the collective title *Géographie cordiale de l'Europe* his travel impressions of three small countries: the Netherlands, Greece, and Finland. In a long preface to the book Duhamel says:

J'ai fait, pour aimer les divers visages de cette Europe confuse, un effort confiant, presque toujours heureux, presque toujours récompensé. L'idylle d'autrefois n'est plus qu'un parfum mort: l'Europe nouvelle est très malade, le voyageur qui ne se paye point de sourires doit sans cesse côtoyer des précipices, buter sur des tombes, réchauffer des cendres. Si je parle de récompense et d'effort heureux, c'est qu'à visiter ces frères ennemis, on finit par découvrir leur ressemblance intime, on finit par dégager le lien qui survit à leurs querelles dramatiques, on reconnaît que, compromis dans la mêlée, il existe pourtant encore, le trésor familial, le précieux patrimoine, la commune civilisation.[12]

For the most part Duhamel lives up to this noble declaration. When traveling he is not too top-lofty to enjoy tourist attractions. In Greece and Holland he delighted in the picturesque garb of the country people. He took pleasure in the snowbound pine forests of the Karelian isthmus. He appreciated Holland's old masters and admired the cleanliness of the towns and the political freedom everywhere apparent. A few years later, in 1934, he returned to the theme of Dutch virtues in another essay, called "Eloge d'une petite nation."

In Finland Duhamel went hiking and enjoyed the national pastimes. He embarked on country excursions and sleigh rides. He met many eminent men, among them the composer Sibelius, with whom he spent an evening. In his summary he characterized Finland as "the land of harmonious culture . . . [where] . . . civilization substitutes prudence for folly and finds its views tempered as are its works by a climate that, happily, recalls man to sobriety."[13]

In Greece he was less admiring. He did not much care for her rocky promontories and sun-drenched, arid landscapes, although he was happy to discover that French literature was popular in Athens. Like Renan, he was moved by the sight of the Acropolis, and he wrote some melancholy words about the fate of the small nation in the modern world.

Among the countries that Duhamel alludes to frequently is Switzerland, which he salutes as a sanctuary of true civilization. He tells us that he travels there often because he feels it to be a sort of "earth" with which, like Antaeus, he must renew his contact in order to maintain his strength.

England he nowhere treats in an extensive essay, although he has visited the country a number of times. His attitude as he writes about the British varies from fear of their "pressure" on the citizens of French Canada, to sincere sympathy for the British people during the Second World War. In *Mémorial de la guerre blanche* he hailed Great Britain, "her great culture, her philosophers, poets, novelists, learned men, administrators, and navigators, her inventive genius, her immense empire, her five hundred million souls, her traditions and methods."[14] But he has not given either a travel book on England or a journal of his day-by-day impressions there.

A little before the stock-market crash of 1929, Duhamel made his first visit to the United States. He came on a freighter that docked at New Orleans. From there he proceeded to Chicago, and thence to New York, with stops at nearby points, returning to France within a few months. Shortly after his return home he published the most controversial of his commentaries on his travels, *Scènes de la vie future.*

The book opens with a graphic account of the traveler's being roughly handled by American immigration and quarantine authorities who, he alleges, poked him in the eye looking for traces of trachoma, thrust a thermometer between his teeth, and then forced him to answer a long and irritating questionnaire. After this disagreeable beginning he landed at New Orleans, where he went to see the Mississippi River "crossing the dull plain between two immense earthen dikes, like a shameful prisoner." He also saw the French quarter, where he sympathized with the "French," subjected as they were to "continued pressure by the Anglo-Saxon wave." He visited a Negro school and implied later that this brief contact had made the race problem clear to him.

From the South he went to Chicago, where according to acquaintances who still remember his visit, he resisted attempts to get him to visit educational and charitable institutions, or the hospitals, museums, and universities that he generally made a point of seeing during his foreign journeys. Instead he spent much of his time in his hotel room, oppressed by a sense of Chicago's noise, dirt, and size. The climax of his stay, and its crisis, was a visit to the stockyards, where he was appalled by what he saw. From Chicago Duhamel's itinerary took him to New

York, where he observed the mores of the apartment-
dwellers and took a look at the phenomena of the
prohibition era.

He concluded his book with the comment that America
had produced but two kinds of apples and few great men,
and that it was the most horrible example of the publicity-
minded, money-mad, mechanized civilization of our times,
which, if not checked, would spread to Europe and destroy
the cultural values and traditions of her ancient peoples.
"By what frightful miracle," he asked, "is this country,
so vast and so varied, which goes from the tropics to the
frozen north, this country, perhaps without grace, but
not without nobility, by what miracle has it been made
so vile and ugly?" And he concludes: "I could not love
America."[15]

At once a storm of protest arose, and a battle of the
critics began. Some French reviewers applauded Duhamel's frankness, saying that he had expressed what many
Frenchmen thought but had not dared to say. Some
reviewers in America thought that his strictures were well
deserved and pointed out that American realistic novelists
were equally outspoken concerning our defects. Others,
in both countries, denounced Duhamel bitterly, calling
him a wrecker of an international friendship of one hundred and fifty years' duration. Meanwhile, the book
enjoyed a tremendous popularity both in France and in
the United States.

In the midst of the controversy, Duhamel refused to
budge from his position. He was willing at most to try
to clarify it. In the introduction to *Géographie cordiale
de l'Europe,* he wrote:

Que si donc on me reproche d'avoir fait en Amérique un
séjour trop rapide, je ne juge pas la critique pertinente et je
ne l'admets pas à considération: en matière de connaissance,

le temps ne confère aucun droit. . . . Depuis bien des années, je souhaitais une bonne chance d'exprimer mon sentiment sur certains phénomènes ou événements, sur certains développements et certaines déviations de la civilisation dite occidentale. Je voulais écrire un ouvrage sur le cinéma, le phonographe, l'automobile, l'industrie «rationalisée,» le sport, les assurances, la publicité, les divers excès de l'étatisme, que sais-je encore? En me faisant visiter un pays où tous ces phenomènes se manifestent de manière en quelque sorte paroxystique, le sort a précipité les choses et m'a procuré mon modèle.[16]

From the subsequent discussions of the abuses of mechanical civilization, not only in America but in Europe, which Duhamel provided in later books and essays, it is plain that civilization as a phenomenon and not America as a country is the real object of the attack that he launched in *Scènes de la vie future*. Still, the manner of his attack left much to be desired, to put it mildly. The irony and even petulance that crept into his pages had a most unfortunate effect. Even Americans who agreed that the status of the Negro in society, the crowded conditions of our cities, and the high-pressure methods of some of the advertising fraternity—to name but a few of the problems of the day—needed attention and study, were reluctant to accept criticism from so hasty and so apparently hostile a visitor. In particular it was asked why the man who in Russia had been careful to avoid irony, who had tried to encompass all aspects of Soviet society in his view, should have deluded himself as to the validity of observations made in haste and almost in anger. In Russia he had sought earnestly to maintain an impartiality he was far from feeling. In America he had been bitterly sarcastic about everything American but still maintained that he intended no malice toward those who had produced the civilization he found so irritating.

Apparently his self-deception on this point was all but complete. He was therefore unprepared for the reception that his book received. Still he refused to budge in the face of critical reactions, a fact that astonished his friends no less than his severer critics.

After the Second World War Duhamel came again to our shores. In 1945, when travel was still difficult, he made a far more extensive journey than his first one, going mostly by air and including California and French Canada in his itinerary. His description of this trip is contained in his war journal of the years 1944–1946, which contains an allusion to his previous and more famous visit. He praises American tolerance for having taken his scolding so magnanimously, and he declares that on this occasion no new *Scènes de la vie future* is to result. In 1945 the hideous and inhuman skyscrapers of 1929 have become "new buildings, beautiful in their very plainness, in their very enormity."[17] The death of Franklin Roosevelt called forth from him a moving and heartfelt tribute. The United States is called "this democratic folk," and he everywhere felt himself surrounded by "guardians of culture," who showered him with affection. He saw with his own eyes the wrapping of parcels for CARE, and he was filled with gratitude. He called America generous and powerful.

Perhaps we should be content with this belated change of view and raise no questions. But did we actually deserve the kind sentiments of 1945 any more than we had deserved the ringing denunciation of 1929? The America of 1945 was still America and, despite appearances, had not changed much since his first visit. The aspects of civilization that Duhamel had criticized in those days were still with us, meaner, uglier, and more deserving of condemnation than ever. The stockyards had doubled and redoubled their capacity. Megalopolis was bigger and noisier than ever. But the Duhamel who visited our continent in 1945 had just emerged from occupied Paris, and his account of his travels was cast in the nature of a diary rather than an essay. As he promised, no brilliant but harsh attack on the dehumanization of twentieth-century civilization was included. He chose to write instead about America within the pattern of the friendly travel books of two decades before. If he did not actually retract any of his previous remarks or apologize for the stinging manner of their presentation, he did at least honestly attempt to see and appreciate another side of the country that had just fought its second world war at the side of France.

As might be expected, Duhamel greatly enjoyed his visit to French Canada. Reversing an earlier provincialism, he urged young French Canadians to learn English, and he advised the Canadian government to send promising young French Canadian scholars and artists to Paris. He expressed the belief that the future of Canada is wrapped up in the continued solidarity of her English- and French-speaking citizens. Referring to his own country, he affirmed his belief in democracy and hoped for positive political results from the newly established suffrage for women. Though self-government is difficult, he averred, it is to be preferred to demagogic or totalitarian rule. He noted with concern that many French citizens abstained from voting, and in strong contrast to his former strictures on popular government, he appears to have embraced a new political realism.

As the memory of the war and the occupation began to fade, and the groundswell of anticolonialism began to make itself felt, Duhamel decided to renew his contact with Africa. In the spring of 1947 he and his wife set out on a journey through North and East Africa to study the Pan-Arab movement and its effect on French possessions. His inquiry was conducted by his usual methods: wide travel, followed by generalizations based on personal conversations, but this time he paused frequently for prearranged interviews with political leaders in an attempt to get at the facts. The book that resulted, *Consultation aux pays d'Islam*, is sober in tone, for the investigations it describes were made in a sincere effort to find out what North Africans were thinking and feeling. Duhamel did not shrink from talking to Arab hotheads both in French North Africa and in Egypt, and he faithfully recorded their ill-concealed contempt for France. He noted their determination to be free of French control even though freedom might mean civil strife and a loss of European technicians and techniques. He listened to violent harangues against French policy as regards both administrative controls and land distribution. He heard the accusation that France had deliberately impeded industrial development in Africa. Most of these accusations he dismissed as the extreme, even fanatical point of view of the colonial and ex-colonial peoples most of whom, he believed, had a severe inferiority complex, accompanied by a desire for self-government quite unmatched by the necessary skills for the job.

After he had listened to and analyzed the attitudes of the indigenous peoples, Duhamel left Egypt, the center of Pan-Arab ferment, and traveled on to Lebanon, Tunis, Algiers, and Morocco, where among other things he continued his investigations of the French contributions to African well-being. He pointed with pride to the fact that French colonists get a greater crop yield than the uneducated local peasants. He cited schools and hospitals, and the sanitary and irrigation engineering that the

French colonial enterprise had brought to the Arab countries. He felt that freedom achieved by the removal of French control not only would open the way to strife but would lead to the cancellation of the reforms in education and sanitation that France had instituted, and ultimately to the enslavement of Africa by another European power. As to which power, Duhamel left no doubt, for almost in the same breath he characterized communism as an alert foe of western Europe, watching for European mistakes and ever ready to take over in the name of Marx and Lenin. In view of the local unrest and the communist danger, Duhamel advised France to reform her administration of the North African protectorates immediately, and to take them into a union with France under a federal constitution. Abdicate he would not. France, he said, had rights as well as duties in North Africa, rights won by French blood, and a long and enlightened colonial policy.

This is a far better book than any other that Duhamel has written on a foreign culture and its relation to France. In it he shows an awareness of current trends that he has never hitherto demonstrated. If he is inclined to dwell on French rights, he also indicates an awareness of Great Britain's similar problems and of her analogous desire to revamp her colonial policy and make of it a force for the improvement of backward nations. He knows that splendid isolation no longer exists, and he shows that his concern for French interests in the lands of Islam is bound up with the fate of western European culture as a whole. At the time of writing he still hoped that with good will and intelligent action France might find acceptance as a natural leader in North Africa. He thought that French culture, with its adaptability and its absence of color-consciousness, was admirably suited to the role of guide and adviser to Africa's millions. Foreign readers of his

text are likely to feel that if Duhamel does not exaggerate
the French contribution to Africa, he is decidedly inclined
to gloss over all the shortcomings of her colonial policy,
shortcomings that objective French observers themselves
have pointed out. Still, the picture of North Africa is for
the most part a sober and realistic one.

Somewhat less satisfactory is *Le Japon,* a book that
resulted from a five-week trip to Japan in 1953. As was
often the case with his travel books, Duhamel attempted
too much. His visit was too short, the culture too different
from his own, for his observations and generalizations to
have much value. He had himself once said: "The only
thing that counts, the only thing that exists, is a real,
profound, and intimate knowledge of something, and this
can be achieved only by a long and close communion with
men and things."[18] This remark was presumably intended
to apply to the background necessary for writing fiction,
but it does not seem out of place to apply it to the equally
complex problem of evaluating a foreign culture. *Le
Japon,* which lacks any such background of "long and
close communion" between the author and his subject,
consists mainly of superficial judgments on Japanese art,
music, and religion as they relate to the author's continued
preoccupation with the inhumane aspects of our modern
world. In conclusion Duhamel expresses the hope that
France may be for Japan a cultural beacon in a materialistic age.

A year later another trip of a few weeks' duration led
to the writing of *La Turquie nouvelle,* which, like the
books that preceded it, reviews briefly the recent history
of the country in question. The reforms of Kemal Ataturk
are described and Turkey's progress in all fields is warmly
praised. The book is readable and thought-provoking,
although little of the material is new. Once again Du-

hamel pointed out, as he had done in North Africa, that French cultural leadership is being lost to the Anglo-Saxon nations, and he begged for a larger appropriation for the cultural relations program of the Ministry of Foreign Affairs.

Similar considerations were uppermost in Duhamel's mind a few years later when he traveled in Israel. There his enthusiasm at becoming acquainted with a new nation was slightly dulled by the scarcity of persons able to converse with him in French and the handicap of his rusty and imperfect English. The observations made on this journey were recorded in the book *Israel, clef de l'orient* (1957). The book received fair reviews, for as usual Duhamel had been an alert and sensitive observer. He showed, as he had before, that he has an eye for detail, and an even enhanced ability to write a good travelogue. He commented on the use of Hebrew and praised the new University of Jerusalem. He noted the dynamism of the Jews and their pleasure in their national progress. As usual, he ended the book on a note of hope, expressing the wish that the new nation might live up to its aspirations.

Duhamel has been a tireless traveler, but the titles of his travel books do not furnish a complete roster of the countries he has visited. He has, for instance, given no account of his visits to Latin America, although his travels there have been extensive. Europe, especially the countries in the immediate vicinity of France, has been his favored region, however. In the manner of Goethe, whom he mentions in this connection, he has tried above all to be a good European. North Africa and the Near East, because of their long connection with French foreign policy, have also been favorite objects of his foreign travels. The Anglo-Saxon countries interest Duhamel far less than many nations that are farther removed in spirit from France, but he does not appear ready to make common cause with us, although of late he appears to feel more sympathy than formerly for Britain and America as part of that western European culture whose values appear to him to be in danger. Even his role as president of the Alliance Française, which must have led him into fairly frequent contacts with American intellectuals, does not seem to have affected his attitude greatly. In other words, as a result of his travels Duhamel has not become, has not attempted to become, a cosmopolitan. As a French author he appears to regard it as his duty to remain proudly and incurably French. One of his principal concerns as a traveler has been his self-imposed mission to further the interest abroad in French literature and language. He also wants man to become more humane, and he sincerely believes that a worldwide interest in French cultural values will help to accomplish this result.

9

CRITIC OF CIVILIZATION

IN THE MIDST of battle, during the First World War, Duhamel gave the following description of civilization, which by implication is also a definition: "If civilization is not in the heart of man, then it is nowhere at all."[1] It is, therefore, his profound conviction that the technical developments of which man is capable must be centered upon man and must be controlled by him. It is the humane spirit, and not the elaborate machines and inventions that man produces, that distinguish him from the lower animals. Anything tending to enslave or to repress the individual must, *ipso facto,* be considered evil. Rousseau had said this in his essays, but Duhamel distinguishes carefully between his own conclusions and those of Rousseau. "Order," says Duhamel, "is a conquest made by experience and the human will over natural disorder. Order, health, morality, peace and beauty, are the very desirable fruits of the slow and patient effort of men against nature."[2] Such a point of view is far from Rousseau's belief that nature is man's infallible guide.

Duhamel points out that the skills learned by one generation are not susceptible of transfer to the next, and for this reason it is important that humane attitudes and a humane concern for the individual should pervade our teaching as each generation imparts its knowledge to the next. He would have us look upon civilization as the sum total of "formulae, methods, beliefs, doctrines, customs, traditions, laws, facts, instruments, monuments, and works that, by their presence, their action, and their interaction work together toward the maintenance and development of our species."[3] Elsewhere Duhamel states that a dichotomy exists between the part of civilization that is moral and that which is purely mechanical or Baconian, since it rests entirely on the application of the inductive method.[4]

Though confessedly not of an orthodox religious persuasion, Duhamel diagnosed the ills of our century as stemming primarily from the backwardness of man's spiritual and moral development. He was troubled as he contemplated the ever-widening gap between the elaborately tooled, material objects contrived by inventors and the low state of man's social and moral outlook, which, all too often, blandly and uncritically equates material possessions and spiritual well-being. The scientist and inventor he found a thousand years ahead of our social institutions. As he put it, "The legislator comes panting in the wake of the inventor."[5] And he set himself to study and to comment on this cultural lag with all the

174 CRITIC OF CIVILIZATION

eloquence and persuasiveness that he could command. As an admirer of Pasteur and all that he stood for, he confesses that it took him some time to cease rejoicing automatically at the triumphs of science. Then when he turned his weapons of preachment, persuasion, satire, and outright denunciation against the sacred cows of "progress," "comfort," and "labor-saving miracles," he was attacked on all sides as a pessimist, an antiscientist, a reactionary, and a back-to-nature visionary.

Duhamel's campaign for a human rather than a materialistic attitude toward life was well expressed early in his career. Writing in *La Possession du monde*, in 1918, he said:

> Il faudra s'efforcer d'apprendre aux hommes étonnés que le bonheur ne consiste point à parcourir cent kilomètres en une heure, à s'élever dans l'atmosphère sur une machine, ou à converser par-dessus les océans, mais bien, surtout, à être riche d'une belle pensée, content de son travail, honoré d'affections ardentes.[6]

The daily tasks of the surgeon, as he performed amputations and bound up gaping wounds made by the shiny steel products of the factories, resulted inevitably in his losing completely his admiration for industry per se. Nor could he continue to revere the intelligence that created the matériel and then put it to such devilish uses. He says:

> Le civilisation scientifique et industrielle, basée sur l'intelligence, est condamnée. Elle a, depuis de longues années, accaparé et affolé toutes les énergies humaines. Son règne aboutit à un immense échec.[7]

Only by tricks of dialectic and by propaganda has the world made the idea of progress appear synonymous with the development of the mechanical, chemical, and biological sciences. True progress concerns the soul alone, Duhamel believes, and it is independent of the expedients and practices of science. Quite frequently, he thinks, when science and industry appear triumphant, real progress—that is, the movement of humanity toward happiness —is being for the time interrupted if not actually set back. This point of view may be called the ideological basis of all of Duhamel's subsequent writings on civilization: that spiritual values must be kept uppermost, and that such values must not be confused with intellectual standards, since the latter can be and often are perverted to serve the nonhuman and material procedures of science, as the mass murder of war so amply demonstrates.

Duhamel's visits to Russia and the United States and the books that resulted, different as they are in their manner of presentation, were part of a campaign that he has never ceased to wage against the purely material aspects of western civilization. Seen in retrospect they are part of the protest against war that he launched with the publication of *Civilisation* and *Vie des martyrs*. What he said there in the guise of fiction he continued to say in his travelogues, his satires, his essays, and his speeches.

As we have already seen, *Le Voyage de Moscou,* although unsatisfactory to the Russians, seemed to western readers a fairly innocuous book. In his preface Duhamel had proclaimed his dislike of sarcasm. He wrote:

Je n'aime pas le sarcasme, dont l'empire est grand chez nous et l'usage toujours facile. Je ne le souffre surtout pas quand il s'agit de l'avenir d'un grand peuple et, qui sait? peut-être d'un monde. On trouvera, dans mes peintures, quelque malice parfois, jamais de la raillerie.[8]

This sane pronouncement was followed, as Americans

winced to discover, by a satiric picture of modern civilization as exemplified by America, in which sarcasm played
a not inconsiderable role. Still, Duhamel's denial that he
had intended an attack on America as such, farfetched
as it may have seemed, had a foundation in fact. In the
U.S.S.R. he had observed the almost frantic attempts of
a revolutionary government to bring an underdeveloped
country into the twentieth century, and with that effort,
however unattractive its methods, he felt much sympathy.
In writing about America he chose deliberately to write
about the soulless and inhuman aspects of what was
admittedly the most scientifically advanced, the most
machine-dominated nation in the world. Was he not
aware, he was asked, that America had poets and artists
as well as skyscrapers? He was. In 1923 he had already
said that America's greatness consisted less in canned
goods, tall buildings, and machines than in Emerson,
Whitman, and Thoreau. Was he not aware that Paris too
had its stockyards? He was, he replied, but what Frenchman urges you to visit them? He was attacking, he said,
a way of civilization, not the people who made it.

The crux of this argument is that the European tradition, which America believes itself to represent, is in
actuality deformed in America. Of this Europe should
be aware. During his visit to Finland, which antedated
his visit to the United States, he had adjured the Finns
"not to imitate America." Rightly or wrongly, therefore,
Duhamel had decided before his visit here that America
would display some of the worst features of the industrial
civilization and the pecuniary society. To reach this conclusion without leaving home, all that he had to do was
to read the more flamboyant of our naturalistic novels,
essays, and plays. If this is kept in mind Duhamel's
analysis of civilization as observed here, marred though

it is by flashes of chauvinism and petulance, is but a part of his broad attack on modern maladies at home as well as abroad. We must remember that *Scènes de la vie future* was followed by the biting but funny satire of *Les Jumeaux de Vallangoujard,* in which France and Frenchmen are seen to be no less bitten by the microbe of modernism than are the Americans. And if he was especially tender toward France in his book on America, he planned and carried out an attack on his own country's foibles in his satiric *Querelles de famille* (1932).

In this book Duhamel amplified his attack on modern times, reiterating his scorn for many of the phases of American life that he had previously subjected to criticism, and in so doing he added ruefully:

Je vais peut-être, une fois de plus, fâcher des amis lointains qui, songeant à mes critiques, s'imaginent dans leur orgueil qu'il n'y en aurait que pour eux. Tant pis, parlons de nous.[9]

The first chapter of *Querelles de famille* dealt in mock-serious fashion with a proposal to create a national park of silence, where for a price one could escape from the unwanted noises that surround us in contemporary life. Duhamel said that some such unorthodox means would have to be found if we are to escape from the cacophony of sounds that assaults our ears. He found that even in the small towns of France, once a refuge from the turmoil of the city, the din was unbearable. To the noises of trains, cars, and airplanes had been added the all-day radios, phonographs, and juke-boxes, and the public, apparently indifferent to the racket, went its way happily, even adding to the output of decibels by purchasing and operating more and more machines.

In his second chapter he deplored the refuse dumps and automobile graveyards that deface the countryside and clog the outskirts of the city. He urged that these kitchen-middens of our culture be hauled away and dumped into the English Channel.

The third chapter contains what is probably a tongue-in-cheek proposal for a periodical moratorium on new inventions. By such a device, he suggested, man might conceivably be afforded the time to enjoy the inventions that he has already. He might learn their proper use and digest them, as it were, before rushing out to buy a newer model of one he already owns.

The next chapter urged the Catholic Church to resist the pressure for loudspeakers and public-address systems in the pulpit. By their use he felt that religious services were cheapened, and he foresaw the day when, if such encroachments were not resisted, there would be mechanized confessionals, recorded sermons, and an expanded and quite improper use of motion pictures.

Other chapters treated satirically of persons who have introduced machines into every phase of their lives, who have become connoisseurs of nothing more important than movies, or who expend all their energies on automobiles that are in every particular carbon copies of those of their neighbors.

The best chapter of all is entitled "Grégoire ou le nouveau malade imaginaire," in which, with a verve unmatched elsewhere in this volume, Duhamel poked fun at a man whose solicitude for the motor in his car, for the vagaries of his electric iron, and the rheumatism of his electric pump, had made him the modern equivalent of Molière's famous hypochondriac. Last and almost as good is a chapter in which the author told of riding about in his car looking for old landmarks, which, with the march of "progress," have now disappeared and been replaced by weed-grown lots or ugly refuse piles. He wondered, as well he might, if this were progress.

The critical comment that greeted the appearance of *Querelles de famille* was not uniformly favorable. Obviously, Duhamel had put his finger on a number of sore spots, but he was again taken to task for his method. There was little of the rollicking humor that had helped to carry *Les Jumeaux de Vallangoujard*. The satirical approach in this case can be said to be marred by an over-use of exaggeration and a mood that seemed to imply as much personal frustration as righteous anger. Even so, as time passed, the public became more receptive to this sort of criticism, probably because the evils that Duhamel attacked were reaching so critical a stage that even the most enthusiastic users of mechanical devices were becoming aware of their drawbacks. Still Duhamel disclaimed pessimism. Into the mouth of his character Grégoire he put these words:

> Je suis triste . . . et cependant ma tristesse porte en soi-même ma consolation. Il n'y a que les pessimistes incurables pour être contents de tout. Mais moi, je ne suis pas désespéré, du moment que je me rebelle. Si je cherche querelle au monde, c'est que, jusqu'à nouvel ordre, je lui fais encore confiance.[10]

Duhamel did not allow the matter to rest there. His concern for man, his conviction that man was in danger, his belief that machines can do the world great harm if not sanely used, and his awareness of the indifference of his fellows to all these problems—all conspired to lead him to a more lengthy and reasoned statement of his convictions. He realized that his satire amounted to little more than a hit-and-run attack on the machine. It could not carry with it the burden of a critical analysis of the matter. The time had come for a reasoned exposition of his views, and this exposition he provided in *L'Humaniste et l'automate* (1933). In this book Duhamel tried to dispose of the silly accusation that in criticizing the machine and its misuse he was in any way proving himself a latter-day Rousseau or a European disciple of Ghandi. He wished to dissociate himself from this false impression, and he tried to do so in these words: "I wish freely to know, to understand, to judge, to criticize, the times in which I live. . . . I fear and hate fanatics and cranks; that is to say, I do not imitate them."[11]

Duhamel has maintained stoutly that he has no wish to halt progress, even progress of the mechanical and scientific sort. He owns and uses a car, makes use of the radio and telephone, and travels in planes. Misuse, not use of these machines, is his concern, and in talking about the subject he has had to struggle not only against the astonishment of those who take every new invention for granted, but also against those who have woefully misread his intentions.

The invention and use of tools, says Duhamel, is a peculiarly human achievement. These tools, in themselves neither good nor bad, tend to make men abandon their powers, make men likely to entrust to the machine what was formerly achieved by individual effort, effort that called for the use of the muscles or the functioning of the mind. For our legs we substitute the car, for our brain an adding machine, for the violin the phonograph, for the family doctor the assembly line of the clinic, for human sympathy an impersonal mechanical world. This frightening prospect first presented itself to him during the First World War, when thousands of men were killed by guns triggered miles away by practically anonymous marksmen. Then the victims were brought into the hospital, where they were operated on by surgeons who in many cases did not even see the victims' faces. From a dislike of the impersonal kill and cure of the war to an analysis of impersonal entertainment was but a step. For

Duhamel the substitution of a reel of movie film for the live stage is a backward step, and the movies became for a time his peculiar *bête noire*. In *Scènes de la vie future* he had given a merciless caricature of the Hollywood creations of the year 1929, and he then consigned them to the ash heap with these words: "I would exchange all the cinematographic library of the world, including what the professionals pompously call their 'classics,' for one of Molière's plays, one of Rembrandt's pictures, or a fugue by Bach."[12] His later pronouncements on the cinema have shown little change in attitude. For him the movies have little appeal, and he says in his memoirs that he is quite unable to understand why they appeal to others.

The radio and phonograph have received a similar drubbing at his hands. He dislikes the invasion of his privacy by the ill-timed and usually loud radio and record playing of his neighbors. On this subject he has been vehement, and perhaps it was at least partly because of his reiterated complaints against the unwanted sounds of modern life that Paris began some years ago the noise-abatement campaign that has made it a quieter and pleasanter place to live.

His chief fear regarding the radio and phonograph was that they might eventually eliminate live music. At best he feared that recorded music and radio programs might absorb a disproportionate share of musical talent that might be better employed. Long before the invention of television made his fears a reality, he anticipated that reading might be widely displaced by listening and that books might be thereby reduced to a second-class medium for the dissemination of ideas. He knew from personal experience that the radio audience frequently gives something less than total attention to the programs that assault its ears, and he saw that good music, jazz, political speeches, and educational programs were all coming to be listened to with an equally indifferent ear by the otherwise occupied listener. He was particularly distressed to hear the music of Bach and other great musicians relegated to the role of background music for a card game, trivial conversation, or worse.

Professionals in radio work, and even some of Duhamel's colleagues who felt less repulsion for radio than he did, reacted unfavorably to these remarks, and so to show that his misgivings were not the products of an artist living in an ivory tower, Duhamel has taken part in commissions or committees charged with the improvement of the French radio network. On more than one occasion he has accepted continuing assignments as a radio lecturer, but he confesses that speaking before an unseen audience gives him little satisfaction.

For the misuse of the automobile he has reserved some of his sharpest reproof. He contends that the coward, the bully, and the merely incompetent have their moment of fatuous glory when seated behind the wheel. Here the man of feeble brain and personality fancies himself the equal of his neighbors, and proves it by driving with ill-controlled speed and a reckless disregard for everyone else. "Superb revenge of the vain and the incompetent," he calls it: "This man, who would not dare to bend a horse to his will, knows that he can demand everything of a machine."[13] In this regard the automobile is a kind of psychograph for measuring personality. From a man's conduct behind the wheel you can tell what manner of man he is. In a gentler mood Duhamel is inclined to acknowledge that the psychological implications of the motor car may not be so damaging as he has sometimes declared. In his memoirs he gives a summary of his

attitude. If properly used, he says, the automobile may be
an excellent adjunct to civilized living:

J'ai, dans maints écrits, blâmé le mauvais usage que l'on fait
trop souvent de l'automobile. Je n'ai pas critiqué l'instrument,
ce qui serait absurde; j'ai, je le répète, mis en garde mes
contemporains contre la tentation que l'on peut avoir d'abuser
d'une telle puissance. Cela ne me met que plus à l'aise pour
reconnaître que, sagement employé, l'automobile est un instrument beaucoup plus précis, beaucoup plus docile et par
conséquent beaucoup moins dangereux que l'ancien équipage-
que l'on dit si comiquement hippomobile.[14]

Such an attitude seems fair enough, but as may be seen
in the pages of *Scènes de la vie future*, Duhamel's campaign against twentieth-century machines and their misuse was at times carried on with considerable fanfare, a
fanfare consisting of irony, exaggeration, denunciation,
the whole skillfully blended with irritation, petulance, and
righteous anger.

It was not to be expected that his apparently in-
transigent attitude would go unchallenged. The hornet's
nest that he stirred up in America was only slightly less
angry than the later outbursts in his own country. Even
friends of his like Jean-Richard Bloch attacked his views.
Duhamel responded to these attacks, but it may be sur-
mised that in the main he knew exactly what he was
doing. He was too astute a publicist not to realize that
attack and counterattack were of real value in getting
his ideas before the public. He refused, however, to
accept the more extreme charges that were hurled at him.
He complained that he was a victim of silly and even
willful misreading of his point of view, and he has constantly sought to redefine and explain his position.

In recent years Duhamel has turned away from day-today attacks on the machine and its problems to a discussion and examination of the theoretical basis of civilization. He has asked himself, as did Rousseau, but in a far less doctrinaire manner, just what are the techniques that man has used in forming himself into societies, and the how and why of tools and inventions. The Second World War caused him to reflect on these matters as had the first, and in his war diary for the 1940–1945 period, *Chronique des saisons amères*, he attempted a brief analysis. He separated civilization into component parts, called "receptacles," "bonds (fraternal and other)," "cloth," "music," and "light." Under these headings he tried to classify the major human achievements in order to discover a rationale of civilization. He wished above all to put aside appearances in order to see behind them the basic elements of human action. He divided the peoples of the world into three groups: those who truly invent new ideas, ideas that take form as radio, or atomic fission; those that take ideas and make practical applications of them but do not contribute to the basic theory; and finally those peoples whose stage of development permits them to use but not to improve or change what has been invented by others. France he rightly included in the first category. But scientists tend to reject Duhamel's theory as unproved a priori reasoning. In reply to Duhamel it has been pointed out that although most of our modern inventions represent a basic idea, in nearly all cases that idea has been modified, redirected, and applied by subsequent thinkers and tinkerers until the final theory or product is a truly international phenomenon. No one in these days is the sole inventor of anything.

With the passing of the years and the increasing difficulty and frustration of life in Europe in the postwar period, Duhamel has returned in two additional volumes to his mood of protest. In fact, he called his first volume *Le Manuel du protestataire* (1952), a title that sets the mood of his commentary. The second he entitled *Problèmes de l'heure* (1957). In these books he broke little new ground. In the first he reverted to many of his favorite themes: the encroachment of the state upon the individual, the degradation of the landscape by the proliferation of billboards, the use and misuse of machines. The second also retraced familiar steps. France and the French cuisine were praised anew. Government, national and foreign, was drubbed again for its interference with the individual. And, as before, the only hope for the future that our author saw was in the emergence of an "elite." Altogether these are rather disappointing volumes. Not only has Duhamel furnished us with no truly comprehensive statement of his overall position, but he has frequently cast patience aside to assume a posture of mere fault-finding.

The chapters on the political realities of our times are forthright but inconclusive. Totalitarianism and its grim effects turned Duhamel into a supporter of political democracy, but the inevitable failure of postwar politicians to find practical yet humane solutions to Europe's problems was disillusioning. Thus although Duhamel is well aware that many of the things that he wishes to see done can only be done by state intervention, he so abhors bureaucracy that he would sometimes rather see a continuance of the status quo than appeal to the state. In this conservative position he is not without company on both sides of the Atlantic.

In summary it may be said that Duhamel's lifetime of tilting at the windmills of modern life has been of distinct service not only to his country but to the world. From the first cry of anger and anguish of the *Vie des martyrs* to his latest somewhat uninspired commentary on postwar life in Europe, Georges Duhamel has performed a useful function. His warnings as to what may happen if inhumanity and selfishness continue to dominate man's actions have acquired new timeliness since the invention of the atomic bomb. We can no longer be indifferent to his belief that civilization is sick, that the strife, hatred, and greediness of man are reprehensible. If Duhamel frets at the ugliness of modern architecture, the absence of greenbelts, the surfeit of gasoline vapor, smoke, and noise, it is because these things are but the outward signs of a deeper problem: man's indifference to his own collective welfare.

The question then, as we try to evaluate Duhamel's sometimes ill-tempered but always well-timed attacks upon the misdeeds of his contemporaries, is as to the extent of his contribution to our awareness of our human dilemma. Undoubtedly he has drawn the attention of the world, and especially that of his fellow countrymen, to the necessity for focusing man's attention upon himself. He has harped endlessly but necessarily on the need to distinguish between material progress and human progress, and he has done so at a time when materialism appears to be well in control of the situation. By his extreme and often bitter campaigns he has made the decline of humanism a live issue in an epoch when the spokesmen for the nations have often registered their contempt for man, at a time when men have put their trust in the test tube and the assembly line rather than in the mind that created both. For this he deserves our thanks.

10

THE DOCTOR DEFENDS
HUMANE LETTERS

DURING HIS long career as a writer and critic of belles lettres, Duhamel has not forgotten that he was trained as a biologist and doctor of medicine. In his writing we find also the indelible mark of the *lycée*, with its rigorous training in the methods and practices of the arts and sciences, a mark made visible in him, as in all who bear it, by a concern for his mother tongue and a lifelong devotion to the things of the mind. Duhamel's years of specialization were laid upon this solid foundation. Few Frenchmen, as he has observed, ever completely escape the imprint of those years of consecration to study. Although he himself does not practice medicine, he remains a scientist and physician in his thinking. He has consistently defended the medical profession against its critics, and in the postwar years, when the state has assumed a larger place in men's lives, he has defended medicine against what he regards as encroachments upon its prerogatives. He has been a leading member of the Academy of Medicine, and as its unofficial publicist he has tried to inform the public of the purpose and achievements of modern medicine.

Duhamel believes that science and humanism need not contradict each other. For him the poet, the playwright, and the essayist are one with the scientist and physician. He thinks that the test of humanism is its disinterestedness and, as a corollary, that medicine, alone of the sciences, can never do other than serve the cause of true civilization.

In his purely literary works Duhamel has given an important place to doctors and to the healing art. The war books, *Civilisation, Vie des martyrs,* and *Lieu d'asile,* were of necessity permeated with medical concerns, but in his other works also we find evidence of the medical point of view. Yet he has always resisted the temptation to write case histories. Of this he remarks:

> J'ai reçu, dans mon jeune temps, une culture scientifique. J'y ai pris le goût de la méthode et même certaines disciplines de travail. J'ai fait effort pour appliquer ces disciplines à mon œuvre littéraire—oh! sans aucune confusion, on voudra bien le penser, mais au moins dans les rites élémentaires du labeur et dans les contraintes imposées à la carcasse.[1]

When the Salavin series was being evaluated, some critics attributed Salavin's oddness to the author's fondness for clinical analysis, and they appear to have been disappointed when Duhamel flatly denied that this approach was valid for a comprehension of his hero. Similarly, in the *Chronique des Pasquier,* where so much of the narrative deals with the medical studies and laboratory experiences of Laurent Pasquier, we are often reminded that Duhamel is a doctor. In fact he readily admits in his memoirs that he borrowed many an episode from his own student days. He has, however, tried to avoid seeming like a doctor writing a novel. He wants to be the novelist always, a novelist with medical training, but a novelist first and foremost. Medicine is for him a reservoir of experience upon which to draw. Medicine and its concerns may be a part of the canvas on which he is painting, but his novels are not characterized by a "medical attitude" or by a "medical point of view." What he strives to do is to blend personal experience, in his case a medical experience, with the imaginary experience of his characters. As a realist he has tried to picture the whole man, and he has not allowed his area of specialization to interfere with his creative powers. Medicine as experience is a valid ingredient in his writing, but medicine as a theme he rejected as too confining for his purpose.

Of Duhamel's creative works only the play *La Lumière* has a plot making use of a physical disability, blindness, and even in this instance the medical and pathological aspects of the case are subordinated to emotional and psychological considerations. In the same fashion, in *La Nuit d'orage* the illness of the heroine, which could easily have furnished an excuse for a clinical approach, was deliberately described in vague terms.

The situation is altogether different with Duhamel's writings on civilization and his essays and travel books. In these less formal productions his medical and scientific point of view is constantly to the fore. During his journeys to other countries he has always visited hospitals and clinics and talked to physicians and administrators. On his visits to North Africa his continued preoccupation has always been with French efforts to improve the health and sanitation of the region. French success in this field he firmly believes to be one of France's chief claims to glory as a colonizing power. The name of Pasteur comes frequently to his lips, and the achievements of Charles Nicolle, a friend in the profession whom he considers a worthy successor to Pasteur, are often praised by him.

Before the Second World War Duhamel had already begun to talk about the future of the medical profession. In his view the fate of civilization may well prove to be intertwined with the development of medicine. And because the relation between a patient and his physician appears to him as one of the noblest and most fruitful of human developments, he deplores the disappearance of the general practitioner in favor of the specialist or the team approach of the clinic. For Duhamel, sympathy is the touchstone of medical practice, and he is not ready to accept improved operating techniques or improved medication as a substitute for this basic quality. He knows that medicine must maintain its standards, must broaden its knowledge, must work with and improve its X-ray machines, fluoroscopes, pumps and sterilizers, and all the rest of the life-saving devices, but these things, soulless robots that they are, can never be anything more than a means to an end. As Duhamel sees it, medicine is the only science that was developed for man's sake, and he will not allow his colleagues or the general public to forget that fact.

Fear that some kind of a national health program might replace the family doctor led Duhamel to register his opposition to a proposal for state medicine as early as

1934. He called his article "Les Excès de l'étatisme et la responsabilité de la médecine," and he has returned to the attack repeatedly, particularly in *Manuel du protestataire*, where concern for the medical profession underlies many of his criticisms of contemporary life. In *Problèmes de l'heure* he continued his discussion with a chapter entitled "Médecine et problèmes de l'heure." In his first article he was ready to champion a program for compulsory vaccination against smallpox, but this was about as far as he would go. Certainly he was unwilling to take the leadership in demanding a more equitable distribution of medical care. Like many of his colleagues he was fearful lest bureaucracy and red tape should achieve a strangle hold on medicine through some kind of state-imposed system. He foresaw the irreplaceable patient-doctor relationship sacrificed as a result. He imagined, as a *reductio ad absurdum*, the formation of doctors' trade unions, which for him would be an unthinkable contradiction of the Hippocratic oath.

By far the most notable exposition of Duhamel's attitudes on medical matters is to be found in *Paroles de médecin* (1946), a book in which he reprinted many of his previous statements and added many new ones. As the title indicates, this work was not a systematic treatise but a miscellany, in which Duhamel discussed a variety of medical problems. He reiterated his belief that medicine is and must remain one of the liberal professions. It must be concerned with the life of the mind and with that humanism that alone can save man from himself. In a chapter entitled "Sur la formation médicale," he summed up what he believes a medical education should undertake to do, and what a civilized medical man should owe to that education. He reiterated his belief that the classics should be studied because of the disciplinary value of this study, among other reasons, and because they "accustom the mind to certain difficulties and prepare it for finding solutions to various problems."[2] A medical education, over and above its rigorous scientific training, should demand the acquisition of humane knowledge and humane qualities:

La médecine contraint l'homme à regarder l'homme, à le regarder de près, à le toucher, à explorer les replis, les cavités et les blessures de son corps infirme et c'est ainsi qu'elle développe et qu'elle entretient dans le monde misérable le nécessaire miracle de la sympathie rédemptrice. . . .

L'empreinte médicale est indélébile. Elle est marquée aussi profondément que l'empreinte ecclésiastique «*Sacerdos in aeternum.*» Je ne connais point de défroqués de la médecine. Le clerc qui a quitté la maison y retourne toujours avec aisance et avec plaisir. Il sait qu'il ne peut pas, quoi qu'il en pense et quoi qu'il fasse, ne pas agir et penser en médecin.[3]

Modern medicine, moreover, is a cooperative venture among the civilized nations of the world. A doctor in Boston, Massachusetts, discovered the use of ether. Frenchmen, Italians, and men of many other nationalities have each contributed their share. As a pilgrim of Hippocrates, Duhamel declared that he was assured of a welcome everywhere he went. If he had chanced to lose his way in a civilized country, he would only have needed to say the word "medicine" to be assured of friendly treatment and a fraternal welcome. This provable theory that medicine is international is in strong contrast to his more parochial notion, which we have just examined, that inventions can be the monopoly of one nation. But if he has noticed this inconsistency, he has nowhere acknowledged it.

Another chapter in *Paroles de médecin* devotes several pages to a eulogy of Charles Nicolle, the discoverer of

typhus vaccine. Duhamel was proud of his friend's contribution to medical science, and proud that Nicolle was
the director of the Pasteur Institute of Tunis. He said
that he once remarked to an Arab that as far as he was
concerned, hygiene and morality are one. He thought
that if ancient Islam refused to consider certain ele-
mentary rules of health, it might cease to exist, and he
said that philosophy was not above cleanliness and
sanitation.

Of equal interest are several chapters on the problems
faced by French medical practitioners during the German
occupation. He described with feeling their heroic efforts
to improvise synthetic or substitute materials to replace
everyday medical necessities like cotton, glycerine, vase-
line, and rubber. He described the grimness of the un-
heated hospitals, where patients who were critically ill
had to bear the additional hazard of cold, damp rooms.
He paid tribute to the work of the physicians who treated
the men of the Resistance, and he gave also some interesting accounts of his own temporary service as a doctor.

It is plain that medicine has always been for Duhamel
a beloved second calling, and although medical practice
has never served him as a means of livelihood, he has
always thought of its concerns as his own. Many of his
books that are quite unrelated to medicine have titles
with a medical connotation. *Au Chevet de la civilisation*
can be roughly translated "At Civilization's Bedside," and
Consultations aux pays d'Islam calls to mind, as it was
meant to do, the atmosphere of the physician's office or
consulting room. As he has the right and presumably the
duty to speak as a medical man, Duhamel is always
indignant at the encroachment of the layman upon the
medical field. Journalistic forays into medicine have his
particular disapproval. He resents the premature publica-

tion of medical discoveries, and he feels that journalists actually hinder the physician when they try to "scoop" the profession to describe to the public a new drug or a new operative procedure.

This ardent love for his profession made Duhamel's decision to leave it for literature a difficult one, but once his mind was made up, he wasted no time in regret. Only when a national emergency arose, during the two world wars, did he consent to put on the hospital smock that he had resolutely put away in order to become a writer. To his second field he has devoted all the skill and intelligence that he has. No aspect of writing, mechanical, linguistic, or even commercial, has escaped his attention. He is always ready to talk or write about writing. To be a writer and ignore the writer's problems Duhamel regards as a betrayal of the profession. He has never turned away a young writer who has sought his advice, nor does he refuse a colleague who asks his help in an enterprise that aims at elevating the writing profession or solving its material, ethical, or technical problems. He has often accepted the role—an unwelcome one for a shy man—of spokesman for the group, and in his essays and articles he has examined the contribution of belles lettres to the civilization of our times.

In undertaking his defense of letters Duhamel has not shrunk from the sometimes dismal and unrewarding tasks of chairing literary committees and prize juries. He has not assumed a pompous pose about writing, as did so many of the Romantics, yet he has held no less exalted a view than theirs of the writer's importance for his generation. In the characteristic fashion of youth, however, he tended at the beginning of his career to regard himself as a member of an elite, a small but learned company, writing for the "happy few," once addressed by Stendhal. In an early critical essay (1914) he took the poet Paul Fort to task for taking part in a campaign against the attackers of literature. What if dolts attack literature? he asked. That is to be expected. One must always distinguish between the poets and the philistines.

In recent years Duhamel has modified this view without completely abandoning it. Dictatorship proved itself so much worse in reality than in prospect that Duhamel came to realize that democracy, with all its faults, was preferable. He has therefore been taking sides on public questions, clearly implying that a writer cannot remain indifferent to public debate on current matters. As a consequence, his polemic writings on a variety of subjects are addressed to all who will listen.

The assumption of an active role as a publicist might well mean for a writer the end of his creative output, but of this pitfall Duhamel is well aware. He makes a careful distinction between creative and noncreative writing. The first deserves and must receive the writer's primary attention. Creative writing, he believes, is a high calling whose demands are severe. Its burdens are not to be assumed lightly. When asked how one becomes a writer, he answered:

On ne se destine pas à la carrière des lettres. Un homme porté par ses goûts, par les traditions familiales, par les nécessités de son milieu, se choisit une profession ou mieux encore un état. . . . Il peut, à un certain moment, opter pour la vie des lettres. Mais on ne s'y destine pas dès le commencement de l'âge. La seule introduction aux lettres, c'est l'expérience de la vie et l'expérience d'un métier. L'écrivain, par la suite, demeure immanquablement ce qu'il était au départ: journaliste, professeur, avocat ou médecin.[4]

Journalism is by implication a possible preparation for creative writing, but Duhamel does not want a writer to work for the newspapers while he is engaged in serious work. Meeting a deadline, he says, is not good for the creative spirit. He counsels the aspiring writer to find some kind of employment that does not call upon his writing skill. To write to live is to write poorly, he says, and he quotes Rousseau, who said that "it is difficult to think nobly when one thinks only to make a living." Yet poverty too can be an obstacle to high thinking. The young writer must assure himself of a modest income by taking a job, but only in the hope that recognition and financial success will finally free him from drudgery and allow him to give all his time and energy to creative work. He reserves his scorn for those who say that they too have thought of becoming writers but have been prevented by circumstances from doing so. By so saying, such persons seem to imply that one can become a writer simply by willing it. Writing, as Duhamel sees it, is not a skill to be acquired by study or determination. The ability to write is a gift possessed by few, and only a few can make of writing a successful profession.

Although fully mindful of the writer's social function, as "one who helps us think our own thoughts," Duhamel would not have the writer feel that he is bound to try to uplift society by espousing a cause or preaching a gospel in his creative work. To the question of whether the established writer should have a message, he replies with an unequivocal "no." In any case, creative work is incompatible with reform. The writer is entitled to his opinions, but they must be kept separate from his creativity. Only man's eternal concerns are worthy of a serious writer's attention as a part of his creative work. He writes in this connection:

Un écrivain joue à mon égard sa fonction sociale quand il nous aide à mieux comprendre l'homme et le monde, quand il s'applique selon la formule de Paul Claudel, à «transformer l'inconnu en connu,» quand il est vraiment un découvreur, un inventeur, un détecteur. . . .[5]

In this role the writer is the sane realist whom Duhamel prizes above all men.

On the subject of writing Duhamel has been articulate at all times. He even welcomes interviews, which he generally dislikes, if the discussion has to do with the writer's craft. But signing manifestos drawn up by others he believes to be a fairly futile business. "Let the writer write what he thinks and let him sign his name proudly," he says. "Let him beware of collective signatures."[6]

Of highest importance to a writer, whether in his creative or his polemic role, is the language that he uses. For this reason the French language, its excellence, and its use and misuse are among Duhamel's favorite themes. He has aspired to be a master craftsman in French, and no one who has read widely in his works is likely to deny that he has succeeded. Grammar, vocabulary, and syntax have been a lifelong interest with him, and he has dealt with them both humorously and seriously in his essays and in his novels and stories. In one place he made fun of the users of the word *mais,* "but." By their fondness for this word he suggested that they displayed "a need for restriction and compensation, and a lack of confidence and generosity."[7] He mocked the penchant for long, compound words, which, if not checked, he thought might result some day in a word like *réceptionnementationner.* He talked about the use of tenses and their names, the agreement of past participles, and the difference between words like *an* and *année.* He criticized foreign inventions like *Komintern* and French coinages like *autochir.* He mentioned the well-known French distaste for repeating a word in a single paragraph or even on the same page. He remarked by way of conclusion in *Au Chevet de la civilisation* that France's true wealth is her language and literature. Yet this was no systematic treatise, and into it Duhamel put little of his knowledge of style and its importance for literature. His own style, which is noted for its ease and fluidity, has left unexplored no nuance of irony or pathos, no source of charm or persuasiveness.

This is not to say that Duhamel's style is devoid of idiosyncrasies. Of these he has several that are worth noting. One is the restatement of a single idea in different words several times in succession, a trick of dialectic he may have borrowed from the lecture platform. Another is the frequent use of English words, whose presence in French he often deplores. Yet another is his self-conscious use of words that he dislikes, like *autochir*, accompanied by the deprecatory phrase "if one must use the word." He is also fond, when in a jocular mood, of creating words of his own. In the *Chronique des Pasquier*, Joseph, in one of his characteristic poses, was qualified by his brother as "Josephissime," and a gesture by Sénac was called a "Sénacisme." The *Chronique des Pasquier* also demonstrated Duhamel's considerable knowledge of slang. In one place he listed more than ten dozen cant words for *woman*. He also likes to compare French to other languages. He regrets that Joseph Conrad did not choose French instead of English for his medium, for French could have offered him more past tenses than English, and therefore greater flexibility for expressing his ideas.

As a traveler, and as a longtime president of the Alliance Française, Duhamel has been interested to observe the fate of French as a world language. He harks back to the day when French instead of English was the truly international tongue, and thus in 1945 he was aghast at the rumor, subsequently proved false, that French would not share equal status with Chinese, English, Russian, and Spanish at the United Nations preparatory conference in San Francisco. He is always pleased when he observes that French is holding its own, distressed when he finds that English is taking its place. He observed wryly on his visit to Moscow:

Il est naturel que dans un monde voué tout entier au trafic et au lucre, on voit décroître l'influence d'une langue admirable et riche en monuments, mais parlée par un peuple dont l'industrie est médiocre et le commerce denué de larges ambitions.[8]

Duhamel has not been entirely parochial, however, in his desire to promote French language and culture. He has cooperated with the leaders of the English Council. He has participated in international conferences and has evidently learned more English. In Canada, just after the Second World War, he strongly advised young French Canadians to learn English both for the vistas it would open and in the interest of national solidarity.

Closely related to Duhamel's linguistic interests is his belief in the value of Latin studies for the formation of the intellect. He emphasizes their usefulness in teaching Frenchmen the etymologies of native words. He believes that in a world where practical concerns orient most men and motivate their actions, the study of the classics furnishes a compensatory discipline, one which by its very lack of practicality is a training in disinterestedness. This in turn is the foundation stone of humanism. He said in *Chronique des saisons amères*:

Prié de fournir, il y a quelques années, une définition de l'humanisme, j'ai donné celle-ci, à laquelle je ne saurais rien reprendre aujourd'hui: «L'humanisme moderne est l'ensemble des notions qui ne semblent pas susceptibles d'application immédiate.» Cela signifie que la culture occidentale me paraît fondée sur le désintéressement, d'abord.[9]

And elsewhere:

Il m'a fallu bien des années pour saisir le sens de la gymnastique humaniste, pour comprendre que l'étude assidue de deux langues mortes est, dans un siècle sordide, preuve de désintéressement et que le désintéressement est le principal ressort de la civilisation véritable. Cette suprême vertu de l'acte inutile, qui ne semble pas intelligible aux esprits médiocres quand ils abordent les problèmes de la culture intellectuelle, leur semble tout à fait évidente dès qu'il s'agit des activités de jeu et singulièrement des sports.[10]

Remarks like these might have been dismissed as special pleading had they been uttered by a professor of classics. Coming from a biologist and doctor they were listened to respectfully, although inevitably Duhamel's fondness for Latin and Greek has been dismissed in some quarters as a mere aberration.

Knowing of Duhamel's interest in the classics, a publisher asked him to write an introduction to a new edition of the Iliad and the Odyssey, to be illustrated by his friend Berthold Mahn. The times were not propitious, but Duhamel set to work. Shortly thereafter the German occupation of Paris occurred, and because he was not permitted to publish even so unpolitical a document as an essay on Homer, publication was delayed until the end of the war, although a secret printing of his remarks was made available to a few friends. The essay thus produced has been published separately as *Homère au vingtième siècle* (1947). Once again Duhamel takes occasion to point out how useful the perusal of Homer is and should be for a nation whose language is rooted in the classics. For himself Homer has been a constant companion.

Next in importance to his interest in the classics is Duhamel's passionate defense of the printed word. To that subject and related problems confronting the professional writer he devoted an entire book, entitled significantly *Défense des lettres* (1937). In this work he demonstrates that every phase of the manufacture and distribution of books has captured his attention. As already noted, one of his principal complaints against radio and movies is that they compete all too successfully against books for our time and attention. He has even feared for the future of the printed word in our harassed century. He says:

Le XXe siècle est brutal et hagard. Il ne semble pas favorable à la lecture. En attendant le moment où il ne lira plus du tout,—ce à quoi on ne songe pas sans frémir, l'homme du XXe siècle lit peu, lit mal.[11]

This he believes is because civilization and its contrivances are forever aimed at sparing our energy, whether physical or intellectual. For this reason he sees the replacement of books by audiovisual aids in the schoolroom as a pernicious trend. Pictures, whether in books or projected on the screen, he says, must never take the place of the absorption of ideas through the printed page. Much of *Les Jumeaux de Vallangoujard* conveys this same message in satirical form. "These little mechanical contrivances," he warns teachers solemnly, "can bring amusement and relaxation into a schoolroom, but you alone can give the little ones true work, fruitful effort, and a taste for them."[12] Work is essential. Fruitful effort and true learning do not consist in eliminating obstacles, but in learning how to overcome them. For himself he knew books not only as a reader and writer but as one who during the days of the Abbaye had become an expert printer and typesetter.

The importance that Duhamel ascribes to books in the field of education he extends by analogy to the intellectual life of the nation. Books, he says, are the best "liaison agent between the members of the [world's] community of intelligent people." Libraries are the repositories of civilization's achievements. They are her blueprints. By the same token the literature of France is her most important export. During the days of Hitler's rise in Germany, Duhamel noted with dismay that the republican governments in power before the fall of France were not making a serious effort to counter German propaganda abroad by subsidizing the export of French books. Everywhere in the world the output of the French presses had to compete in the world market with de luxe editions of German and Italian books exported by subsidy and sold at a loss. France, he feared, was losing the battle of propaganda by her shortsighted policy.

A little later, during the German occupation, the implications of the French book shortage became even clearer to him. In a miscellany entitled *Semailles au vent* (1947), he gives his wartime views on the subject. German policy was to discourage the printing of French books, and it was Duhamel's conviction that by this means the occupying authorities were aiming deliberately at bankrupting the French intellect. Trash they printed gladly, but the classics were kept from the presses by an alleged shortage of paper. Duhamel's remedy was to redouble his efforts in behalf of the Alliance Nationale du Livre, an organization of publishers and booksellers that sought to save the situation. Real paper shortages and the difficulties of book distribution also claimed Duhamel's attention. In his war journal, *Tribulations de l'espérance*, he comes back to these questions again. He expressed his gratitude to

Canada and the United States for printing French books during the years of the occupation, but he believed that as soon as possible France should resume the publication and exportation of her classics. He worked also to free book exports from punitive taxes, and he rejoices that his intervention resulted in a reduction of the rates.

To the question as to how the position of books is to be maintained in our modern world, Duhamel has given some positive answers. In the *Défense des lettres* and in *Semailles au vent*, he described the way that books are advertised, sold, and preserved, and he had something to say about each process. He had long been impatient with the high-pressure salesmanship that treated books as if they were ordinary merchandise, and he deplored the intrusion into bookselling of ad-men and hucksters. He called attention to the flamboyant or sexy titles that are used to attract the naïve buyer, and to the authors with an eye for business who coldly calculate their chance of outselling their rivals. He saw bookstores being turned into tearooms, where writers appear to autograph books and shake the hands of crowds of bores. As a legitimate method of book advertising he pointed to the *journée des livres*, or national book day, as an effective and dignified way of attracting the book-buying public.

Second to radio and motion pictures as rivals for the attention of the reading public Duhamel placed newspapers and magazines. Toward the newspaper he was particularly resentful. Because it purveys many things beside news, including literary features of many kinds, Duhamel felt that it swallowed up the talents of young men who might otherwise make their mark in literature. But despite this unfavorable view he has himself frequently written for the daily paper, being aware that the newspaper can furnish a public not reached by books.

Toward magazines Duhamel is more tolerant. France,

he says, has many magazines of exceptional literary
quality. Of these none is more distinguished than the
Mercure de France. Duhamel's connection with this
magazine began long before the First World War and
has continued to the present. Upon the death of its
founder in 1935, Duhamel, as a kind of heir apparent,
assumed the post of editor. A goodly portion of Duhamel's
articles first appeared in this periodical, later to be
gathered in books that, in their turn, usually bear the
imprint of the *Mercure de France*.

Duhamel's conception of the social role of an intellectual periodical is a lofty one. He believes that a
reputable magazine, without becoming the partisan or
exponent of any cause, should provide a forum for young
writers who might not otherwise reach the public. When
so edited, a journal of opinion will bear the trace of all
the notable world events that have occurred during its
lifetime. An editorship so regarded is a public trust. It
is also a time-consuming activity, and Duhamel warns his
fellow writers against assuming editorial responsibilities
before their fiftieth year. Until then, he believes that a
writer should be exploring his mind and talents. An
editorship undertaken too soon may keep a man from
living a full life, and this he must have if his writing is to
have depth and variety. Duhamel himself looks back
with nostalgia upon the days when he and his friends
struggled to find an outlet for their material, and he
compares his own precarious situation in youth with that
of the younger writers today. The latter seem to need but
to decide where they want their articles published.

Duhamel has also touched on literary criticism, of
whose function he has a high opinion. He calls it "one of
the last manifestations in the great press of generosity
and disinterestedness."[13] Censorship too he touches in

passing, and he says jocularly: "Of course we are all in favor of censorship for each of the fine arts . . . provided that the scissors be placed in our own hands."[14] In actual practice he thinks censorship is unworkable as well as inconsistent with individual freedom.

Since the Second World War Duhamel has viewed with increasing distaste the amount of paper work that is demanded of all citizens. There seem always to be forms to fill out, questionnaires to answer, coupons to tender, numbers to remember, and rolls of red tape to contend with. Postwar conditions in France were grim. Coincident with the prodigal misuse of paper by the bureaucracy, the world faced an acute shortage of paper, a shortage so discouraging that it was sometimes necessary to decide whether republishing a classic might not deprive some new and deserving work of the light of day. The slowing down, and in some instances the complete stoppage, of the presses during the war had meant that the libraries of schools, institutes, and universities were practically worn out. Duhamel feared that unless book stocks were quickly replenished, teaching and research would suffer. He urged the branches of the Institut de France, like the Académie des Sciences and the Académie Française to devote time and energy to the solution of the book shortage.

Since Duhamel's election to the French Academy in 1935, he has taken a prominent part in its deliberations, serving from 1942 to 1946 as its secretary. As a young man he had not felt kindly toward the venerable association. On the occasion of Henri de Régnier's election he wrote: "M. de Régnier had to choose between our love and the Academy. He has chosen the Academy."[15] When Alfred Vallette, the editor of the *Mercure de France*, read these words in one of Duhamel's manuscripts, he urged him to withhold them from publication. Duhamel did so, and he tells the story as a sample of his youthful intolerance. Years later he told Régnier the story. The latter flushed angrily at first; then he saw the humor of the situation and laughed heartily. Nowadays Duhamel misses no opportunity to uphold the dignity and worth of the Academy. She is not, he declares, the useless and rich old spinster that people imagine. To those who point to the Academy's failure to take to its bosom many of France's most illustrious writers, Duhamel replies that the Church too has sometimes failed to recognize her saints.

By far the most spectacular if not the most important business that engaged the attention of French writers in and out of the Academy immediately after the Second World War was the treatment to be meted out to writers who had collaborated with the Germans. The controversy over this complex problem assumed almost the proportions of a civil war of literature. Duhamel reluctantly let himself be drawn into the debate. His own activities during the occupation had consisted of apparently passive resistance. In reality he had secretly participated in every sort of literary activity that ingenuity could devise for the discomfiture of the Gestapo. This work, in which he risked his life, had brought him into contact with the unpleasant realities of collaboration. He well knew which of his colleagues had been willing to dip their pens in vitriol and put them at the service of the conqueror. He repeatedly expressed his contempt for traitors, but after the expulsion of the enemy he refused to join in a national witch hunt. Like all patriots he was disgusted by the sudden repentance of erstwhile collaborators who exhausted themselves trying to prove that their disloyal activities had been but a mask for patriotism. He expected the guilty to be tried and sentenced without delay. Then when the courts proceeded to act with infuriating slowness, when the judges could think of no penalty but death, whether the crime was great or small, Duhamel lost patience and protested.

The reactions of the fanatical, who thirsted for bloody vengeance, were immediate. The extremists castigated Duhamel for his moderation. Claude Morgan heaped vituperation on him in an article entitled "To Refuse to Judge Is to Refuse to Be a Man."[16] To this extravagant piece Duhamel replied in *Tribulations de l'espérance*:

J'ai dit que cette justice est d'une lenteur désespérante et qu'elle manque d'imagination; j'ai dit qu'elle distribue au hasard, comme une machine mal réglée, la mort, les travaux forcés et la prison; j'ai dit que cette justice frappe avec une aveugle indifférence des criminels notoires et des gens qui n'ont fait que des fautes vénielles. J'ai dit que cette justice, monotone et profuse, risquait de contribuer à la démoralisation de notre peuple épuisé.

J'ai dit tout cela et je vois bien qu'il me faudra y revenir dans quinze ans, si je suis encore en vie et si on ne m'a pas, d'ici là, réduit au silence, ce que les Allemands ont déjà fait une fois.

Je me suis abstenu de parler de charité et de miséricorde, faisant d'ailleurs observer que nos sociétés ne sont pas, actuellement, en état d'entendre des paroles d'apaisement.

Là-dessus, plusieurs personnes ont commencé de pousser des clameurs. On m'a reproché mon «humanitarisme,» Je vous demande un peu![17]

In Duhamel's opinion the ostracism voted upon collaborators by the learned societies should have been lifted after one year. By then the real criminals would have been punished. For lesser villains public disapproval would have been adequate to the purpose. For this degree of moderation Duhamel was roughly handled as a sentimentalist.

In a lifetime of activity in his chosen profession, Duhamel has spared no pains to elevate the dignity of his calling. In his country's darkest hour he was steadfast in his opposition to totalitarianism. A word from him would have sufficed to place him in the forefront of the conqueror's showcase. That word was not forthcoming.

In his postwar collections of essays, like *Manuel du protestataire,* Duhamel has continued to battle for French language and literature. For sixteen years, beginning in 1942, he was president of the Association au Service de la Pensée Française. From 1937 to 1949 he was world president of the Alliance Française. These tasks have taken time and energy. They have entailed self-sacrifice. But Duhamel assures us, and we must agree, that they have not been allowed to interfere with his creative work. What he has done he has done because he feels that every man owes something to his profession. He says of his willingness to assume these responsibilities:

J'ai, la cinquantaine atteinte, ou presque, accepté souvent, du moins quand il m'apparaissait que je pouvais défendre une cause juste, rendre service à mon pays, à l'humanité, à la civilisation.[18]

11

PORTRAIT: SUBJECTIVE AND OBJECTIVE

AT ABOUT the beginning of the Second World War, Duhamel decided to reconsider his earlier declaration that he would not write memoirs, and the resulting work, in five volumes, has delighted his admirers the world over. It is pure Duhamel. To its composition he brought all the charm and candor that he has displayed in his creative writing. There is also an occasional dash of the pepper that seasons his work as a traveler and critic of his times. For its autobiographical aspect alone the work will be seized upon eagerly by future biographers, since in it he not only clarifies and amplifies his opinions but elucidates many points regarding the proportion of imagination and reality in his fiction.

The first volume, *Inventaire de l'abîme*, dealing with the years 1884–1901, was written during the years 1941–1942 and was published in Canada in 1944, following a clandestine French edition in the same year. Perhaps the most striking feature of this volume is its preoccupation with the city of Paris. Duhamel knows every inch of the city and a considerable portion of its history, but he avoids the usual parochial enthusiasms. He is seldom concerned with possibilities of modernization or improvement. He never says of an ugly and unhealthy tenement that it ought to be torn down. The Paris that he relishes is the old city, with all its dinginess and poverty. No reformer's zeal interferes with his enjoyment of the city as it is: crowded, musty, and smelly. His very pleasure in the old quarters is inextricably mingled with the status quo. Here is a description of one of his favorite quarters:

Le narrateur du *Père Goriot,* le poète des *Misérables* pourraient, s'ils sortaient de la tombe, se promener dans les venelles de ce quartier de Plaisance sans éprouver le dépaysement douloureux que le temps nous procure plus sûrement encore que le voyage.

C'est, en pleine capitale, c'est, en plein vingtième siècle, un grand village suranné. Par les portes charretières, le passant aperçoit des cours que l'on dirait abandonnées et qui ressemblent aux fondoucks de l'Orient, avec leurs remises poussiéreuses, leurs échoppes d'artisans, leur pavé cahoteux, leurs monceaux de détritus, leurs charrettes et leurs écuries dans lesquelles il arrive qu'on aperçoive, triste et osseuse, une haridelle toute semblable à celle de l'illustre hidalgo.[1]

In these humble sections Duhamel found an echo of his own youth. He had grown up among humble people and amid humble surroundings. He was accustomed to teeming streets. As he peers into windows and courtyards, he is not looking to catch a glimpse of the rich bourgeois at

his expensive desk, lighted by his ultramodern lamp. He
is thinking rather of the undistinguished, heavy carved
furniture that accompanied the Duhamel family on its
many moves. As an adult, and particularly as his travels
have taken him far from these humble places, he looks
back on them with nostalgia. He does not remember the
Paris of the Louvre or the Champs Elysées but the narrow, picturesque streets of the Latin Quarter:

> . . . quand il m'est arrivé d'être loin de ma ville natale et
> d'y rêver avec nostalgie, ce n'est pas ces lieux illustres que je
> revoyais les plus volontiers. J'appelais, du fond de mon exil,
> les ruelles odorantes de la montagne Sainte-Geneviève, ou
> les faubourgs populeux, ou les boulevards extérieurs, avec leur
> décor disparate, enfin non pas le Paris achitectural, le riche
> Paris de l'orgueil et du succès, mais bien plutôt le Paris du
> travail et de la souffrance, celui de la chair et du sang.[2]

It is with this Paris as a background that the first
volume of memoirs introduces us to the Duhamel family.
In its pages we follow young Georges as he moves from
neighborhood to neighborhood and school to school. We
are present at family crises and separations. We suffer
with young Duhamel as he has his first attack of laryngial
spasm, and, as in the Pasquier chronicle, it is the father
in his role of physician who appears most frequently. We
conclude the story with Duhamel the proud possessor of
the *baccalauréat*, a moment he thus describes:

> A l'instant où je suspends mon récit, le garçon a dix-sept ans
> et voilà qu'il se croit un homme! Il faut du temps, beaucoup
> de temps pour faire un homme, et une bonne exposition, de la
> pluie et du soleil, des liens, des coups de sécateur, des chances
> miraculeuses.[3]

Biographie de mes fantômes (1944) brings Duhamel's
account down to 1906. During this period of his life

he was, like Laurent Pasquier, detached from his family and living in bachelor quarters. This was a time of friendships and amours, of summer journeys, and of serious studies in the hospital and laboratory. He was learning about human nature, too. As a student he observed the strengths and weaknesses of his teachers. He mentions Renon, for instance, who stopped prescribing a certain drug because he always stuttered when he tried to pronounce it, and who, on seeing the dissected heart of a heavy smoker, remarked absent-mindedly: "And how is the patient?" These were happy days. The students of the period shared with their teachers the belief that the world's time of trial and tribulation was over. Scientific optimism had captured much of France along with most of the rest of Europe. Those who protested and talked of the possible bankruptcy of science could be heard only sporadically. Duhamel himself, though already a skeptic in religion, still held to his illusions about all-powerful science. He had found at least a tentative religion in the healing art. The war was to turn him to doubt once more, for he then came to realize, as he worked as a surgeon, that the science that saved the lives of the wounded was a branch of that same science that inflicted the wounds in the first place.

The long summer vacations came as a welcome change at the end of each scholastic year. Regular hours and the routine of the laboratory were put aside. Duhamel and his friends organized excursions into the country that have remained for him the brightest of memories. He became interested in nature then, and since that time nearly all his writings give evidence of his love of the out-of-doors. We also are told that in more recent years, whenever he is able to do so, he spends months at a time at his country property at Valmondois. He calls this time in the country among the happiest hours of his life. Paris, though still the city of his predilection, has become increasingly identified with the many and inescapable chores of the Academy and the public personality.

Duhamel's most memorable summer trip was a visit to the home of his friend Alexandre, in Auvergne. There, amid rustic surroundings, the city boy learned to appreciate humble but staple foods like bacon and eggs, and he acquired a taste for the mild wines of the locality. There for the first time he learned to enjoy walking tours with a knapsack and no fixed destination. This was his happy introduction to the open air and the unlimited horizon of the hiker. From Auvergne he returned to Paris renewed in vigor and enthusiasm, with a store of energy to support the grind of his medical studies. This first real taste of the country merely whetted his appetite for more, and so, during another summer, he set out with his brother Victor, his friend Gabriel Adain, and several others for a long hike through Switzerland, down into Italy, and back through the Grimsel Pass to Meiringen, Interlaken, and Bern. This was a carefree, joyous trip, despite a nearly empty purse. Duhamel tells how after a long and weary hike they reached Bern, penniless, as they supposed, only to have the irrepressible "Biel" Adain take a gold piece out of a knotted corner of his handkerchief and announce that he had been saving it for a rainy day.

On still another journey the itinerary through the Alps led by way of Switzerland and Lake Constance to Lindau, Munich, and Innsbruck, ending with a visit to Karlsruhe, Mannheim, and the cities of the upper Rhine. This too was a happy journey, but Duhamel's first contact with Germany found him ill at ease and not moved to affection for the country or its people. Some of the customs he saw repelled him. His attendance at one or more *Volkfeste* left him disgusted with the drinkers' capacity for beer and sausages. He was annoyed at the smugness he detected everywhere, and he remarked how self-sufficient the Germans appeared and how confident of their national genius. The language too was a barrier, but he did not take seriously the task of learning it. His brother did so, and Duhamel says that he has since relied on him when he has needed help in understanding or translating a book or article in German.

The German journey did not leave Duhamel totally pessimistic. He saluted German genius and observed, as has many another, that a Germany content to conquer the world through science, literature, and music would be more successful in peace than she could ever be in war.

Of all these travel experiences Duhamel seems to have been most impressed by his first trip through the Alps. This journey, more than all his subsequent ones, opened his eyes to vistas beyond the borders of France. In one form or another, in fiction and in essay, this trip lives again. "Biel," the cheerful comrade of hiking days, became a part of a score of characters in fiction, and he used and reused incidents from the trip. This friendship with Gabriel Adain he characterizes as an "amitié douloureuse," and this too was useful in *Deux hommes* and other books where friendship is a prominent theme.

It was the walking tours of his student days rather than the de luxe travels of later years that Duhamel most cheerfully recalls. The youth with the tender feet, light haversack, and empty pockets was still free of the ideological burdens that have made subsequent travels a mere extension of his life in Paris. One thing is certain, the fondness for walking he then acquired has not deserted him. After marriage he managed to communicate some of his enthusiasm to his wife, but he complains mildly that his motor-minded sons have not always shared their father's passion for hiking.

Not the least instructive aspect of Duhamel's story of his years of study is his description of his orientation toward a career in literature. Throughout this second book of memoirs, and especially in the last chapters, he describes the friendships and associations with other young writers, some of them fellow medical students, which gradually turned him away from the medicine he was already beginning to like toward a professional interest in writing. Conspicuous among these friends was Charles Vildrac. When the two men met, Vildrac was already a determined *vers libriste,* and this common interest in poetry led, as we have seen, to their collaboration on a book of poetry criticism called *Notes sur la technique poétique.* René Arcos, a fellow medical student and future poet was also a member of the group, and with him and Vildrac, Duhamel planned the retreat that became the Abbaye de Créteil. Jules Romains, whom he calls a phenomenon, was also a friend and associate engaged in studying biology and philosophy simultaneously. These young men and some others went about Paris, manuscript in hand, knocking on the doors of editors. Looking back on these days, Duhamel characterizes them as a time when no clouds appeared in the sky.

The third volume of memoirs is entitled *Le Temps de la recherche* (1947), a title more prosaic yet more descriptive than those given to his first two. Its meaning is double. It refers in the first instance to Duhamel's decision to work in laboratories for a few years, a decision made with full knowledge that by so doing he was turning his back on a medical career. He had few regrets, for within him the conviction was deepening that literature must be his first choice. He knew that the endless cares of the general practitioner would leave little or no leisure for writing. To convince himself that this was so, he served a brief term as a doctor's replacement, an experience that clearly demonstrated to him that though he could live without medicine, he would not be able to live without literature. Journalism in the ordinary sense tempted him not at all. Yet he had to earn a living. At this juncture a friend offered him a job as an industrial researcher. The equipment was of the best, the pay excellent, the hours flexible. Duhamel accepted and thus began the "time of research," research in the laboratory, research in the field of writing. This apprenticeship in writing and in science ended only with the beginning of the First World War.

Both sorts of research were necessary to Duhamel. He needed first of all to earn his living. He needed also to grope and experiment as a writer. Only by trial and error would he be able to determine his real literary bent. In his opinion the public is intolerant of the apparent idleness of the young writer. The need for years of preparation and experience is understood in the case of the scientist, the doctor, or the lawyer. The byproducts of their apprenticeship are visible in tangible form as a contribution to society in the menial but indispensable capacity of laboratory assistant, interne, or process-server. Not so the writer. His first scribblings are usually unsaleable, unpublishable, and apparently useless; yet experience he must have. It was with this in mind that Duhamel chose the industrial laboratory as a not-too-difficult taskmaster during his years of experimentation as a young writer.

A major portion of this third volume is also devoted to amiable reminiscences of the early years. We follow the apprentice writer through his experiments with free verse and the publication of four books of poetry, and we are introduced to the friends he met along the way. The days of the Abbaye, long the subject of study and discussion by the critics, are here given full, authoritative treatment, and the respective roles of Arcos, Vildrac, Gleizes, and the rest of the band are clearly defined. Duhamel flatly declares that *Le Désert de Bièvres* owes little more than its framework to the actual Abbaye. For Duhamel the Abbaye demonstrated among other things how difficult it is, even for a group of friends, all of them idealists and men of good will, to find a satisfactory life while sharing a common existence. Thus, finally, the Abbaye ceased to exist.

In addition to being a chronicle of his literary beginnings, this third volume of memoirs is the story of his affections. During one of the Sunday afternoon gatherings at Créteil a young actress from Paris came to the Abbaye with some friends. Her name was Blanche Albane, and she became Duhamel's wife. The progress of their love and courtship is told with charm and discretion. Duhamel attributes to his fortunate marriage a great deal of his success. Since Madame Duhamel is less retiring than her husband, she has lent him her strength, particularly as he has been led, in spite of himself, to assume a public role as a speaker, lecturer, and radio commentator. Whenever he can properly do so, it is Duhamel's custom to pay sincere and heartfelt tribute to his wife for her sympathy and support in their common endeavors.

After their marriage the Duhamels continued their separate careers for a while, he in the laboratory and study and she on the stage, where she acted under the direction of the aging but still energetic André Antoine. In his spare time Duhamel often sat in the empty theater listening to rehearsals in which his wife was taking part.

In this manner he became acquainted with theater people like the experimenter Copeau and the actor-managers Jouvet, Baty, and Dullin. Through Jules Romains, rather than through his wife, he met Antoine himself. Thus he came to the theater as a writer, and this too, as he implies, was in the nature of research. He praises the work of Antoine, who retired from the Odéon, France's second state theater, just as Copeau was founding his experimental Théâtre du Vieux Colombier. A trip to England with Copeau for a very brief stay gets equally brief mention, after which the memoir takes up again his more personal concerns.

Duhamel's greatest opportunity as a young writer was not, as he sees plainly in retrospect, the acceptance of his early plays by Antoine, but his introduction to that truly distinguished editor, Alfred Vallette, of the *Mercure de France*. The latter offered him the post of poetry critic for the small sum of sixteen francs per issue, in all about thirty-two francs a month. This was small pay, but in addition to the encouragement the appointment gave him, the work required him to write regularly, like the journalism he sought to escape. The articles produced for his bimonthly column became *Les Poètes et la poésie*, a book he now thinks little of, but at least he was writing and being paid for it. This was a short but essential step on the way to fame.

In the closing pages of *Le Temps de la recherche* Duhamel tells us about the days immediately preceding the First World War. When hostilities began, he was resting in Avignon with his wife, who had been taken ill during a summer theater season. The startling news meant an end to holidays. He describes in detail and with much feeling his ride back to Paris, his farewells to the family, and his induction into the army. The somber concluding page of this volume of memoirs begins with these words:

Car voici le temps de l'affliction qui commence.

Car les hommes de notre âge peuvent renoncer aux purs jeux de l'esprit, aux limpides œuvres de la paix. Ils n'auront désormais de souffle que pour souffrir et pour combattre.

Car les mots vont changer de sens et les idées de pouvoir.

Car le plus précieux de tous les biens imaginables, la vie, va, pour de longues années, tomber dans le mépris et dans l'avilissement.[4]

Volume four, *La Pesée des âmes* (1949), deals with Duhamel's participation in the war. This was the time of his greatest personal sacrifice as well as the time of his first great literary triumph. From many points of view this is the best volume of the memoirs. In it he told without bitterness and even with occasional humor the story of his frustrations and misadventures as a medical officer, and he narrated in straightforward fashion his adventures in the field hospital, adventures of which he had written so tellingly in the war sketches.

Even for the wartime surgeon there was time for friendships, for writing and leisure activities. Not only did he find time to write much and well, but he began to learn to play the flute and to study music seriously. The mysteries of military protocol amused when they did not annoy him. He recalls that when General Pétain made an inspection of his ambulance unit, he did not once remember to address him as "mon général." Years later Duhamel mentioned this to the old man, who seemed amused and commented, "Well, it wasn't my job to indoctrinate you."

Of greatest concern to Duhamel as an active participant in the war was the attitude that he encountered among the civilians. He was annoyed by the super-patriotism of Maurice Barrès, writing hate-filled editorials in Paris. He was equally dissatisfied with the humanitarian detachment of Romain Rolland, who preached pacifism from his exile in Switzerland. Each man seemed to him to be mistaken in his own way.

As a memoir of the war, personal this time instead of general, *La Pesée des âmes* is a most satisfactory book. Its introduction is a valuable exposition of his view of the world. It must be remembered that the sentiments here expressed were written just as the Second World War had concluded. In Duhamel's view it was time for a world inventory. As he evaluated the war as a human phenomenon and tried to assay its cost it seemed to him that the greatest loss of all was the permanent loss of prestige suffered by the white race of western Europe. Though he is no white supremacist, or petty hater of nonwhite races, he found himself appalled by the thought that Europe, by its fratricidal conflict, had lost its leadership in the world. Here is how he saw the situation:

> Pourrais-je, avouant ainsi mon anxiété, laisser le moindre doute sur mes sentiments profonds? Il se tromperait lourdement celui qui me croirait consterné parce que les hommes de la race blanche vont devoir abandonner leur position de régents tyranniques. Non, non! Que l'on m'entende bien! Tout observateur de sang-froid sait que l'équilibre est, dans les choses humaines, ce qu'il y a de plus nécessaire et, toutefois, de plus difficile à trouver et à maintenir. La mission de la race blanche, en admettant qu'elle fût vraiment consciente de ses dons intellectuels, de ses vertus, de son hoirie, était de trouver, pour le monde, un honnête système d'équilibre et, l'ayant trouvé, de s'y tenir.[5]

The Second World War appeared to him as a point at which mankind turned away from civilization. The third

might well spell the end for all mankind. The prospect
was hardly consoling, and with this somber note Duhamel
set out to chronicle the comic, tragic, boring, yet intensely
interesting events of his more than four years in the army.

With *Les Espoirs et les épreuves* (1953) Duhamel
brought the story of his life down to the year 1928. This
is as far as he intends to go. Except for the possible
publication after his death of some notes now in preparation, he says that he does not intend to offer the public
any more memoirs. Judging by the note of hope in the
title of this volume, and judging by the rise in Duhamel's
literary fortunes that it chronicles, the reader expects to
encounter a happy outlook in its pages. In point of fact
he does not. In the period after the First World War
the trials seem to have outweighed the hopes. Duhamel
was troubled by many things. His attempts at Franco-
German *rapprochement* began to be frustrated by the rise
of National Socialism. Materialism seemed to be in the
ascendant. Even in the literary field he found himself
occasionally out of joint with the times. He did not stay
his full time at the writers' conference that he attended
at Pontigny. He was equally ill at ease at the meetings
of the P.E.N. Club. To his distress he found his time
more and more taken up with serving on prize juries and
the writing of prefaces, all of which kept him away from
his creative writing. He began to be increasingly impatient with hearing himself referred to as an optimist.
In reality he was deeply worried. He had become aware,
long before the Second World War, of the incipient
conflict between the Russian and American political and
economic systems. He feared that all the civilized world
held dear might be doomed to destruction in a confrontation of the two materialisms, as he called them. He was
skeptical of the ability of the French government, torn by

internal conflicts as it was, to save the situation. He was
almost certain that the efforts of intellectuals like Leon
Blum to bring order out of chaos were going to fail. The
world seemed without salvation. The book was, of course,
written with the benefit of hindsight, but one has only to
read Duhamel's essays and fiction in the period between
wars to realize how accurately he gauged the situation
that confronted Europe, and how few were willing to lay
aside their fatuous optimism to listen to what he had to
say.

Six years later, in 1959, we have from Duhamel's pen
an excellent short summary of his career. As an introduction to an anthology of selected pages from his writings,
entitled *Travail, ô mon seul repos,* he gives a rapid sketch
of his life and works. Nothing that any of his biographers
has done is as good as this. Each of the major productions
is discussed briefly, and some of the background for
writing them is explained. The book is useful as a capsule
autobiography.

This summary, together with the five volumes of memoirs, are the extent of Duhamel's published autobiographical writings, but in his other books there are innumerable
passages that throw light on him as a man and as a
thinker. Prominent among his interests is music, of
which there is frequent and eloquent mention in his
pages. We have already seen how this interest was used
to advantage in the *Chronique des Pasquier* and to a
lesser extent in his other novels. In *La Nuit d'orage*
the character François Cros is a talented amateur. Duhamel is aware of the large part he has given to music
in his narratives. He has told us of his pleasure in
learning to play the flute at the age of thirty-two and of
the satisfaction it has given him, though he had loved
music for years. He has described his participation in

chamber music groups and of his assiduous concert-going. In 1921 he was persuaded by his friend Albert Doyen to make a speech at the Fêtes du Peuple, and he published his remarks under the descriptive title *La Musique libératice*. This essay is noteworthy for its affirmation of the doctrine that a love of good music, and taste in its appreciation, can be acquired.

In 1925 Duhamel again associated himself with Doyen, this time collaborating with him on an operetta to be entitled *Voix du vieux monde*. He describes how he composed the libretto feverishly at his house in Valmondois and then bicycled over to the nearby home of Doyen to work with him. He thoroughly enjoyed this work, and he says ecstatically that music can make manifest for those who will listen the true dimensions of mankind.

This theme was developed at even greater length in a second book on music, entitled *La Musique consolatrice* (1944), published after the liberation of France. Beginning with a statement of the power of music to move him deeply, to lighten his burdens, to make him sometimes gay and sometimes sad, he called it a palace of dreams. Yet he rejected the thought of music as mere escape from reality. Great music, he said, makes us see and understand life. He described his own introduction to the appreciation of music, the thrill he experienced on hearing a military band play snatches from *Die Walküre*. After that the young Duhamel began to sing and to listen to Wagner's music with his friend Schuller and later with Albert Doyen. He has since always listened to Wagner with pleasure, but he confessed that as he has grown older, Bach has supplanted Wagner as his musical idol. Of all the great musicians, Bach, the man of bourgeois origins and humble life, is for him the greatest master. As contributions to his own musical education, the experience of playing the flute and his participation in ensemble-playing were of greatest importance. He advised all who wish to cultivate a taste for music to acquire personal experience with it. Singing or playing an instrument, even if one is far removed from virtuosity, does much, he believed, to make listening to great music more enjoyable and more intelligible.

The remainder of the book is made up of a discussion of the role of music in modern life. As we already know, Duhamel condemns the juke-box because he feels that even good music, if the boxes play any, should not be desecrated by too frequent rendition. His severest comments he reserved for the prostitution of the great masters by restaurant and steamship orchestras that play medleys of Bach and Beethoven interspersed with trash, served up to an audience that is eating, talking, or playing bridge. He was irritated by concert-goers who, like the opera fans of the past, spend their time in endless, trivial gossip while the performers are on stage. He was also afraid that if mechanical music, of the record or tape recorder, becomes too perfect, it might supplant the living artist.

Duhamel gives a rapid analysis of polyphonic music. For him its invention and development is one of the touchstones of our Western democratic civilization. Of all the forms of polyphony, he likes best the string quartet because of its intimate quality. *La Musique consolatrice* is a calm and reflective book, and for the reader of Duhamel it has the advantage of giving full expression to the love of music that he has elsewhere often referred to but never before so clearly defined.

Music is not alone among the arts in claiming Duhamel's attention. In the days of the Abbaye he was the friend of the painter Albert Gleizes, and in *Le Temps de la recherche* he pays tribute to him as well as to Henri Doucet, a promising young artist who was killed in the First World War. But his closest friend among the artists has been Berthold Mahn. It is Mahn who has given us the best sketches of Duhamel, and it is he also who has provided the drawings of Salavin that come closest, their creator says, to his conception of him. During the course of their long friendship Duhamel and Mahn have been much in each other's company. A trip that they took in 1931 became the subject of a charming book they wrote together, *L'Alsace entrevue, ou l'aveugle et le paralytique.* They set out in Duhamel's car and, leaving their families behind, drove through the little towns of the old province, ending up in Strasbourg. The alternative title is a reference to an old fable in which a blind man is led by a cripple. In their version of it Duhamel represents the blind man because he is unable to perceive the beauties immediately apparent to the artist. Mahn made some sixty pen-and-ink drawings for the book and Duhamel wrote the text. Little that he says is in a serious vein. He jokes about Mahn's foibles and his own reactions to them and occasionally provides a commentary on one of the drawings.

Sixteen years later Mahn and Duhamel collaborated again. Mahn accompanied him on a trip to Greece while he was collecting material for his essay on Homer. The volume they published jointly contains Duhamel's essay together with Mahn's drawings and commentary.

Duhamel has twice attempted a more serious discussion of art. He has written two appreciative essays on the work of artists with whom he is acquainted. The first, *Henry de Waroquier* (1925), talked of the artist's work and also declared the author's preference for an art centered upon man. He declared also that he demands of an artist a finished work and not a mere preliminary sketch. The second essay, *Maurice de Vlaminck* (1927), dealt with his friend and neighbor of Valmondois. Duhamel had ample occasion to know well both the man and his work. In his essay he praised his technical mastery and his vigor. He also wrote humorously of his friend's robust tastes and heroic stature. Neither of these essays is pretentious, and therein lies their charm.

Many another of Duhamel's tastes and preferences as we find them out contribute to our knowledge of him as man and author. We learn for instance by chance references that he likes fishing but not hunting, that to his fondness for walking he adds a fondness for swimming and rowing, but that he has little interest in competitive sports. He tells us that he learned to cook, and one of his biographers, René Arcos, has painted a glowing picture of him as a chef-gourmet. In his memoirs Duhamel repudiates this account of himself, declaring that he has really had no time to become a gourmet.

Religion has been one of Duhamel's constant preoccupations throughout his life. For him it has failed of consolation. He tells us that since he lost his faith, as he was passing from youth to manhood, he has never been able to replace the absolute verities of the Church with any others. His belief in the omniscience of science and of the reason that directs its activities was shaken by the horrors of the First World War. Since that time, although he rejoices over the discoveries of medicine and of pure science, he does not look to them to provide man with any sort of salvation. Happiness, as he said in *La Possession du monde*, is not induced by the material possessions of an individual or of society. As for the Church, her demands upon us as the price of salvation are, as he phrases it, beyond his reach. Duhamel is outside the

Church, but he is sympathetic toward those who find salvation inside. He has described his position in these words:

Je n'ai pas la foi religieuse. Je suis, présentement, ce que j'appelle, pendant les heures d'amertume, un agnostique désespéré, ce que j'appellerai plus tard, ayant pesé les idées et les mots, un agnostique chrétien. A ce monde incompréhensible, il s'agit, pour les hommes d'une certaine sorte, de donner quand même une explication qui laisse l'esprit en repos et l'empêche de s'enfoncer dans des layons sans issue. Accepter une métaphysique et la déposer aussitôt dans «l'arche sainte» pour se donner plus librement aux œuvres de la vie, c'est une solution de sagesse, tout au moins en apparence. Par malheur, je ne suis pas en état d'accepter. . . .

Non, je n'ai pas la foi religieuse; mais, de ce manque, je me garde bien de tirer orgueil. J'envie, et je ne m'en cache point, ceux qui, ne souffrant pas du vide majeur, peuvent consacrer leur capacité de souffrance à d'autres blessures, à d'autres sujects d'amertume.[6]

This is quite the opposite of the antireligious zeal of some of the characters Duhamel has created, such as the scientist Nicolas Rohner in *Les Maîtres,* whom the author attacked grimly. Rohner would have had his students reject every human attribute except reason, which he called the "one faithful and serviceable attribute" which man has at his disposal. Duhamel has turned his back as resolutely upon such a belief in the infallibility of science as he has upon his faith in religion, yet he declares that most men, even in this day and age, are actively seeking a church,—that is, a formula for personal happiness and salvation. He writes:

Le passant qui vous arrête et qui vous demande du feu, laissez-le seulement parler: au bout de dix minutes, il vous demandera Dieu. Tous, qu'ils le sachent ou non, veulent une loi, une règle, une direction, une contrainte. Tous demandent à se délivrer sur quelqu'un du soin d'évaluer ou de choisir, du soin de décider, de trancher et de conclure. Tous, pour finir, veulent, obscurément, Dieu et la vie éternelle, même s'ils sont, par ailleurs, cyniques, sceptiques, grossiers, insensibles.[7]

With this groping for certainty Duhamel has vast sympathy, but he refuses himself the role of prophet or seer. He claims only to be a writer who confesses that his own search for salvation is no less agonizing than that of his fellow men. Yet it is his conviction that faith cannot be achieved by merely wishing for it. His heroes Laurent Pasquier and Louis Salavin tried, each in his own way, to find a faith, but their attempts were unsuccessful. Death came to Salavin and middle age to Pasquier without their having found an adequate substitute for religion. For his own part Duhamel feels that there is no adequate substitute, but he has kept on looking for tentative conclusions as to the meaning of the universe. His most ambitious attempt was, as we have seen, his plea for a systematic search for happiness, in *La Possession du monde,* but his quest for a valid philosophy of life did not stop there. Equilibrium is a word he often uses in this connection. Laurent sees the world as a disordered place, and Duhamel has him declare that he wants to find a balance. It is not always clear just what form this equilibrium, or balance, advocated by Duhamel, is expected to take, but from the general tenor of his writing it appears that he is striving for a world in which the forces that make for human happiness will at least counterbalance those that make for bitterness and despair. Despair he has always wished to combat, but the eternal skeptic in him, fostered by his early scientific training, requires that his views remain tentative. When necessary he discards yesterday's truth as incompatible with today's knowledge, and he is even willing to hold simultaneously two theories that might to another man seem mutually exclusive.

Of one thing Duhamel is certain: Pascal was right in assigning to the feelings a preponderant place in the scheme of life. Reason, though not subordinate to emotion, must work in harmony with the nonrational forces in man, and in this collaboration reason will not always be the senior partner. Because of the misuse of reason in the invention and manufacture of engines of destruction, the relief of misery and suffering will remain for some time one of man's chief goals. It would appear, therefore, that our habits and methods of reasoning are in urgent need of reform. Reason tells us that material progress saves us from toil and travail, but the existence of war shows the contradiction in our thinking. Materialism, in Duhamel's view, is one of the principal causes of war, for rival materialisms strive against each other. Even in a time of peace we see it demonstrated that riches and material possessions are not synonymous with happiness. Duhamel has thus been unable to convince himself that an improvement in our economic status will inevitably result in our greater happiness. For this reason he has never evinced any passionate interest in labor unions, social legislation, or political and collective methods of improving the economic status of the average man. To this extent he is out of step with the times, but only a utopian dreamer could declare that his point of view is totally wrong. War and materialism are still with us. Happiness is frequently as elusive as ever.

In the midst of the suffering of the First World War one of Duhamel's chief consolations was friendship. Like most shy men he declares that it is not possible to have a large number of friends, yet his memoirs and other writings of a personal nature show that he has given and received the gift of friendship in large and generous measure. There is hardly a literary man of any importance in France with whom Duhamel has not had an acquaintance varying from cordial to intimate. Alfred Vallette of the *Mercure de France* and André Antoine of the Odéon theater were elder statesmen whose advice and encouragement he appreciated during his literary beginnings. Henri de Régnier, Jules La Forgue and René Ghil, and later Paul Claudel, Emile Verhaeren, and Max Jacob were his friends among the poets. Among contemporary men of letters he esteems Roger Martin du Gard, François Mauriac, Paul Valéry, Georges Chennevière, Luc Durtain, Charles Vildrac, and René Arcos. He makes one of the characters in the Pasquier chronicle comment thus half-seriously on friendship:

> On ne choisit pas sa famille—et c'est bien regrettable—. Je commence à comprendre qu'on ne choisit non plus ses amis. On les a reçus, on les garde, on les porte, on les subit, et c'est comme cela.[8]

Friends are inescapable, yet real communication between oneself and one's friends is frequently difficult if not impossible. We face the problem of communication in our dealings with all men, but in the case of our friends the problem is most acute because it is most exasperating. He makes Salavin say in *Confession de minuit*:

> Comment affirmer que l'on n'a pas fait souffrir un homme alors qu'on l'a regardé, fût-ce une fois, alors qu'on a traversé sa vie, même en pensée.[9]

Yet Duhamel does not despair. Friendship is indispensable to man. Its difficulty and fragility, a theme to which he returns again and again, is but another of the many human problems that are always with us but which we must ever try to solve. This problem had already been noted by the Romantics. In our century it has been reechoed by Maeterlinck and many others. Of this Duhamel is aware, but he carries somewhat farther than most writers the notion of the fragility of the bonds that hold men together. He is in complete agreement with Montaigne's statement that every man must reserve for himself an *arrière-boutique* for his private thoughts, but friendship must also have its place in our lives.

During his long career Duhamel has striven to be a leader of humanistic thought, but he has also explicitly stated that he has had no wish to found a school of writers or to become the head of any sort of organized movement. He defines his role as a writer in the following terms:

Je donne ce que j'ai. Je dis ce que sais. Je suis un écrivain dans la force de l'âge. J'ai vu beaucoup d'hommes et quelque peu voyagé. Je suis, en outre, médecin, et j'ai tiré de la médecine un large enseignement humain. Voilà mon domaine. Il n'est pas trop petit. Je peux répondre à beaucoup de questions. Plus nombreuses encore sont les questions qu'il me faut laisser sans réponse, qu'un honnête homme se doit de laisser sans réponse.[10]

Duhamel has also frequently discussed his methods of work. He has given us his views on inspiration and has explained how he determines the orientation of new novels and stories. He relates in his memoirs that the habit of work is strongly fixed in him. Relaxation does not mean freedom from writing, but an indulgence in its lighter forms. His conscience makes him take a dim view of days when he has managed to keep busy with no more important tasks than writing speeches, correcting proofs, or answering correspondence. If during such a day he has not turned his hand to creative writing, the writing that is his real work, he counts that day lost.

When creative work begins, the blankness of the sheet of paper on his desk is a torture to him. An irrational fear seizes him, a fear that no inspiration will come. And inspiration cannot be summoned; it is not the product of determination or desire. It is the fruit of long meditation. To induce the proper mood, he says:

Il va falloir mettre en branle la déconcertante machine intellectuelle. Il va falloir, par un exténuant effort d'incubation, amener l'âme à une certaine température qui est indispensable à la genèse créatrice.[11]

Then ideas come flowing. "To invent is to find"—*invenire, c'est trouver*[12]—to find within oneself the source of one's ideas. From this point to the finished work there intervenes all the anguish of creative toil, a toil not quite distinguishable from physical pain. The writer may be led gradually to the point of actual writing while he is walking, alone or in the company of friends, or while listening to others talk, but when the day comes that he must actually confront the empty sheet of paper and begin to work, his anguish is greatest. This feeling of acute misery is progressively relieved as the work progresses. When the book is finally finished and laid aside, he begins to think about his next book. Yet he is never wholly satisfied with what he has accomplished, and he despairs of not being able to put down on paper more than a sixth of what he would like to write during his lifetime.

The products of this toil and struggle have won the praise of readers and critics. Their source is the life that has been described in the memoirs, the thoughts that have resulted from the friendships, the activities, the meditation of Georges Duhamel. His view of that work is modest, yet he knows his own competence. There are, as he has said, many questions that he can answer.

NOTES

CITATIONS from Duhamel that are given in French in the text are translated below into English. Correspondingly, where short citations have been given in English in the text, the French is given here. All translations are by the present author. Publishers and dates of publication of works cited herein are given only when the edition differs from the one listed in the bibliography.

EPIGRAPH TO PART I

Before the moment of oblivion, I must count, weigh, evaluate all the mountains, all the rivers, the forests full of fragrance, and the teeming cities where my beloved brothers, my bitter brothers, my terrifying brothers, my fellow men rejoice, work, and suffer. —*Le Bestiaire et l'herbier*, in *Les Livres du bonheur* (Mercure de France, 1950), p. 320.

CHAPTER I

[1] *Le Temps de la recherche*, chap. V, *passim*.

[2] Basically, the idea of a human association to be sought after rather than borne, even accepted with joy, is not absurd. We are intellectuals —we are, that is to say, hard to get along with. Our failure proves nothing for the rest of mankind. —*Le Désert de Bièvres* (1963), p. 280.

[3] Nowadays persons who defend regular verse with the shrill and dogmatic stubbornness of a Dorchain are either blind or imbecilic. —*Notes sur la technique poétique* (Champion, 1925), p. 3.

4 While admitting that in this prisonhouse *incomparable* masterpieces have been created, we cannot measure without astonishment the mousehole that a Baudelaire, winged though he was, had to pass through.
—*Notes*, p. 2.

5 If there is a spot
Where you have lived violent hours,
And where the air still bears your imprint,
Do not leave it.
—*Compagnons* (Nouvelle revue française, 1918), p. 104.

6 And these ordinary events
Which frame your existence,
Which are for you events of considerable importance,
Which are for you the only important events in the world,
Shall I find them altogether negligible?
—*Compagnons*, p. 24.

7 You, my companions! O you, all men!
Let me seize this lost happiness,
Let me be, and if my outstretched hands are not enough,
Help me then to attain it and possess it.

Help me then, and when it is conquered,
This joy that for you perhaps
Scarcely resembles joy.
I want to give back to each of you,
Under the guise that you prefer,
Ten times the weight of this happiness
That I agree to owe you.
—*Compagnons*, p. 96.

8 He resisted twenty long days
And his mother was beside him.

Florentin Prunier resisted,
For his mother doesn't want him to die.

As soon as she found out that he was wounded,
She came from the ends of the old province.

She crossed the thundering land
Where the immense army crouches in the mud.

Her face is stern under the starched bonnet.
She is afraid of nothing and of nobody.

She brings a dozen apples in a basket,
And fresh butter in a little jar

. . . .

He resisted for twenty long days,
And his mother was beside him,

Like an old swimmer who goes into the sea,
Holding her weak child above the water.

Now, one morning, when she was very tired,
After twenty nights, spent God knows where,
She allowed herself to nod,
She napped for just a moment;

And Florentin Prunier died very quickly,
Quietly, so as not to wake her up.
—*Elégies,* suivies de *Quatre ballades* (Mercure de France, 1920), pp. 75-76, 78-79.

[9] . . . un «sujet» devient poétique entre les mains d'un artiste, qui ne l'était pas particulièrement auparavant, et qu'il peut cesser de l'être dans la suite. —*Propos critiques* (Mercure de France, 1924), p. 157.

[10] Mais j'éprouve quelque gêne à ratiociner quand il s'agit d'un pòeme et que j'aime. —*Propos critiques,* p. 230.

[11] . . . ressentir quelque chose, penser quelque chose, et serrer sa pensée d'aussi près que possible. —*Les Poètes et la poésie,* p. 95.

[12] I think I have shown as much partiality in dispraise as in praise. Instead of taking myself to task for this, I am tempted to insist that it is so, so sure am I that in literary matters a subjective and relative opinion is the only valid one. —*Les Poètes et la poésie,* p. 6.

[13] *La Lumière* est bien le spectacle le plus ennuyeux qui soit. —*Mercure de France,* XCI (1 mai 1911), 193.

[14] Struck by the beauty of the work, I did not hesitate to announce publicly before the performance that a writer of first magnitude had appeared. . . .   —*Revue de la Capitole* (1927), p. 21.

[15] Les trois pièces de théâtre qu'il fait jouer avant 1914 . . . n'annonçaient encore qu'un jeune écrivain touché par tous les courants de la sensibilité moderne, mais précieux, obscur, cherchant sa voix et sa forme—sa vocation aussi. —*Georges Duhamel* (Editions du temps présent, 1946), p. 26.

[16] *Revue de la capitole,* pp. 25-27.

[17] . . . il y a plus de vraie philosophie et d'originale profondeur dans dix lignes de Spinoza, de Spencer ou de Bergson que dans quatre ou cinq actes écrasants. —*Essai sur une renaissance dramatique,* p. 54.

[18] His work was not written for the footlights but for the light of the study lamp. —*Georges Duhamel,* p. 81.

CHAPTER II

[1] Since then I have often thought that there is a truly international language, a universal language. I wonder whether even animals are deaf to it. It is the language of suffering. Do you really think there are men incapable of understanding it? —*Entretiens dans le tumulte,* p. 68.

2 If this sacrifice is to run its full course, and be fully understood, it must be bitter to the end; the cup must be drained to and including the dregs. We must not become accustomed to it. —*Entretiens*, p. 113.

3 When my fingers come close to his punctured eye, Croin pulls away a little.

"Don't be afraid," I say.

"Oh, I'm not afraid."

And he adds with quiet pride:

"If you have been on Hill 108, you aren't afraid of anything anymore."

"Why do you pull away then?"

"My head pulls away by itself. I don't even think of it." —*Vie des martyrs* (Mercure de France, 1945), pp. 57-58.

4 They all tell the same story. The war hasn't changed them much. You can recognize them all.

"Are you sure you can? You who have just looked at them, are you sure you have really seen them?"

Under the surgical dressings there are wounds you cannot imagine. Deep within these wounds, within the mutilated flesh, an extraordinary yet furtive soul moves and is exalted, a soul that does not show itself readily, although it expresses itself innocently, a soul that I would very much like you to feel. —*Vie des martyrs*, pp. 6-7.

5 Mercier is dead. His pupils dilate solemnly over a glassy void. It is all over. He will not be saved.

Then from the dead man's eyes flow great tears, which run down his cheeks. I see his features contract, to weep for all eternity.

For long minutes I continue to hold the dead man's hand in mine. —*Vie des martyrs*, pp. 109-10.

6 Alas, I have met hate; not here but elsewhere, far from these thundering battles, far from the flame and anger of combat. I have heard cries of hate: those who uttered them were almost always far from action, suffering, and danger. Were they play-acting? Were they trying to make excuses? Did they hope to fill the emptiness of their existence and of their soul with these outcries? Did they think this would cause their uselessness to be forgotten? I do not know. Certainly they were to be pitied. —*Les Sept dernières plaies*, p. 213.

7 The grumbling of war, the noise of moving convoys, the convulsive shaking of the cannonade, all the hissing and panting of the killing machine reached the windows and shook them with spent fury, just as the vain echoes of a thunderstorm at sea reach a little harbor. But this noise was as familiar to the ear as the very pulse of the wretched world. There was no boredom in Revaud's room. —*Civilisation* (Mercure de France, 1925), p. 11.

8 Vous êtes bien heureux d'oser faire des projets en une pareille époque.

—N'est-ce pas déjà faire un projet que de laisser battre son cœur?

Et puis, il faut défier l'avenir si l'on ne veut pas être réduit à le redouter. —*Civilisation*, p. 86.

[9] It seems that Dauche was buried in the little cemetery shut in by the branches of the birch trees and the dead firs that can be seen from the village of C— in a desolate field of white sand. I could not make myself go and visit his grave. I carried with me a deeper and less empty tomb. —*Civilisation*, pp. 96-97.

[10] Perhaps discipline is not a French virtue. God be praised, we have other virtues, and one of them—our critical sense, for example—is so fine, so incisive, so delicate that it is worth as much as all the heavy qualities of our enemies, if I may say so. —*Civilisation*, p. 218.

[11] I hate the twentieth century as I hate this rotten Europe and the whole world over which this unhappy Europe has spread itself, like a blot of axle grease. I know it is a bit ridiculous to come out with high-sounding phrases like that, but, Lord, I don't say these things to everyone, and after all, this sort of ridiculous talk is no worse than any other kind! —*Civilisation*, pp. 257-58.

[12] I looked at the monstrous sterilizer on its throne. I tell you in truth, civilization is not in that object, any more than in the shining forceps of the surgeon. Civilization does not consist of this awful bundle of things; if civilization is not in the heart of man, well, it isn't anywhere. —*Civilisation*, p. 272.

[13] . . . le but de ma vie, comme il est le but de toute l'humanité, comme il est le but de tout le monde vivant. . . . Le bonheur n'est pas que la fin, la raison de la vie, il en est le ressort, l'expression, l'essence. Il est la vie même. . . . O Bonheur, tu es bien mon but et ma raison d'être, je le reconnais à mes larmes. —*La Possession du monde* (Mercure de France, 1927), pp. 17, 19, 21.

[14] . . . car le monde est proposé à tous les hommes pour être possédé en totalité par chacun d'eux avec l'aide de tous. —*La Possession*, p. 56.

[15] Mais il est sûrement riche, celui pour qui la vie est une perpétuelle découverte. —*La Possession*, p. 111.

[16] M. Bergson has said of the intelligence, that it is "characterized by a natural incomprehension of life," and one might add: by a complete incomprehension of happiness, which is life's goal. —*La Possession*, p. 244.

[17] The Anglo-American peoples, although receptive to all the moral and religious revolutions, have applied themselves to changing simple well-being from its original meaning and identifying it with comfortable luxury. This is a way of giving a moral aspect to self-indulgence and of compromising honestly with the corruption of money. —*La Possession*, p. 261.

[18] *Le Temps*, 6 mars 1919.

[19] *Mercure de France*, CXXXV (16 septembre 1919), 312.

[20] *Revue universelle*, VIII (15 mars 1922), 738-61.

[21] . . . the selfish instincts rooted in man's flesh are not so easily spirited away. But no matter. What had to be understood, and what the readers of 1920 did understand in this generous book, and what still gives it deep appeal, is its passionate yet lucid condemnation of the pride of man, the maker of machines, its condemnation of "calculating, demoralizing intelligence"; it is its invitation to lower scientific civilization from its place as an idol to that of a servant. —*Georges Duhamel*, pp. 31-32.

[22] I am sorry to stir up these memories again. They are too simple, too bare, too true, to move a society that wishes not to be cured of its wounds but only to forget them. Why talk about the war again? What is the use of talking about something that no longer interests anyone? —*Les Sept dernières plaies*, p. 214.

[23] I am quite certain there will be other wars, inexpiable wars, in the not far distant future. I am no longer at the age when one hopes to reform the world. But I intend to reform myself, to hold back my simple and primitive impulses, and I shall reasonably establish my disavowal of war, of all wars without distinction and without pious sophistry. —*Anniversaire*, p. 265.

[24] La paix à tout prix, voilà ce qu'il faut dire et répéter. —*Délibérations*, p. 62.

[25] There is nothing changed about the way nations settle important human affairs. I repeat, Sleep peacefully; your Europe has not been remade. It is still the Europe of the Cimbrians and Teutons, the Europe of the Saint Bartholomew massacre and the Spanish Inquisition. —*Entretiens*, p. 267.

[26] Works of art arouse curiosity and maintain affection. It is above all through Dickens, Hardy, Wells, Kipling that I know England. If I love Russia, it is because of Moussorgsky, Borodine, Turgenev, Dostoevski, Gorki. —*Délibérations*, pp. 96-97.

[27] If communism appears to me, individualist that I am and intend to remain, susceptible of many improvements, if communism in many respects wounds and outrages me, I bow before the revolution. I accept and acknowledge it.

. . . .

If communism should one day spread over the face of the earth, it will be because millions of men have wanted it with all their might, and because other men, by their excesses, have acted in such a way as to make it inevitable. —*Voyage de Moscou*, pp. 245, 251.

[28] . . . you can change what is called the regime, you can replace the class in power, you can change everything; but if you do not change me—me, Salavin—well, you will not have changed anything. —*Le Club des Lyonnais*, p. 188.

[29] It must not be forgotten that the first act of the National Socialist

party was to burn books on the public squares. A regime that burns books has sinned against the mind. It is right for the mind to turn away from such a regime. —*Mémorial de la guerre blanche,* pp. 84-85.

[30] We reason like philosophers of the past when we say that a courageous people, sure of its cause and firmly resolved upon martyrdom, cannot be conquered. We must yield to the evidence: with airplanes, poisons, tanks, and machine guns, everything can be conquered, because everything is within reach of destruction. —*Mémorial,* p. 132.

[31] If I may permit myself to make a personal statement on this subject, it is to say that true pacifism must change its character and methods with changing events. I am pacific not only by philosophy, experience, and taste, but for many personal reasons. I have sons of combat age. My old mother lives with me and cannot be moved. I live most of the time in a large, unprotected city. I am vulnerable from every direction. In any case war will not only defeat the thought of my whole life, it will not only be the negation of my life's work, but it will certainly touch everything I hold dear. That is why I say that pacifists must resist, must arm themselves to resist. All else, at the moment, is sophistry, nonsense, bad strategy, and tragic error. —*Positions françaises,* pp. 59-60.

[32] . . . les Allemands étaient au petit nombre des peuples qui ont contribué à construire la civilisation occidentale. —*Positions,* p. 189.

[33] . . . des fous et des malades qui la conduisent au désastre. —*Positions,* p. 74.

[34] . . . le plus lointain passé, l'homme préhistorique, l'homme des cavernes, l'homme encore prisonnier de l'animalité primitive. —*Positions.* p. 102.

[35] . . . c'est pour restituer l'Allemagne à son génie véritable, pour la réintégrer de force dans le concert des peuples cultivés. . . . —*Positions,* p. 207.

[36] When I saw her on her stretcher, Madame Camile Pochet presented me at first glance with the dreadful sight of someone in death agony. She wore, pinned to her dress, a medical tag with this alarming diagnosis: fractured pelvis. Furthermore, Madame Pochet seemed to be plunged into the depths of grief: it was impossible to get a word out of her. But it was not difficult to make her scream. This she demonstrated readily. —*Lieu d'asile* (Mercure de France, 1955), p. 112.

[37] M. Krauset is suffering from a big abscess on his hand, for the insane suffer from their flesh as other men do. I opened his infection and dressed it. He walks about ceaselessly, holding his bandaged hand straight out in front of him. With a clumsy but obstinate gesture he tries to untie and tear off his bandage.

I have a feeling that M. Krauset, from this time on, will never leave us. He will continue to complain and to stumble through my thoughts, the ridiculous and tragic phantom of these eccentric times. —*Lieu d'asile*, p. 63.

³⁸ Peter, you are a rock and upon this tiny rock we will rebuild our country. . . .

"For unto us a child is born," born as the new France will be reborn, born of a wounded, broken, and bleeding creature, a creature still proud withal, still strong and resolved to triumph over her misery. —*Lieu d'asile*, p. 142.

CHAPTER III

¹ I love the humble, stale odor that the drafts send through the bowels of the tenement. If I come back to life five hundred years from now, I shall recognize that smell among all the smells in the world. Don't make fun of me. Perhaps you are fond of less clean and less admissible things yourself. —*Confession de minuit* (Fayard, n.d.), p. 23.

² Yes, the gutter sings its little song all the same. It makes me think of green fields, and rivers, and lands I shall never see. It is civilized water, foul water, but water, water none the less. It is the sea, great lakes, and mountain torrents. If you go through Lhomond Street fairly late at night, when all the sounds of Paris are subdued in slumber, you will hear beneath your feet all the sewers of Mount Sainte Geneviève singing as sweetly as distant waterfalls. These are the waterfalls of my travels. —*Confession*, p. 53.

³ Night had long since come. The lamp had been lighted, and the coolness of evening was upon us, when, without any intelligible reason, a new sensation came upon me.

There was a precise moment when I noticed that I was a little less happy than I had been the moment before. That was it exactly. I can't put it any more clearly than that. . . .

I felt like crying out and shouting for help, like a sailor in distress in a drifting boat. It was quite useless; solitude engulfed me, black, impenetrable, mortal solitude. —*Confession*, pp. 44-45.

⁴ Je ne pose pas à l'original, je ne suis pas fait autrement que les autres. . . . . . . je passais la nuit à me mépriser et à me haïr. —*Confession*, pp. 19 and 47.

⁵ Salavin is a modern man, any man, but in him men of good faith from all points of the moral horizon, of different occupations and all ages, of differing social positions, nationalities, and races, can at certain times find something humbly or mysteriously common to them. —*Confession de minuit* (New York: Appleton-Century, 1933), p. 2 (Preface written by Duhamel for the American text).

⁶ As a physician I do not consider Salavin a sick man. Above all, he is not a paranoic. I maintain that Salavin does not need treatment.

Otherwise we would have to treat in psychopathic wards all who suffer from their thoughts. *—Deux patrons,* suivi de *Vie et mort d'un héros de roman,* p. 137.

[7] Don Quixote's grand-nephew. *—Deux patrons,* p. 93.

[8] I have never asked anything of you. You have made me accept everything. So that you might be yourself, I had to take everything you offered. You forced me to be weak so that you might be strong. . . . Under the pretext of giving me everything, you have taken everything from me, even my rare hours of freedom and friendship. *—Deux hommes* (Montreal: Editions variétés, 1944), pp. 205, 206.

[9] In spite of everything, we are two intelligent and generous men, good despite our weakness. We want to see concord and harmony rule the actions of all peoples, yet we have not been able to blend our two voices.

Well, it must be begun again.

I must start over again. To be entirely frank, entirely loyal, entirely honest is my greatest, my only wish. And I must believe that this wish for purity is not the only human purity. *—Deux hommes,* p. 242.

[10] Sir, you are probably going to get a false idea of me. You are going to think that I have a hateful disposition, that I am a misanthrope. I, a misanthrope! That's absurd! I love my fellow men, and it is not my fault if I cannot stand them most of the time. I dream of concord, of a confident, harmonious life, as charitable as a universal embrace. When I think of men, I find them so worthy of affection that tears come to my eyes. I should like to have nothing but kind words for them. I should like to pour my heart into theirs. I should like to join them in their plans and their actions, to have a place in their lives, to show them how capable I am of constancy, fidelity, and sacrifice. But there is something touchy, sensitive, and irritable about me. *—Confession,* pp. 57-58.

[11] Tel je suis et, pourtant, tel je ne m'accepte pas. Je ne prends pas mon parti d'être Salavin pour l'éternité. Il faut que l'on m'aide et que ça change. *—Journal de Salavin* (Montreal: Editions variétés, 1944), p. 166.

[12] *Revue hebdomadaire,* XXXVI, 2 (12 février 1927), 229-37.

[13] *Revue universelle,* XXVIII (15 février 1927), 492.

[14] The truth is that the *Journal de Salavin,* if it forces us to think and to argue with ourselves, is none the less a work carved from life itself, with a gallery of portraits so lifelike and so close to us that I defy you not only not to close the book before you have read the last page, but not to reopen it immediately in order to reexperience some scene that continues to haunt you. *—Georges Duhamel,* p. 102.

[15] I have all my faculties. You must understand that it is not a question of exchanging souls with Peter or Paul. This is a reasonable experiment. My soul consists of forty years of habits, of little events, thoughts, and gestures, forty years of words, always the same words.

What I call my soul is a carcass, already more than half worn out, with hair, wrinkles, scars, and callouses. It is a couch that you do not know, but which is not devoid of experience. —*Le Club des Lyonnais*, pp. 210-11.

[16] But I rarely put my thoughts into action. To act or not to act upon one's thoughts! It took me years to reach this humble definition of virtue. "Verily, he who has looked upon the wife of his neighbor with desire has already committed adultery in his heart." No, no! I have suffered for twenty years because of that accursed phrase! Everyone looks with desire upon his neighbor's wife. Virtue consists in locking all that up in one's heart with other uncleanness. —*Le Club*, p. 84.

[17] *Opinion*, 9 novembre 1929, pp. 9-11.

[18] *Annales politiques et littéraires*, XCIII (1 décembre 1929), 498.

[19] Everything happens . . . as if Salavin at last realized man's powerlessness to surpass himself by the force of nature alone. His story is the drama of the redemption of man by man, or of redemption without a mediator, or of salvation without grace: it is also the story of a failure. —*Georges Duhamel*, p. 113.

[20] *Mercure de France*, CCXL (15 novembre 1932), 170-73.

[21] There is a little bit of Salavin in M. Duhamel. —*Revue universelle*, XXXIX (1 novembre 1929), 368-69.

[22] *L'Europe nouvelle*, XV, 2 (22 octobre 1932), 1256-57.

[23] *Mercure de France*, CCXL (15 novembre 1932), 172-73.

[24] Je crois même que le plus important de leur vie s'accomplit en dehors de ces instants laborieux, dans les longs intervalles de songerie et d'attente. —*Deux patrons*, p. 114.

[25] Les cinq années d'attente, je le vis tout de suite, l'avaient fortifié, nourri. Le fantôme avait pris de la densité, de la couleur. Dès cet instant, il m'apparut tel que je devais longtemps le voir à côté de moi. —*Deux patrons*, p. 116.

[26] A peine en présence les deux héros de mon futur livre, je découvris avec étonnement qu'un de ces deux personnages était Salavin. —*Deux patrons*, p. 120.

[27] Je n'ai pas même prévu que, le dernier soupir poussé, la dernière ligne écrite, j'éprouverais le besoin d'élever tout à coup la voix, moi le confident silencieux, et de m'adresser au mort, à mon frère misérable, au compagnon de tant d'années, pour lui dire adieu avec déchirement. —*Deux patrons*, pp. 133-34.

[28] L'histoire de Salavin est, en gros, l'histoire d'un échec et, si l'on tient aux apparences, l'histoire d'un échec obstiné, réitéré, on dira peut-être même incurable. —*Deux patrons*, p. 141.

[29] . . . a work devoid of deep significance, but lively in scene, in which I should like to see some man other than the wretched Salavin. —*Correspondent*, CCCXX (10 juillet 1930), 147-49.

CHAPTER IV

[1] The supreme goal of the novelist is to make us sensitive to the human soul, to cause us to know it and love it in its greatness as in its wretchedness, in its victories as in its defeats. Admiration and pity, this is the motto of the novel. *—Essai sur le roman,* p. 61.

[2] I like works of imagination, of course, but I always prefer books that reflect a personal experience, a heartfelt experience full of human truth. A gifted novelist, if he took the trouble, could always invent a host of poignant, interesting episodes on the life of political prisoners in Siberia. But what is the use of inventing in our unhappy times? What fiction would not seem weak by contrast to our monstrous reality. *—Positions françaises,* p. 161.

[3] Il nous reste nous, l'homme. Il nous reste un pathétique purement, étroitement humain. *—Remarques sur les mémoires imaginaires,* p. 93.

[4] L'essentiel est qu'il ne perde pas de vue le but de son travail: la recherche de l'éternelle vérité humaine. . . . . . . je tiens l'alliance mesurée du réel et de l'imaginaire comme la meilleure et la plus féconde forme d'art en matière de romans. *—Essai sur le roman,* pp. 52, 65-66.

[5] . . . nous sommes fondés à portraire nos contemporains. Notre devoir est de témoigner devant l'avenir. . . . *—Essai sur le roman,* p. 55.

[6] A character is not a representative human being at the outset, but he may become one. A great innocence is doubtless necessary to the creation of a representative character. The true novelist does not say, I am going to depict the moderately well-educated Frenchman of the early twentieth century. The true novelist draws the portrait of a "particular chap." Then it sometimes happens that this man comes to represent the Frenchman of the early twentieth century very well. It even happens, though more rarely, that this man simply represents mankind, that is, man of all times and all places. *—Défense des lettres,* p. 254.

[7] The action of works of imagination, or, rather, the plot, is something we forget immediately, as soon as we have closed the book. *—Remarques,* p. 79.

[8] What we have left forever is a face tortured with hope, two white hands that fold and unfold, a little square of light on the floor of a room. An odor, a taste, even less perhaps. *—Remarques,* p. 80.

[9] Cela n'empêche pas . . . les meilleurs d'entre leurs écrivains d'explorer avec audace les profondeurs de l'âme humaine et d'y jeter de fulgurantes lueurs. *—Essai sur le roman,* p. 56.

[10] If the rich United States dreams of becoming one day a leading nation, she must hasten to raise up and inspire a greater number of free and noble souls. Whitman, Poe, Emerson, and Thoreau are all very well, but this is not enough for a nation of 100,000,000 people and two centuries of history. *—Géographie cordiale de l'Europe,* pp. 205-206.

[11] Lacking these, people begin to read American novels, and even to read them in English. Now what is this American novel? It is a good brand of novel conceived according to the formula or the methods of Balzac, Zola, and Maupassant. You see, America has a genius for imitation, even in literature. She gives there, as elsewhere, an honest merchandise that will, if we are not careful, make the whole world forget exceptional quality. —*Les Nouvelles littéraires*, 6 mai 1948.

[12] A remark made to the present writer, December, 1949.

[13] The Scandinavians, in particular, who have given us philosophers of first rank, great poets, admirable dramatists, were still, as far as the experience of realism was concerned, playing scales and arpeggios. They had scarcely emerged from the epic and the legend. —*Chronique des saisons amères* (Mercure de France, 1949), p. 33.

[14] *La Nouvelle revue française*, XXVI (1 juin 1926), 748-51.

[15] *Les Cahiers du mois*, No. 21/22 (1926), pp. 236-37.

[16] *Revue de Paris*, XXXV, 2 (1 avril 1928), 688-93.

[17] *Revue hebdomadaire*, XXXVII, 2 (18 fevrier 1928), 360-68.

[18] . . . nous avons peu de chances de comprendre l'événement. —*Revue de Paris*, LIX (avril 1952), 145.

[19] *Mercure de France*, CCCXIV (1 fevrier 1952), 310.

[20] One of the themes that has haunted his works for many years is here grasped, and becomes the center of the novel. The sharpness and bitterness that sometimes could be seen through his smile, his good humor, and his purposeful confidence, break through the dam. Politics, so long contained, breaks through, face to face. —*Mercure de France*, CCCXI (1 fevrier 1951), 301.

[21] *Revue des Deux Mondes*, 1 janvier 1957, p. 185.

[22] . . . a little treatise on morals and esthetics abandoned to the vagaries of a romanesque dialogue, a philosophic tale, in effect. —*Mercure de France*, CCCXXVII (1 mai 1956), 87.

CHAPTER VI

[1] I have already said that I can recall my own life but imperfectly. But I can recall day by day and minute by minute the life of Laurent Pasquier, my creature, my imaginary comrade. —*Remarques sur les mémoires imaginaires*, p. 58.

[2] To have had in plain sight for nearly fifty years a model as striking as Pierre Emile Duhamel and to have let him disappear without a trace for doctrinal or esthetic reasons, would have been absurd. I declare then, without hesitation, that in creating the characters of the father and mother in the *Chronique des Pasquier*, I borrowed many elements from my family models. I must add also that as my story grew, my sketches departed in many ways from the originals. I will add further that the Pasquier children have absolutely no connection with my

brothers and sisters. Cécile, Suzanne, Joseph, and Ferdinand are creatures of my imagination. —*Inventaire de l'abîme* (Montreal: Editions variétés, 1945), p. 53.

[3] Je me suis beaucoup diverti avec le Docteur Pasquier. Mon père était moins gai que ne l'est, dans la *Chronique*, le mari de Lucie-Eléonore. Il était moins gai, moins brillant. —*Inventaire de l'abîme*, p. 94.

[4] And since the poet has discretionary powers, I decided many years later to give my dead friend the life he never lived, to have him endure, enjoy, and suffer an ample and rich existence under the name of Justin, one of my fictional characters, and to share with him in imagination all that deep affection of which his death deprived us. —*Inventaire de l'abîme*, p. 136.

[5] The vast reading public has a tendency to believe that a writer's stories correspond exactly to reality ("So that's how it happened!"), or that a thing is wholly invented. These conflicting views are equally childish. All the tales of a story-teller have a germ of reality. As in biology, *omne vivum in ovo*. All our stories have their seed and their roots in what is roughly called the real. —*Chronique des saisons amères*, p. 51.

[6] I told in the *Désert de Bièvres* a story somewhat like the Abbaye. The imaginary house immediately began to hide the real one from me. When I think of the Abbaye, it is Bièvres that I first perceive. To return to the banks of the Marne, and remember our seasons, our quarrels, our hopes, our disagreements, I must first put aside my familiar fantasies with determination, and I cannot always do so. —*Inventaire de l'abîme*, p. 22.

[7] Mieux vaut donner le sentiment de vérité avec un récit fictif que le sentiment de fiction avec un récit «réel.» . . . Mon plus vif désir, quand je compose un récit, c'est que le lecteur, frappé par l'accent de vérité, s'écrie, songeant à moi: «C'est bien évidemment son histoire.» —*Remarques*, pp. 58-59, 67.

[8] The greatest tyrants of the people are almost always of humble origin. The most determined anti-Semites often have Jewish blood in their veins. And it is those of mixed blood who speak of the Negro with the cruelest of scorn.

"I don't quite see—"

"Excuse me, I was preoccupied. Do you think it is easy to be a Jew? I have all the cares of other men plus a constant and major care. I am a Jew. Once again, pardon me." —*Le Combat contre les ombres*, p. 214.

[9] . . . sa bouche se tordait de manière spasmodique. —*La Passion de Joseph Pasquier*, p. 12.

[10] My father, for example, could not stand anything ugly. He could not tolerate the sight of something ridiculous in someone else. His reaction was frank, immediate, and quite unexpected. We were in a

bus once when a middle-aged gentleman, perhaps even decorated with the rosette of the Legion of Honor (in those days practically a mark of distinction), started yawning. My father, coming out of his silence, spoke up. His attack was usually direct: "Come, sir," said he, in a voice at once unctuous and rasping, "Aren't you ashamed of showing us everything you've got in your mouth?" —*Le Notaire du Havre* (Montreal: Editions variétés, 1943), p. 113.

11 When I think that there are unfortunates who live on Rue Pirouette or Cité Vacheron, it's enough to make me cry. Rue Fessart is at least comical; it sounds well; it has a certain something. But Passage Gatbois? What is Gatbois? What did he do? A palace, you hear? A palace. You could give me a palace on Rue Cossonerie or Rue Biscornet, and I wouldn't want it. You've got to have the courage of your impulsions and repulsions. —*Les Maîtres* (Montreal: Editions variétés, 1943), p. 13.

12 Mon père, dans ses emportements, avait quelque chose d'un artiste. —*Le Notaire du Havre*, p. 117.

13 . . . but that night, as on every other night, every time he went down into his hiding place, he felt himself gripped by an incomprehensible weariness, and he began to doze, a thread of saliva in the corners of his mouth, his big hairy hands resting on his stiff knees. —*La Passion de Joseph Pasquier*, p. 76.

14 . . . if I come to life someday, a sightless ghost, I shall recognize the land of my childhood by the things I smell. Odors from the fruit store, fresh and acid, which toward evening grow sharp and seem to bring a breath of the swamp, or faded greenery and dead nourishment. Steam from the hand laundry, smelling of wet clothes, the steaming iron, the perspiring laundress. Scent of the butcher shop, which sells beef bouillon, a faint and terrible perfume of murdered animals; the resinous whiff, with its woodsy note, of pine sawdust spread upon the tile floor. —*Le Notaire du Havre*, p. 88.

CHAPTER VII

1 During his first year, Cuib was a very brilliant thumb-sucker. His digit held tightly, his hand folded back, the index finger pressing his nose to maintain his position—such was his manner. It was not without elegance and hid fairly well the intimate and delicate part of the procedure. —*Les Plaisirs et les jeux*, in *Les Livres du bonheur* (Mercure de France, 1950), p. 68.

2 The night is so black now that it seems to have fallen for good and all.

But the house breathes, gently and insensibly, like wild creatures in their winter sleep, curled in their furry coats.

Sometimes a light sound comes from the depths: a sigh from the little sleepers, a laugh, or a word drawn from them by a dream.

The oldest piece of furniture creaks one last time, severely. It is all over. Everything is still.

Silence and night are come together. —*Les Plaisirs,* p. 141.

3 Gymnastics in this remarkable institution was called mecanotherapy. The students sat on a very curious apparatus that shook them from head to toe and from right to left, and made them turn, pivot, and jump; it stretched their arms, bent their knees, and scratched the soles of their feet.

After that came the swimming lesson, which was done with a motion-picture demonstration, the driving lesson and the radio lesson in which they learned to distinguish Radio Buda-Pest at once from among fifty stations.

There were also, according to the day, lessons in illuminated advertising, industrial rationalization, submarine navigation, and interplanetary aviation.

"This is the twentieth century," explained M. Pepinsky proudly. "The twentieth century in all its force and all its beauty. We are preparing the man of the twentieth century."

"Exactly," continued Professor Pipe. "Man of the latest model, whom we shall render mathematically happy. This is an admirable illustration of my method, the Pipic method." —*Les Jumeaux de Vallangoujard,* pp. 85-86.

4 "Here, sir, we make preserves for their odor only, the rest is of no importance. When the preserves are done we throw them away."

I said this in a lyric impulse to bedazzle my learned interlocutor. It is not quite true. We eat our preserves, in memory of their perfume.

—*Fables de mon jardin,* in *Les Livres du bonheur* (Mercure de France, 1950), pp. 193-94.

5 René Daumal, *La Nouvelle revue française,* XLVI (1 mai 1936), 799-801.

EPIGRAPH TO PART II

The work of my life, I mean my written work, which I see on a wide shelf in my library, is, everything considered, a long cry of alarm. I have hardly ever spoken except of suffering, wretchedness, illnesses, intellectual aberrations, war, and death. Nevertheless, I enjoy a surprising reputation: that of an optimistic writer. This is probably because I am also, by nature—that is, without much willing to be so—unendowed with a certain venom, a certain spirit of aggressiveness. Today this famous spirit is the pepper and the mustard of works that, like the praying mantis, devour those whom they delight. —*Les Espoirs et les épreuves,* pp. 17-18.

CHAPTER VIII

[1] *Civilisation française,* p. 62.

[2] Et c'est pourquoi l'empire colonial de la France ne ressemble à nul autre. Ce n'est pas, au principe, une création de banquiers et de trafiquants, c'est une entreprise de missionnaires, de pédagogues et de guérisseurs. —*Civilisation française,* pp. 59-60.

[3] Elle a souvent pu se reprocher ses erreurs et ses fautes, elle a commis très peu de mauvaises actions et cet éloge d'apparence modeste est, pour une nation, un éloge majuscule. —*Civilisation française,* p. 33.

[4] Mais la France a toujours été le pays de l'initiation et de la révélation. —*La Possession du monde,* p. 267.

[5] . . . naïve grandeur d'âme disculpe toute l'humanité de son plus grand crime et la relève de sa plus profonde déchéance. —*Vie des martyrs,* p. 243.

[6] A ce seul trait, je reconnais et j'admire le génie de ma patrie, à ce seul trait, je comprends qu'elle ait produit tant de grands hommes en toutes carrières. —*Scènes de la vie future,* p. 231.

[7] The sentiment of home and country continues none the less its irresistible invasion. It comes to me—how shall I say it?—from my loins and mounts gently to my heart. A mystery.

"What are you thing of?" asks Arnauld affectionately.

"Of France," I reply softly. "Yes, of France, and in a curious fashion. To say that I am thinking of France is probably an exaggeration. But there is something here that recalls my country, and I do not even dare to tell you what part of my anatomy the sensation is coming from."

"France!" murmurs Blanc. Suddenly, turning his head, he said: "Did you know that this road we are speeding over was built by the French during the Great War? It is not very well kept up and even . . ."

I am no longer listening. I have understood everything. —*Géographie cordiale de l'Europe,* p. 162.

[8] I know many things, many beings, many landscapes; but having attained and passed my forty-sixth year, I must declare that to live for a long time outside France is no longer possible for me. If I should chance to incur someday a mortal punishment, I privately admit that exile would suffice. I have traveled a good deal, each time with enough enthusiasm, enough energy and enough confidence for me to admit today this passive attachment to my native soil. I admire hearts that can beat anywhere with the same rhythm. I know that my heart is not like that. I am neither proud nor ashamed of the fact. That is the way it is. —*Géographie cordiale,* p. 24.

[9] Etudier nos voisins est notre devoir, si nous souhaitons d'être éclairés sur nous-mêmes. Etudier, aimer, célébrer les vertus des nations étrangères, c'est travailler à notre enrichissement, prendre conscience de toute grandeur humaine. —*Discours aux nuages,* p. 70.

10 Il n'y a pas deux heures que nous sommes à Prague, mais nous avons l'impression de pénétrer, du premier coup, bien profondément dans l'âme de ces gens. —*Délibérations,* p. 76.

11 For a man who is interested in his fellow man, a visit to Russia is above all an exceptional opportunity to meditate profitably on social experiments, to cultivate his opinion on the conduct and the future of the human race. —*Le Voyage de Moscou,* p. 9.

12 I have made a confident, an almost always successful, almost always rewarded effort to love the several faces of this confused Europe. The idyllic days of the past are but a memory: the new Europe is sick. The traveler who is not deceived by smiles must skirt many a precipice, stumble over graves, and stir up dying embers. If I speak of having been rewarded and of my efforts having been successful, it is because while visiting these enemy brothers, one finally discovers their intimate resemblance; one finally discovers the bond that has survived their dramatic quarrels; one realizes that although it has been compromised in the struggle, the family treasure, the precious inheritance, our common civilization, still exists. —*Géographie cordiale,* p. 22.

13 . . . le pays de la culture harmonieuse; la civilisation n'y est point folle, mais prudente, toujours tempérée, dans ses vues et dans ses œuvres, par un climat qui, heureusement, rappelle l'homme à la décence. —*Géographie cordiale,* p. 242.

14 . . . sa haute culture, avec ses philosophes, ses poètes, ses romanciers, ses savants, ses administrateurs, ses navigateurs, son génie inventif, son empire immense, ses cinq cent millions d'âmes, ses traditions et ses méthodes. —*Mémorial de la guerre blanche,* p. 117.

15 Par quel affreux miracle ce pays si grand, si varié, qui va des tropiques à la banquise, ce pays, peut-être sans grâce, mais non sans noblesse, par quel miracle se trouve-t-il avili, enlaidi? . . . que je savoure encore un peu cette amertume ineffable de n'avoir pu aimer ce que je vois. —*Scènes de la vie future,* pp. 115, 247.

16 If you reproach me and say that my stay in America was brief, I do not consider the criticism relevant and do not admit it to consideration. When it comes to knowing a country thoroughly, time confers no rights. . . . For years I had been looking for a good opportunity to express my opinion concerning certain phenomena or events, concerning certain developments and certain deviations of so-called occidental civilization. I had long wished to write a book about the movies, the phonograph, the automobile, rationalized industry, sport, insurance, advertising, various excesses of statism and that sort of thing, and by visiting a country where all these phenomena are manifest in a sort of furious fashion, fate played into my hands and gave me a model. —*Géographie cordiale,* pp. 38, 39.

17 . . . de nouveaux buildings, beaux de leur seule nudité, de leur seule énormité. —*Tribulations de l'espérance,* p. 245.

[18] Seule compte, seule existe la connaissance réelle, profonde, intime que l'on gagne par une longue et étroite communion avec les hommes et avec les choses. —*Essai sur le roman,* p. 85.

CHAPTER IX

[1] Si la civilisation n'est pas dans le cœur de l'homme, eh bien, elle n'est nulle part. —*Civilisation,* p. 125.

[2] L'ordre est une conquête de l'expérience et de la volonté sur le désordre naturel. L'ordre, la santé, la morale, la paix, la beauté, tous ces biens si souhaitables sont le fruit d'un lent et patient effort que l'homme poursuit contre la nature. —*Les Confessions sans pénitence,* pp. 34-35.

[3] . . . un ensemble de recettes, de méthodes, de croyances, de doctrines, de coutumes, de traditions, de lois, de faits, d'instruments, de monuments et d'ouvrages qui concourent, par leur présence, par leur jeu, par leur action, à la subsistance et au développement de l'espèce. —*Civilisation française,* pp. 3-4.

[4] . . . baconienne, puis qu'elle repose tout entière sur les applications de la méthode inductive. —*Scènes de la vie future,* pp. 12-13.

[5] Le législateur s'essouffle sur les pas de l'inventeur. —*Défense des lettres,* p. 12.

[6] We must try to teach men (to their astonishment), that happiness does not consist only in going sixty miles in an hour, in rising in the air upon a machine, or in conversing across an ocean, but rather, above all, in being rich with great thoughts, content with one's work, and honored by warm affection. —*La Possession du monde,* pp. 255-56.

[7] Scientific and industrial civilization founded upon intelligence stands condemned. It has for many years seized upon and misled all human energies. Its reign ends in an immense defeat. —*La Possession,* p. 244.

[8] I do not like sarcasm, to which the French are addicted, and which is so easy to use. I especially dislike it when the future of a great nation and, who knows, perhaps even the future of the world is at stake. In my descriptions you will find malice at times, but mockery, never. —*Le Voyage de Moscou,* p. 15.

[9] Perhaps once again I shall anger distant friends who, considering my strictures, imagine in their pride that my remarks were aimed at them. So much the worse. Let us talk about ourselves. —*Querelles de famille,* p. 7.

[10] I am sad . . . and yet my sadness has within itself its own consolation. Only incurable pessimists are satisfied with everything. As for me, as long as I rebel I am not desperate. If I quarrel with the world, it is because, until further notice, I still have confidence in it. —*Querelles de famille,* p. 247.

[11] . . . je veux librement connaître, comprendre, juger, critiquer le

temps dans lequel je vis. . . . Je redoute, j'exècre les fanatiques et les illuminés. C'est assez dire que je ne les imite pas. —*L'Humaniste et l'automate*, p. 12.

[12] Je donne toute la bibliothèque cinématographique du monde, y compris ce que les gens de métier appellent pompeusement leurs «classiques,» pour une pièce de Molière, pour un tableau de Rembrandt, pour une fugue de Bach. —*Scènes de la vie future*, p. 60.

[13] Superbe revanche des vaniteux et des incapables! Cet homme, qui n'oserait pas signifier sa volonté à un cheval, sait qu'il peut tout demander à une mécanique. —*Scènes de la vie future*, p. 97.

[14] In many of my writings I have criticized the misuse that is too often made of the automobile. I have not criticized the instrument itself, which would be absurd. I have, I repeat, warned my contemporaries against the temptation to misuse its power. This but makes it the easier for me to admit that the automobile wisely used is a more precise instrument, and a much more docile one, than the old equipage comically called the hippomobile. —*Inventaire de l'abîme*, pp. 150-51.

CHAPTER X

[1] In my youth I acquired a scientific culture. In so doing, I acquired a taste for method and even certain disciplines of work. I have attempted to apply these disciplines to my literary endeavor—Oh, quite without confusing them, you know—but at least in the matter of working habits and the constraints imposed upon the body. —*Biographie de mes fantômes*, p. 13.

[2] [Ils ont] l'avantage de rompre l'esprit, de l'accoutumer à certaines difficultés, de le préparer à trouver des solutions à divers problèmes. . . . —*Paroles de médecin*, p. 59.

[3] Medicine forces man to look at man, to look at him closely, to touch him, to explore the recesses, cavities, and wounds of his weak body. Thus it develops and keeps alive in this wretched world the necessary miracle of soul-saving sympathy. . . .

The medical imprint is indelible. It is marked as deeply as the ecclesiastical imprint—"sacerdos in aeternum." I know of no unfrocked physicians. The member of the medical fraternity who has left it returns with ease and pleasure always. He knows that whatever he thinks or does, he cannot stop acting and thinking like a doctor. —*Paroles de médecin*, pp. 63, 65.

[4] One does not plan for a writing career. A man is led by his tastes, family traditions, or necessity to choose a profession or a status. . . . At a certain moment he can decide upon a career as a writer, but he does not plan for it from the beginning. The only initiation into the world of letters is a comprehension of life and experience in a profession.

The writer afterward remains inevitably what he was at the start: journalist, professor, lawyer, or doctor. *—Les Confessions sans pénitence,* pp. 89-90.

5 In my opinion a writer performs a social function when he helps us better to understand man and the world: when he applies himself, according to Paul Claudel's formula, to "transforming the unknown into the known," when he is truly a seeker, an inventor, and a discoverer. . . . *—Défense des lettres,* pp. 181-82.

6 Qu'ils écrivent ce qu'ils pensent et qu'ils le signent, fièrement. Mais qu'ils se défient des signatures collectives. *—Défense des lettres,* p. 179.

7 . . . un besoin de restriction et de compensation, un manque de confiance et de générosité. *—Discours aux nuages,* p. 17.

8 In a world given over entirely to business and gain it is natural that one should see a decline in the influence of an admirable language, rich in masterpieces, but spoken by a people whose industry is medium-sized and whose commerce lacks large ambitions. *—Le Voyage de Moscou,* p. 116.

9 Several years ago I was asked to furnish a definition of humanism, and I gave the following, which I would not change today: "Modern humanism is the sum total of ideas that do not seem susceptible of immediate application." This means that western culture seems to me to be founded first of all upon disinterestedness. *—Chronique des saisons amères,* p. 114.

10 It took me many years to understand the meaning of the humanistic discipline, to understand that the assiduous study of two dead languages is, in a sordid century, a proof of disinterestedness, and that disinterestedness is the mainspring of true civilization. The supreme virtue of a useless action, which does not seem intelligible to mediocre minds when they come to grips with intellectual matters, seems to them quite evident when sports or games are in question. *—Inventaire de l'abîme,* p. 137.

11 The twentieth century is tired yet brutal. It does not seem favorable to reading. Awaiting the time when people will no longer read, a situation one cannot contemplate without a shudder, the man of the twentieth century reads little and reads badly. *—Discours de réception de M. Georges Duhamel à l'Académie française,* p. 37.

12 . . . ces petites mécaniques peuvent apporter en classe le divertissement, le repos, mais que le vrai travail, que l'effort fructueux c'est vous seul qui pouvez en donner aux petits le goût. . . . *—L'Humaniste et l'automate,* p. 189.

13 La critique est, d'abord, une des dernières manifestations de la générosité et du désintéressement dans notre grande presse. *—Discours aux nuages,* p. 140.

14 Eh oui, nous sommes tous, et pour chacun des beaux arts, partisans

d'une telle censure, à la condition que les ciseaux soient confiés à nos mains. —*L'Humaniste et l'automate*, p. 143.

15 M. de Régnier avait à choisir entre notre amour et l'Académie. Il a choisi l'Académie. . . . —*Mercure de France*, CCLXVIII (15 juin 1936), 451.

16 Refuser d'être juge, c'est refuser d'être un homme. —*Les Lettres françaises*, décembre 1946.

17 I have said that justice is of a desperate slowness and that it lacks imagination. I have said that it hands out death, forced labor, and prison sentences at random, like an ill-contrived machine; I have said that justice strikes with blind indifference notorious criminals and persons whose sins were merely venial. I have said that justice, monotonous and extravagant as it is, risks contributing to the demoralization of our weary people.

I have said all this, and I see that I will have to say it again fifteen years from now if I am still alive, and have not been forced into silence by then, as I once was silenced by the Germans.

I have abstained from talking of charity or mercy, having observed elsewhere that our society is not at the moment ready for words of appeasement.

At this several persons began to protest. I have even been taken to task for my "humanitarianism." Can you imagine that! —*Tribulations de l'espérance*, pp. 413-14.

18 Now that I am fifty, or almost, I have often agreed—at least when it seemed to me that I could defend a just cause—to render a service to my country, to humanity, or to civilization. —*Travail, ô mon seul repos*, pp. 102-103.

CHAPTER XI

1 The writer of *Père Goriot*, or the poet of *Les Misérables*, if they were to come from the tomb, could walk the narrow streets of the Plaisance Quarter without feeling any of that uneasy strangeness that time brings us even more surely than travel.

Here in the midst of the capital, in the midst of the twentieth century, is a big old-fashioned village. Through driveway gates, the passerby glimpses courtyards that seem abandoned, like the fonduks of the East, with their dusty sheds, their artisans' shops, their rutty pavements, their piles of rubbish, and their carts and stables, in which one sometimes sees a sad and bony nag like that of the illustrious Hidalgo. —*Inventaire de l'abîme*, p. 8.

2 . . . when I happen to be far away from my native city, and I chance to dream of it nostalgically, it is not the famous place that I recall most gladly. From my exile I call up the odorous alleys of Mount

Saint Genevieve, the populous quarters, or the boulevards on the out-skirts with their ill-assorted ornamentation, in a word, not the Paris of great architecture, the wealthy Paris of pride and success, but rather the Paris of work and suffering, the Paris of flesh and blood. —*Inventaire de l'abîme,* p. 42.

[3] When I interrupt my story, the lad is seventeen and already thinks himself a man! It takes time—a lot of time—to make a man, and a good exposure, rain and sun, some restraint, some pruning, and a bit of good luck. —*Inventaire de l'abîme,* p. 207.

[4] For the time of affliction is beginning. For the men of our age must give up the play of the mind and the bright works of peace. Henceforth they will have only enough breath to suffer and fight. For words are going to change their meaning, and ideas will change their power. For the most precious of all imaginable possessions, life itself, will for many years fall into scorn and degradation. —*Le Temps de la recherche* (Mercure de France, 1949), p. 244.

[5] While thus confessing my anxiety, can I leave the slightest doubt concerning my deep feelings? He would be greatly mistaken who would think me upset because the white race is going to have to abandon its role of tyrant. No, no! Understand me well. Every calm observer knows that in human affairs, equilibrium is not only the most necessary element but at the same time the element most difficult to find and maintain. If the white race were truly conscious of its intellectual gifts, its virtues, and its legacy, its mission would be to discover for the world an honest system of equilibrium and, having found it, to maintain it. —*La Pesée des âmes,* p. 19.

[6] I do not have a religious faith. I am at present what I call, in hours of bitterness, a despairing agnostic—what I will later call, having weighed both ideas and words, a Christian agnostic. Men of a certain kind need to find, all the same, a kind of explanation for this incomprehensible world, an explanation that will leave the mind at rest and prevent it from plunging into blind alleys. To accept a metaphysics and place it forthwith in an "ark of the convenant" in order to devote oneself more freely to life's activities is a wise solution, at least in appearance. Unfortunately, I am not able to accept it. . . .

No, I do not have a religious faith; but this lack gives me no feeling of pride. I do not hide the fact that I envy those who, as they do not suffer from a feeling of emptiness, can dedicate their capacity for suffer-ing to other wounds and other subjects of bitterness. —*Les Espoirs et les épreuves,* pp. 10-11.

[7] The passerby who stops you to ask for a light will ask you, if you'll let him talk ten minutes, to show him God. Everyone, whether he knows it or not, is looking for a law, a rule, a direction, a restraining influence. Each wants to unburden himself and leave to someone else the task of evaluating or choosing, of deciding, judging and concluding.. Everyone,

in short, is dimly seeking God and eternal life, even if he is otherwise cynical, skeptical, gross, and insensitive. —*Défense des lettres*, pp. 122-23.

[8] One does not choose one's family, which is regrettable. I am beginning to realize that one does not choose one's friends, either. They have been given to you, you keep them, you stand them, and you bear them, and that is all there is to it. —*Les Maîtres*, p. 51.

[9] How can you say that you have not made a man suffer if you have looked at him—or even thought of him as your paths have crossed? —*Confession de minuit*, p. 104.

[10] I give what I have. I tell what I know. I am a writer in the prime of life. I have seen much of men and have traveled a bit. Besides, I am a physician, and I have derived from medicine a broad human training. That is my domain. It is not too small. I can answer many questions, but many more must be left without an answer, because an honest man owes it to himself to leave them unanswered. —*Défense des lettres*, p. 123.

[11] One must get the disconcerting intellectual machine into motion. By a wearing process of incubation one must bring the soul to a certain temperature that is indispensable for creative beginnings. —*Biographie de mes fantômes*, p. 14.

[12] *Biographie de mes fantômes*, p. 123.

BIBLIOGRAPHY

DUHAMEL'S policy in publishing his writings, shrewdly calculated to provide him as wide an audience as possible, has posed problems for a bibliographer. It has been his practice to publish in periodicals and in newspapers almost all that he has written before having it issued in book form. Many of his novels have been serialized before publication as books. Of his miscellaneous short pieces, articles, and essays the majority began as magazine articles and later reappeared in books. For the most part he does not change the titles or wording of articles and essays thus reprinted, and it is therefore relatively easy to identify them in books where they reappear as chapters or parts of chapters. But when, as sometimes occurs, he changes both title and lead paragraph, it is less easy to follow the material back to its source. Sometimes there is a lapse of as much as ten years before a given piece is reused, and sometimes the selection is reused in more than one book. Short stories also are shifted around, appearing first in one book and then in another.

A further problem is created by Duhamel's practice of allowing his works to be privately printed in de luxe editions, with unfamiliar titles. When after diligent search an elusive title is found, the work itself may be altogether familiar.

Recently the task of the student has been made easier by the publication of an exhaustive bibliographical study of Duhamel's writings by his friend Marcel Saurin, *Les Ecrits de Georges Duhamel* (Mercure de France, 1951). Though guilty of a few omissions, this work is on the whole quite accurate and performs a useful, nay indispensable task. It is to be hoped that the promised sequel will soon appear to bring us down to a more recent date.

As might be expected in the case of so prominent and so prolific an author, the body of critical commentary is vast and still growing. To attempt even a selective bibliography would be beyond the scope of this study. Below is simply an alphabetical list of Duhamel's published books, including some omitted by Saurin, a fairly complete list of readily available translations of the major works into English, and a list of the more prominent studies of Duhamel's work in English and French, particularly those that have been found most useful in writing this study. Place of publication is Paris unless otherwise noted.

WORKS BY GEORGES DUHAMEL

L'Alsace entrevue ou l'aveugle et le paralytique. In collaboration with Berthold Mahn. Strasbourg: Libraire de la Mésange, 1931.

Anniversaire. Les 49 Ronins du Quai Malaquais. Champion, 1925.

Anthologie de la poésie lyrique française de la fin du XVe siècle à la fin du XIXe siècle, presentée par Georges Duhamel. Leipzig: Insel-Verlag, 1923.

L'Archange de l'aventure. Mercure de France, 1956.

Au Chevet de la civilisation. Flammarion, 1938.

Ballades. Les Ecrivains réunis, 1926.

Le Bestiaire et l'herbier. Mercure de France, 1948.

Chronique des Pasquier
1. *Le Notaire de Havre.* Mercure de France, 1933.
2. *Le Jardin des bêtes sauvages.* Mercure de France, 1934.
3. *Vue de la terre promise.* Mercure de France, 1934.
4. *La Nuit de la Saint-Jean.* Mercure de France, 1935.
5. *Le Désert de Bièvres.* Mercure de France, 1937.
6. *Les Maîtres.* Mercure de France, 1937.
7. *Cécile parmi nous.* Mercure de France, 1938.
8. *Le Combat contre les ombres.* Mercure de France, 1939.
9. *Suzanne et les jeunes hommes.* Mercure de France, 1941.
10. *La Passion de Joseph Pasquier.* Montréal, Editions de l'Arbre, 1944.

Chronique des saisons amères, 1940-1943. Paul Hartmann, 1944.

Civilisation 1914-1917. Under the pseudonym Denis Thévenin. Mercure de France, 1918.

Civilisation française. Hachette, 1944.

Le Combat, pièce en 5 actes. Mercure de France, 1913.

Compagnons, poèmes, 1910-1912. Nouvelle revue française, 1912.

Les Compagnons de l'Apocalypse. Mercure de France, 1956.

Le Complexe de Théophile. Mercure de France, 1958.

Les Confessions sans pénitence. Plon, 1941.

Consultation aux pays d'Islam. Mercure de France, 1947.

Cri des profondeurs. Mercure de France, 1951.

Dans l'ombre des statues, pièce en 3 actes. Nouvelle revue française, 1912.

Défense des lettres. Mercure de France, 1937.

Délibérations. Les Cahiers de Paris, 1925.

Le Dernier voyage de Candide. Fernand Sorlot, 1938.

Des Légendes, des batailles. Editions de "l'Abbaye," 1907.

Deux patrons, suivi de *Vie et mort d'un héros de roman.* Paul Hartmann, 1937.

Discours aux nuages. Editions du siècle, 1934.

Discours de réception de M. Georges Duhamel à l'Académie française. Réponse de M. Henri Bordeaux. Mercure de France, 1936.

Elégies. Bloch, 1920.

Entretiens dans le tumulte. Mercure de France, 1919.

Entretien sur l'esprit européen. Aux éditions des cahiers libres, 1928.

Les Erispaudants. Société de gravure sur bois originale, 1926.

Essai sur le roman. Marcelle Lesage, 1925.

Essai sur une renaissance dramatique. Lapina, 1926.

Fables de mon jardin. Mercure de France, 1936.

Géographie cordiale de l'Europe. Mercure de France, 1931.

Guerre et littérature. A. Monnier, 1920.

Henry de Waroquier. L'Art d'aujourd'hui, 1925.

Homère au XXᵉ siècle. Union latine d'édition, 1947.

L'Homme en tête, poème. Editions "Vers et Prose," 1909.

Les Hommes abandonnés. Mercure de France, 1921.

L'Humaniste et l'automate. Paul Hartmann, 1933.

Israël, clef de l'orient. Mercure de France, 1957.

Le Japon, entre la tradition et l'avenir. Mercure de France, 1953.

La Journée des aveux, comédie en trois actes, suivie de *Quand vous voudrez,* comédie en un acte. Mercure de France, 1924.

Les Jumeaux de Vallangoujard. Paul Hartmann, 1931.

Lettres au Patagon. Mercure de France, 1926.

Lieu d'asile. Mercure de France, 1940.

La Lumière, pièce en 4 actes. Eugène Figuière, 1911.

Lumières sur ma vie
   1. *Inventaire de l'abîme.* Paul Hartmann, 1944.
   2. *Biographie de mes fantômes.* Paul Hartmann, 1944.
   3. *Le Temps de la recherche.* Paul Hartmann, 1947.
   4. *La Pesée des âmes.* Mercure de France, 1949.
   5. *Les Espoirs et les épreuves.* Mercure de France, 1953.

Manuel du protestataire. Mercure de France, 1952.

Maurice de Vlaminck. Les Ecrivains réunis, 1927.

Mémorial de la guerre blanche, 1938. Mercure de France, 1939.

Mon Royaume. Paul Hartmann, 1932.

La Musique consolatrice. Monaco: Editions du Rocher, 1944.

La Musique libératrice. Editions des fêtes du peuple, 1921.

Notes sur la technique poétique. In collaboration with Charles
   Vildrac. Chez les libraires et chez les auteurs, 1910.

Nouvelles du sombre empire. Mercure de France, 1960.

La Nuit d'orage. Mercure de France, 1928.

L'Œuvre des athlètes, comédie en 4 actes, suivi de *Lapointe
   et Ropiteau,* comédie en un acte. Nouvelle revue française, 1920.

Pages de mon carnet. Editions des cahiers libres, 1931.

Paroles de médecin. Monaco: Editions du Rocher, 1946.

Paul Claudel. Mercure de France, 1913.

La Pierre d'Horeb. Mercure de France, 1926.

Les Plaisirs et les jeux, Mémoires du Cuib et du Tioup.
   Mercure de France, 1922.

Les Poètes et la poésie, 1912-1913. Mercure de France, 1914.

Positions françaises. Mercure de France, 1940.

La Possession du monde. Mercure de France, 1919.

Le Prince Jaffar. Mercure de France, 1924.

Problèmes de civilisation (1962), précédé de *Traité du depart, Fables de ma vie, La Médecine au XXe siècle.* Mercure de France, 1963.

Problèmes de l'heure. Mercure de France, 1957.

Propos critiques, première série. Eugène Figuière, 1912.

Querelles de famille. Mercure de France, 1932.

Refuges de lecture. Mercure de France, 1954.

Remarques sur les mémoires imaginaires. Mercure de France, 1934.

Scènes de la vie future. Mercure de France, 1930.

Selon ma loi, poèmes. Eugène Figuière, 1910.

Semailles au vent. Monaco: Editions du Rocher, 1947.

Les Sept dernières plaies. Mercure de France, 1928.

Souvenirs de la vie du paradis. Mercure de France, 1946.

Travail, ô mon seul repos. Mercure de France, 1959.

Tribulations de l'espérance. Mercure de France, 1947.

Trio pour Henri Mondor. In collaboration with Paul Valéry. Imprimérie Gauthier-Villars, n.d.

La Turquie nouvelle, puissance d'occident. Mercure de France, 1954.

Vie des martyrs, 1914-1916. Mercure de France, 1917.

Vie et aventures de Salavin
  1. *Confession de minuit.* Mercure de France, 1920.
  2. *Deux hommes.* Mercure de France, 1924.
  3. *Journal de Salavin.* Mercure de France, 1927.
  4. *Le Club des Lyonnais.* Mercure de France, 1929.
  5. *Tel qu'en lui-même.* Mercure de France, 1932.

Voix du vieux monde. Chansons et chœurs. Poèmes de Georges Duhamel. Musique de Albert Doyen. Heugel, 1925.

Le Voyage de Moscou. Mercure de France, 1927.

Le Voyage de Patrice Périot. Mercure de France, 1950.

Les Voyageurs de l'Espérance. Librairie Gedalge, 1953.

WORKS TRANSLATED INTO ENGLISH

Chronique des Pasquier.

    Cécile Pasquier. Trans. Béatrice de Holthoir. New York: Holt, 1940. (Contains *Les Maîtres, Cécile parmi nous, Le Combat contre les ombres.*)

    Papa Pasquier. Trans. Samuel Putnam. New York: Harpers, 1934. *(Le Notaire du Havre.)*

    The Fortunes of the Pasquiers. Trans. Samuel Putnam. New York: Harpers, 1935. (Contains *Le Jardin des bêtes sauvages, Vue de la terre promise.*)

    The Pasquier Chronicles. Trans. Beatrice de Holthoir. New York: Holt, 1938. (Contains *Le Notaire du Havre, Le Jardin des bêtes sauvages, Vue de la terre promise, La Nuit de la Saint-Jean, Le Désert de Bièvres.*)

    Young Pasquier. Trans. Béatrice de Holthoir. London: Dent, 1936. *(Le Jardin des bêtes sauvages.)*

Civilisation, 1914-1917

    Civilization, 1914-1917. Trans. E. S. Brooks. New York: Century, 1919.

Le Combat

    The Combat, drama in five acts. Authorized trans. Sasha Best. Boston: R. G. Badger, 1915.

Cri des profondeurs

    Cry out of the Depths. Trans. E. F. Bozman. Boston: Little, Brown, 1954.

Dans l'ombre des statues

    In the Shadow of Statues. Authorized trans. Sasha Best. Boston: R. G. Badger, 1914.

Défense des lettres

    In Defence of Letters. Trans. E. F. Bozman. New York: Greystone Press, 1939.

La Lumière

    The Light. Trans. Sasha Best. *Poet Lore,* Boston (1914).

Lumières sur ma vie

    Light on My Days. Trans. Basil Collier. London: Dent,

1948. (Contains *Inventaire de l'abîme, Biographie de mes fantômes.*)

Mémorial de la guerre blanche, 1938
  The White War of 1938. Trans. N. Hoppé. London: Dent, 1939.

Les Plaisirs et les jeux
  Days of Delight. Trans. R. Wills Thomas. London: A. Dakars, 1939.

Positions françaises
  Why France Fights. Trans. Basil Collier. London: Dent, 1940.

La Possession du monde
  The Heart's Domain. Trans. Eleanor Stimson Brooks. New York: Century, 1919.

Scènes de la vie future
  America: the Menace, Scenes from the Life of the Future. Trans. Charles M. Thompson. Boston: Houghton Mifflin, 1931.

Vie des martyrs
  The New Book of Martyrs. Trans. Florence Simmonds. New York: Doran, 1918.

Vie et aventures de Salavin
  Salavin. Trans. Gladys Billings. New York: Putnam, 1936. (Contains *Confession de minuit, Journal de Salavin, Le Club des Lyonnais, Tel qu'en lui-même.*)

Le Voyage de Patrice Périot
  Patrice Periot. Trans. E. F. Bozman. London: Dent, 1952.

CRITICAL WORKS ON GEORGES DUHAMEL

Antoine, André, and others. *Georges Duhamel. Revue de la capitole,* 1927.

Denuit, Désiré. *Georges Duhamel.* Bruxelles: Les Editions de Belgique, 1933.

Falls, William. *Le Message humain de Georges Duhamel.* Boivin, 1948.

Ouy, Achille. *Georges Duhamel, l'homme et l'œuvre.* Les Ecrivains réunis, 1927.

Santelli, César. *Georges Duhamel, l'homme, l'œuvre.* Bordas, 1947.

Saurin, Marcel. *Les Ecrits de Georges Duhamel.* Mercure de France, 1951.

Simon, Pierre-Henri. *Georges Duhamel.* Les Editions du temps présent, 1946.

Thérive, André. *Georges Duhamel, ou l'intelligence du cœur.* Rasmussen, 1925.

INDEX